S. Clark

A new Description of the World

Or, A compendious Treatise of the Empires, Kingdoms, States, Provinces, etc.

S. Clark

A new Description of the World
Or, A compendious Treatise of the Empires, Kingdoms, States, Provinces, etc.

ISBN/EAN: 9783337123000

Printed in Europe, USA, Canada, Australia, Japan

Cover: Foto ©ninafisch / pixelio.de

More available books at **www.hansebooks.com**

A NEW DESCRIPTION OF THE WORLD.

OR, A

Compendious Treatise of the Empires, Kingdoms, States, Provinces, Countries, Islands, Cities and Towns of *Europe, Asia, Africa* and *America*: In their Scituation, Product, Manufactures, and Commodities, Geographical and Historical.

WITH

An Account of the Natures of the People, in their Habits, Customes, Warrs, Religions and Policies, &c.

AS ALSO

Of the Rarities, Wonders and Curiosities, of Fishes, Beasts, Birds, Rivers, Mountains, Plants, &c. With several Remarkable Revolutions, and Delightful Histories.

Faithfully Collected from the best Authors,
By S. Clark.

LONDON,
Printed for *Hen. Rhodes* next Door to the *Swan Tavern*, near *Brides-Lane*, in *Fleet-Street*, 1689.

icenfed,
August the 11th. 1688.

THE Introduction

Addressed to the

READER.

WHEN the great and wise Creator of the Universe thought it in Eternal Wisdom convenient to build the Mansion, all Creatures now inhabited, he left nothing undone that might contribute to the Glory and Magnificence of so great a work; and lest Mankind, the top of the Creation, should grow supine, and neglect the filling or peopling every part of so admirable a Frame, he even compelled them to do it by confounding their Language at Babel, and thereby obliging them as they multiplied, to scatter over the Face of the Earth

The Introduction

Earth, that none of his wonderous works might remain obscure or unobserved to those for whose use and pleasure they were made; by which means the people in sundry Tribes, wandering from place to place, incroaching by degrees, as men began to multiply, planted themselves in the most advantagious Countries, every one striving for the best: however, through Wars, Pestilence, Inundations, and other strange Revolutions and Accidents, it is past all peradventure, that the bad as well as the good found possessors, as at this day. Though, Reader, I shall not trouble you in this place, with entring upon the original Peopling of Kingdoms and Countries, as to particulars; but let you know that my care has been to present you with Geographical and Historical Description of the World, as it formerly stood, and at present stands: and though upon first thought it may seem strange, that in so small a Volume so large a one can be contained, yet upon perusal you will find that nothing material is omitted, that can be required to render satisfaction upon this occasion: insomuch, that by well considering this Work, a mean Capacity may suddenly know how the Worlds mighty Fabrick is disposed, and soon become acquainted with every Country under Heaven, enough to render him capable

Addressed to the Reader.

capable not only of contemplating the Goodness of the Almighty, in his VVorks and Creatures, but readily Discoursing, even with the most knowing Travellers, and without hazarding the danger of treacherous Seas, Winds, Robbers, and a VVorld of Inconveniencies that attend an expensive search into these Affairs; securely Travel in Imagination from Pole to Pole. For to be brief, there is no Kingdom, Province, or Estate, that is wittingly left out of this History or Treatise; and as to what is most material, the Account is considerably large; wherefore recommending it to the benefit of my Country Men, I remain Reader,

Your Friend to serve,

In what I may,

S. Clark.

Of EUROPE, a brief DESCRIPTION.

EUROPE is the least of the Four parts of the World, yet nothing inferiour in Goodness to the rest, in the Generosity of People, Riches, Worth and Vertue, and exceeding them, if we consider the Flourishing of the True Religion; and is said to take its Name from *Europa* the Daughter of *Agenor* King of *Phœnicia*; containing many Flourishing Kingdoms and Provinces; as will appear in the sequel. And is accounted in length 2800 miles; In breadth 1200; bounded on the West, with the main Ocean; on the East, with the *Ægean* Sea, *Pontus Euxinus*, the Fenns of *Mæotis*, and the River *Tanais*; from which a right Line conjecturally drawn from the Bay of *Granvicus*, it is dis-joined from *Asia*; In the North, it is bounded with the *Hyperborean* Sea; and on the South, with the *Mediterranean*, divided into Continent, and Islands, the Continent Intire, and the Islands dispersed, In the *Greek*, *Ionian*, *Ægean*, *Adriatick*, *Mediterranean*, *Cretan*, and *Northern Seas*; divided chiefly into ...ce, Spain, Italy, the *Alps*, *Germany*, *Britain*, ...*ium*, *Denmark*, *Swedeland*, *Hungary*, *Sclavonia*, *Russia*, *Poland*, *Dacia*, and *Greece*; with the dispersed Islands. And in *Europe*, beside the Latin Tongue, which is now rather Scholastical, than National, there are other diversities of Language, besides the *Italian* and *French*, supposed to be corruptly derived from the Latin; and has been Famous by twice giving Laws to the World, during the flourishing of the *Greek* and *Roman* Empires; and at this day, though the least of the four parts, it excels, in what may be called solid good, the other Three, &c.

A Queen she Reigns, upheld by strictest Fate,
Whilst th' other Three, on her as Hand-Maids wait,
With Tribute Glories, to enrich her State.

A Geographical AND Historical Description OF THE KINGDOM OF FRANCE,

In its Particular Countries, Provinces, Cities, Towns, &c.

THE Flourishing Kingdom of *France*, being the nearest part of the Continent on which we border; I have thought, for the observing the most regular method, to begin this History of the World, with the Description of it, and its appendances.

As for *France*, or so much as is generally understood of it, it is bounded on the East with a branch of the Alps, passing between *Dauphin* and *Peimont* *Switzerland, Savoy*, some part of *Germany*, and the *Neitherlands*; on the West with a Branch of the *Pyreenian* Mountains, dividing *Spaine*, and with the *Aquitane* Ocean; on the North with the *British* Seas, and part of *Belgium*, and has on the South the rest of the *Pyreenian* Mountains, and the *Mediteranian* Sea, being in a manner Square; accounted in Length, from *Calais* to *Toulon* 620 Miles, reckoning 73 to a Degree, and in Breadth from the border of *Lorain* to *Brest*, or from *Nice* in *Peimont* to *Bayon* 492 Miles, though of late the Teretories have been much Inlarged by the new Conquests and Acquisitions, but being to speak of them in the Countries where they properly have their Scituation, I willingly here omit them.

This Country is called by the English *France*, by the Italians *Francia*, and so by the Spaniards; by the Germans *Franckreich*, by the Turks *Alfrangua*, and is the antient *Gallia* of *Cæsar* and *Pliny*; lying excellently in Compaction, between the most Flourishing Kingdoms and States of *Europe*, Scituate in the middle of the North Temperate Zone, between the middle Parralells of the Fifth Clime, where the longest Day is 13 Hours; and the middle Parralel of the Eighth Clime, where they extend to 16 Hours and a half: So that the Air is very Healthful, the Country every where Rich and Fertile, and the People numerous; as likewise the Cities and Towns, no less than 4000 being reckon'd of note, especially the greatest part of them, and was Distinguished by four Parts or Divisions, when the Romans (not without great blood-shed) brought it under their Subjection, viz.

1. The *Narbonensis*, or *Bracatta*, containing *Dauphin, Languedock*, and a part of *Savoy*. 2. *Aquita-*

(3)

ally under...o, taking its denomination from the City *Aquæ ...ugusta*, and now known by that of *d' Aeque*, con... ...ining *Gascoigne, Limoisin, Guinne, Sanctogne, Quærci, ...eregort, Bourbonnois* and *Aurergne*.

3. *Celtica*, comprehending the Provinces of *Nor...undy, Britagne, Anjou, Tourain, Maine, Labeause,* ...rt of *Campagne*, the *Isles* of *France*, the Dukedom ... *Burgundy*, and the County of *Lionoise*. 4. *Belgica*, ...ontaining *Picardy*, a part of *Campaigne, Burgundy,* ...d the *Spanish Netherlands*: But in the time of *Ho-...ius* the Emperor, the *Goths* having over-run ...ain and *Italy*, sent their Forces to Invade the ...*rbonensian* Gauls, and having Subdued them, cal-...d their Country *Langue de Goth*, and from thence ...*anguedock*; nor did they stay here, but extended ...eir Conquests to the River *Ligeris*, now the Fa-...ous *Loire*, founding themselves a Kingdom, and ...king *Tholouse* the Regal Residence; nor was it long ...fore the *Burgundiones*, or *Burgundians*, who had ...ated themselves in a part of the Country of *Ca-...bii*, and some of the Teretories of *Brandenburg*, ...yning with the *Vandles* and *Sweths*, seized upon ...her parts of *France*, and grasped them with so ...rd a hand, that they in spight of Opposition ...nded themselves a Kingdom, called the King-...m of *Burgundy*, but afterward reduced to a Duke-...m, and now in the hands or possession of the pre-...t *French* King.

The Kingdom of *France* is Hereditary to the ...les, but not to the Females, who are disabled by ...e *Saliq*; Law, and the Heir or Eldest Son is sti... ...*Dauphin of France*; nor can the Younger Son of ... King, by the Law of *Apennages*, have any part ... the Government with the Elder: And this Mo-...rchy has been upheld ever since the Year 420, ...y the Races of Three Kings, *viz.* the *Moravinian,* ...*rolinian* and *Capitine*, in a Descent of 63 Kings; ...d here the Christian Religion is held to be first

Plant-

Planted amongſt the *Gaules* by *Martialis*, but a-
mongſt the *French*, or the latter ſetled People of
the Kingdom, by *Remigius*, much latter: as for the
Arms Royal, now boren by the Kings, they are
Three Flower de Luces *Azure*, in a Field *Or*, being a Device taken by *Charles* the Sixth.

This Kingdom is compoſed of Eſtates, and Orders
threefold, *viz.* the Clergy, the Nobility, and the
Commons; and here are uſually found 16 *Arch-Bi-*
ſhops, and 106 *Biſhops*, not accounting thoſe of *Ar-*
ras, Tournay, and *Perpignan*; 16 *Abbots* Heads of
Orders and Congregations, and about 30000 Cu-
rate-ſhips: and not accounting other Governments
there are 12 *Peers* chiefly appointed, or ancient
Peer-ſhips, beſides others of new Creation, and the
Order is that of the *Holy Ghoſt.* There are likewiſe 11 Parliaments, 8 Chambers of Accounts, 22
Publick Places of Receipt, or Generalities of the
Kings Revenues.

The Rivers of this Kingdom are principally Four,
viz. the *Rhone,* or *Roſne,* the *Loire,* the *Garonne,* and
the *Siine*; who receive into them many other Rivers, and waſh the Walls of the chief Cities and
Towns, &c. the firſt ariſing about 3 Miles from
the head of the River *Rhine,* the ſecond about the
Mountains of *Avergne,* the third from the *Pyree-*
nian Hills, and the Fourth has its Spring in *Bur-*
gundy.

The Mountains of moſt note are thoſe of *Averg-*
ne, part of the *Alps*, and the *Pyreenes,* on the latter of which Nature ſtrangely expreſſes her ſelf, for
that part of thoſe Mountains toward rich and
wealthy *France,* are altogether barren, but that towards *Spain* exceeding Fruitful, as if it had diveſted
it ſelf to cloath the one, and robbed the other.

In the Year 1614 *Lovis* the 13 convened the E-
ſtates of the Provinces under 12 Heads, or great
Governments, four of which lying towards the North,
bor-

order upon the *Seine*, and the other Rivers that augment its Stream, *viz. Picardy, Normandy*, the Iles of *France* and *Campaigne*, adjoyning towards the middle to the *Loire, Orlenoise, Britagne, Burguudy,* and *Lionoise*; and the other Four towards the South, near the *Garonne, viz. Dauphin, Guienne, Lauguedock* and *Provence*; and under the *Orlenoise* are contained *Maine, Perche* and *Beauce*: on the hither side of the *Loire, Nievernois, Anjou* and *Touraine*; and above this River beyond *Poctou, Berrey,* and *Burgundy,* hath *Bresti*, and under *Lionoise*, are comprehended *Lionois, Auvergne, Burbounois,* and *Marche*; under *Guienne* is *Bearne, Gascogne,* and *Guienne, Saintogne, Perigort, Limosin, Querci,* and *Rovergne*; and under *Languedock* is found *Cevenes*.

The chief Cities are, 1. *Paris*, situate in the Isle of *France*, anciently called *Lutetia*, by reason of the Clayeness of the Ground about it; which for Riches, Stateliness of Building, the many Magnificent Pallaces and Churches, that every where adorne it, and the Fruitfulness of the Soil about it and number of its Inhabitants, may compare with most in *Europe*. 2. *Lions,* or *Lugdunum.* 3. *Orleance.* 4. *Bullogne.* taken by *Henry* the Eighth of *England* 1544. 5. *Amiens.* 6. *St. Quintiens*, where the English Forces under the Command of the Earl of *Pembrook*, in the Quarrel of *Philip* the Second of *Spain*, overthrew the French, Anno 1557. 7. *Burdeaux.* 8. *Roane* or *Rovenyfenlis.* 10 *Rhemes.* 11. *Claremont.* 12. *Tholouse.* 13 *Calais*, which being taken by *Edward* the 3 of *England*, remained in the hands of the *English* 220 Years, and was lost in the reign of Queen *Mary*, soon after the Battle of St. *Quintines*, and the occasion, as many conjecture of hastning her end, she giving out, *That if she were opened when dead, they might find* Calais *written on her Heart*, &c. Many other Cities and Towns there are of note, whose names for brevities sake I must omit,

mit and in general proceed to say; there is no Kingdom better stored with considerable places, nor more abounding in plenty of what ever may conduce, to the Commodity and suport of Humane Life; abounding with almost all the sundry sorts of Fruits that *Europe* produces, as also store of River and Sea-Fish; a great number of Cattle, plenty of Wine, Corn, Salt, Linnen Cloth, Flax, Hemp, Wool, Saffron, Paper, and many other Products and Manufactories, very considerable; for which the Natives, *&c.* as it were command the Commodities, or ready Money of most Countries; as for the Coins those chiefly in use, are the Pistole of Gold, and the Crown of Silver.

As for the people of this Kingdom, they are great pretenders to Antiquity, deriving their Original, as to the Inhabitants of the Country from *Meseck* the sixt Son of *Japhet*, though the first Inhabitants mentioned with any credit in History, were the antient *Gauls*, a people thrifty and valiant; who under the leading of *Bellovessus*, conquered the heither part of *Italy* called *Gallia Cisalpina*, and soon after under the conduct of *Segovesus*, subdued a great part of *Germany*, nor resting there, under *Brennus* another of their Commanders; they discomfited the Roman Army and Sacked even *Rome* it self, and so passed Conquering on into *Asia*, where they fixed a Government, calling it *Gaul-Asia*, since corruptly *Gallatia*, on which the Learned *Dubartas* discants, *viz.*

The Antient Gaul *in roving every way,*
As far as Phœbus *darts his Golden Ray;*
Seiz'd Italy *the Worlds proud Mistriss sack't,*
Which rather Mars *than* Romulus *compact:*
Then Spoils Pisidia, Missia *doth Inthraul*
And midst of Asia *plants another* Gaul.

The

(7)

The present Inhabitants though somewhat fantastick, are generaly of a free and curteous Behaviour, kind to strangers, and extremely given to Complement; the Women are likewise wonderfully familiar even with Strangers especially in Speech, taking it for a great peice of breeding, not to be too Austere or Reserved.

Their Apparel for the most part is rather Gay than Costly, made of light Stuffs and slight Silks, &c. though the Country people are distinguished from others; by the Men's wearing a large pair of Breeches and a Coat to their Knees; and the Womens attireing their Heads, or rather wraping them in Linnen, and these are in a manner Drudges, or Slaves, to the Gentry, especially such as are their Land-lords, they being all of them Tenants at Will, and have their Rent raised as the Land improves, or as the Lord thinks fit; which is the occasion of their great Poverty; for although many of them hold Farms of Wine and Corn, they have scarce the happiness to taste the first, or eat any good Bread made of the latter.

In Arts and Manufactury, the *French* are very Ingenious, and in War very furious, at the first onset, but with the change of Fortune their courage soon abates; though *Cæsar* confessed that he slew 1100000. of them before he could bring them into subjection; yet by a small power of the English, they were frequently worsted; in the Reign of *Edward* the Third, and almost the whole Kingdom, after the Fortunate Battle of *Azin-court*, Conquored and brought under subjection by *Henry* the fifth, who with 15000. men, only overthrew an Army of above 100000. in which the flower of their Nobility were either Slain, or taken Prisoners: Nor is it less the Fortune, or rather misfortune in all Battles, to have the greatest storm of War fall upon their Nobility.

B. 4   The

(8)

The things worthy of Note in this Illustruous Kingdom, are the Cathedral Church of the Blessed Virgin in *Paris*, Vulgarly called *Notrodam*; supported by 120. Pillars, whereof 12. are very great, but the remainder indifferently large, and in the midst of the Church is a Chancel, accounted 71 paces in length, and 60 in bredth; and in the Circuit or Circumference, it hath 45 Chappels, and is closed with Iron Gates, and two double doors in the front, adorn'd with the Statues of 28 Kings; and on the sides are four Towers of Bell-fries of 44 Cubits in height, and a Bell so large called St. *Mary*, that 24 Men are required to Ring it out. The Seven Wonders of *Dauphin*, viz. The burnig Fountain, the Inaccessable Mountain, the Tower of *Sanevenin*, the Wine-fats of *Saffinage*, the Wine Fountain, the Manna of *Briancon*, and the Fountain of *Barberon*; which Rarities see at large in *Allard Sylva*: The Statue of *Joan* the *Peucelle*, who assisted the French against the English, and raised the Seige of *Orleance*, acting many Wonders in feats of Arms, till taken by the English and burnt for a Witch: As for the Building, in Cities and considerable Towns, it is mostly of rough Stone, Plastered and rough cast over flat roofed; and commonly 4, 5, and 6 Stories. And now to *France* I might add the new aquisitions, but more of them hereafter.

The chief Islands are *Rhee* the out-work of *Rochle*, in attempting the Relief of which the English lost many brave men in the year 1627. The strong *Bell Isle*, *Venetica San. Colosus*, *Salt*, *Nermoustier*, *Oleron Vliaras*, where our King *Richard* the Third, as Lord of the Sea, gave those Laws *Marine* so much in request, and known as the Laws of *Olerone*, *Rochle*, famous for the siege it sustained against the whole power of *France*; *Ouissant* over against the *Lizard*, and in the *Mediterranian* are the Isles of *de Eres* by *Ptolemie*, called the *Staechades*.

The

The Discription of the Kingdom of Spain, in its Provinces, &c.

Spain is acknowledged the most Western part of Europe, formerly called by the *Greeks Iberia* and *Hsperia* enviornd on every side by the Sea, except towards *France*; from which it is parted only by the *Pyreenian* Mountains: The Seas that bound it are the *Cantabrian* on the North, the *Atlantick* Ocean on the West, and the Straights of *Gibraltar*, on the South; on the East with the *Mediterranian*; the *Pyreenians* bearing only to the North East, and is formed by *Strabo*, in the shape of an Oxes Hide; containing as well *Portugal* as *Spain*, Scituated in the most Southern part of the Northern Temperate Zone; so that the longest day exceeds not 15 hours, accounted 760 miles in length, and 600 in bredth.

As for the Original of this People in Relation to their possessing the Country, Authors differ; for some will have them to be of the Progeny of *Tubal* Son of *Japhat*, as being the decendants of the *Iberij* who entred the Kingdom under *Pannus*: Others that they are derived from the *Celtæ*, a powerful, people decended from *Alchenaz*, who first peopling it, called the whole Country *Celtiberia*; but more certain it is, that the *Phœnicians* sailing from *Tyre*, planted *Collonies* here, and after them the *Rhodians*; nor did the *Carthagenians* fail in a manner to subdue it, till being worsted in the second Punick War, it became Tributary to the *Romans*, who devided it into 3 Provinces, viz. *Bætica*, *Lusitanica* and *Terraconensis*; the first of these containing the Kingdoms of *Andeluzia* and *Granata*; part of New *Castile* and *Estremadure*, Inhabited by the *Turdulie* Eastward, and by the *Celti* towards the West; *Lusitania*

ſitania contained *Portugal*, and part of Old and New *Caſtile*, and the remaining part was comprehended in *Terragon*; and again they laid it into two parts, comprehending the two firſt Provinces in one; and ſo it remained till the time of *Honorius* the Emperor, when *Gundericus* King of the *Vandels*, broke in and over-run it with a numerous Army, Anno 400; but had not well ſettled themſelves before the *Goths* Invaded, it and drove the new poſſeſſors into *Affrica*; and in the year 720. under the conduct of *Muſa* and *Tarrif*, who were invited in by *Julian*, with a great Army of Moors and Saracens entred warring upon the *Goths* and after a Battle of ſeven days became Victorious dividing the Countrey amongſt them; ſo that at laſt it fell into 12 diviſions, *viz. Leon Oviedo, Navarre, Corduba, Gallicia, Biſca, Tolledo, Murica, Caſtile, Portugal, Valentia, Catalonia* and *Aragon*; and ſo they ſtand at this day: wherefore I proceed to ſpeak of them in their order and due places.

Leon had heretofore the Name of *Auſtria*, and is a very pleaſant Country, yielding Mines of precious Mettal, ſome Gold, Red Lead, and Vermillion, though otherwiſe not very fruitful, as being ſome-what Mountainous, yet gives Title to the Eldeſt Son of *Caſtile*, notwithſtanding few Towns of note are found in it.

Navarr is a Kingdom of great Antiquity, bounded on the Eaſt, with the *Pyreenian* Mountains, on the Weſt with *Iberius*, North *Biſcay*, and South *Aragon*; being a Campaign Country, not ſubject to Woods, or Incloſures, yet abounds with Trees in the nature of Hedg-rows, conſiderably fruitful, and has for its chief Cities, *Victoria, Sangueſſij, Viana*, and *Pampelune*, Gariſoned as the chief defence of the *Spaniards*, againſt the Incurſions of the *French* in time of War, who's King, though wanting the Poſſeſſion, has the Title of that Kingdom, the Revenues whereof has been eſtimated at One hundred Thouſand Duckets.   *Corduba*

...orduba, is a very fruitful Province, accounted and ...ged, (as it is) the richest in all *Spain*, abounding in ...divant Skins, Mallago, Sherry, Oranges, Cattle, ..., Corn, great store of Fowl; and has in it di... fair Cities; as 1*st*, *Corduba* the Principal from ...ch it takes its Name. 2*d*. *Xeres*. 3*d*. *Sevil*. ... *Granada*. 5*th*. *Mallaga*. 6*th*. *Almeria*. 7*th*. ...*dalcanal*, where the rich Mines are found.

...alicia, is a Country very Mountainous, many of ...ch cannot be passed without great difficulty, and ...ers by reason of their Craggyness, held not passi-... yet in this Province are found the Cities of ...*postella*, the Seat of an Arch-Bishop, called ...*Jago*, in Honour of St. *James* the Apostle, whom ... impute to be buryed here; *Bajonna* a place ve-...leasant for its Scituation, and *Corronna*, or *Groynne*. ...s Country is held the Principal in *Spain*, for the ...d of Jennets; and here is found the Promon-...*Nerius*, formerly held to be the *Ne plus ultra*.

...isca, makes a Famous Bay into the Ocean, yet ...y times proves dangerous to Sailers; and al-...igh the Country is Mountainous, yet it has many ...sant Valleys, and is adorned with Cities, and ...ms of note, as St. *Sebastian*, *Toolosa*, *Fonterabia*, ...*a*, &c. And from the Mountains of this Coun-... the Rivers that water the greatest part of *Spain* ... their Springs, being accounted no less than One ...dred and fifty; and great store of Timber for ...ping is found in those parts, with some Iron ...es, &c.

...oledo, a part of *New Castile*, takes its name from ... principal City, scituate on the banks of *Tagus* ...*aio*, exceeding pleasant, and is ordinarily the ...dence of the Nobility, and of Merchants that ...le in these Parts; being the See of an Arch-Bi-..., who is above the rest of the Bishops of that ...dom, his Revenue being accounted Three hun-... thousand Crowns; and here the Kings of the

Goths-

Goths and *Moors* held their Courts: there are likewise found the Cities of *Calatrava* and *Talboia*, one scituate on the *Ava*, and the other on the *Tagus*.

Murica, contains the City *Murica*, the Town of *Alicant*, and *New-Carthage*, being a Country very plentiful, though thinly peopled; and hence come the *Alicant* wines and curious *Earthen Vessels*, with much fine silks: Nor did the *Romans* in their Conquest for some time reap a less benefit than Twenty five thousand drams of Silver a week, from this Country only.

Castile Old and New contain the Towns of *Soria*, *Segovia*, *Valodolid*, *Salamanca*, a University, *&c.* *Madrid* the Kings Principal Seat; *Alcala* and *Alcaltura*, most of them very pleasantly scituate, as being posited in the heart of the Kingdom of *Spain*, abounding with Corn, Fruits, and Cattle; and the latter watered with the River *Tagus* and *Ava*, which much inrich the Country. As for *Portugal* it is now a separate Kingdom, wherefore I intend to speak of it in its due place, as more proper in a work of this Nature.

The Principal Rivers appropiated to *Spain*, are the *Tagus* or *Tajo*, the *Duero* or *Duerius*, the *Guiadiana* or *Anas*, which for a good space Ingulfs it self, and runs under ground, giving the *Spaniards* Occasion to boast, that they have one of the fairest Bridges in the World, on which Ten thousand Cattle feed, and over which an Army with extended Wings may March; the other Rivers of note are *Gualdahquiver*, and the *Ebro*, called by *Strabo*, *Bætis*, and *Iberus*. As for the Mountains they are distinguished into six great Ridges, continued knit together, whereof the lesser are but parts, the chief of which are the *Pyreenians* that extend from the *Cantabrian* Ocean to the *Mediterranian* Sea.

As

As for the People of *Spain*, they are swarthy of Complexion, black-Hair, and of a good Proportion, stately in their Actions, and grave of Deportment, very serious in their Carriage, and Offices, much addicted to Religion, and very Observant and Faithful to their Prince, not prone to alter their Determination, but patient in Adversity, in War they are very Deliberate and Cautious, not much regarding Arts, but adict themselves much to Women, and are generally very much conceited of themselves; As for the Women they carry themselves very sober and discreet, and are tolerably handsome: Those that are marryed are in great Subjection to their Husbands, and extream loving; though the men are naturally Jealous. In matters of Religion, they are *Roman Catholicks*, only there are some Churches of *Toledo*, where the *Muf-Arabick* Office is used. As for the Language, it is not all the same, for in some parts, it has a mixture of *French*, in others much of the *Moorish*, and in some again the *Gothish Arabick*, but generally and vulgarly, the Old *Spanish* is used, which has much Affinity with the Latin; and as for the Civil and Imperial Laws used amongst them, they are intermixed with many Customs of the *Goths*, and the King governs his Provinces by Vice-Roys, or Ministers of State; and though this Country is not very fruitful in Corn and Cattle, yet it generally abounds in Wines, Oyls, Sugars, Rice, Silk, Liquoras, Honey, Wax, Saffron, Annifeeds, Rosin, Almonds, Oranges, Lemmons, Cakes, Soap, Anchovies, Soda, Barrilla, Shumack, Wool, Lamb-Skins, Tobacco, besides the great Treasures of Gold and Silver that comes from *America*, from whence it is conjectured since the first discovery, that above Fifteen hundred thirty six Millions of Gold has been brought into *Spain*.

As for the Buildings, they are every where more solid and durable, than stately and magnificent, unless at *Sevil*; in Relation to which, the *Spaniards* usually say, he that has not been at *Sevil*, has seen no stately Building. As for Apparrel, they affect rather Gravity than Gaudiness; and their Diet is as sparing, consisting for the most part of Herbs, made into Pottage, with minced Meats and Salads; though there is scarcely a Mechanick in any noted Town, but when he goes abroad, has his Cloak on, and his Rapier by his side, and walks in as much State as the greatest *Don* in the Kingdom.

A Description of the Kingdom of Portugal.

THIS Kingdom was in the time of the *Roman* Conquests accounted a Province of *Spain*, but since, been a Kingdom of about Five hundred years standing, bounded on the North, with the River *Minio*, and *Ava*, which parts it from *Gallicia*; on the East with the two Castles, and *Estremadure*; on the South, with *Algarve*; and on the West, with the *Atlantick* Ocean; and was anciently called *Lusitania*, deriving its present Name from *Porto*, a Haven Town, scituate in the mouth of the River *Dueras*, the usual Landing place of the *Gauls*; and thence corruptly called *Portugal*, or the *Gauls* Port; and is accounted to be in length, from North to South, about Six score Leagues, running along the Sea-Coast; and consequently, not answerable in breadth, in which it disproportions, as in some places Twenty five, some Thirty, and in others Fifty Leagues.

This

This Kingdom, especially of late years, has made its self famously known throughout the World, by its Discoveries, and Trafficks, in Navigation; so that no Trading part of the Universe, has escaped its Knowledge. As for the Provinces attributed to *Portugal*, they are principally Six, which are as many General Governments, *Inter-Dueras*, and *Minho*, *Tralos-Montes*, *Beyra*, *Estremadure*, *Aleuteio*, and the Kingdom of *Algarue*; and of these, *Inter-Dueras*, and *Minho*, are the most noted, as being exceeding Fruitful, and well Peopled, that for Eighteen Leagues in length, and Twelve in bredth, it possesses One hundred and thirty Monasteries, One Thousand four hundred and sixty Parishes, Five Thousand Fountains, or Springs of Water, Two hundred Stone-Bridges, and Six Sea Ports: The chief City in these Parts, is *Porto*, called by the *English Port à Port*, from its delightful Scituation, and the Advantage of the Commodities of the Country, there in abundance found; this place contains Four thousand Houses, and is much traded to by divers Nations; the next to this is *Braga*, famed for the many Councils held there.

Tralos Montes, is a part of this Kingdom, stored with Rich Mines, and in it is found the City of *Braganca*, the Capital of the Dukedom of that Title, besides which there are Towns of lesser note, and the Princes who are derived from this Title usually reside at *Villa-Viciosa*, being now in Possession of the Crown; and had before their coming to it, a Prerogative, beyond the Grandees of *Spain*, to sit in publick under the Royal Canopie of the *Spanish* Kings; *Beyra* another part of this Kingdom is exceeding fertile, producing store of Millet, Rye, Apples, Chestnuts, Cattle, Corn, &c. And in it is scituate the Famous City of *Coimbra*, noted for its University, and the See of a Bishop, &c. *Estremadure* abounds in Wines, Oyls, Salt, and Honey, gathered from Citron Flowers;

ers; and in it is seated *Lisbon* the Principal City of the Kingdom, upon five little rising Hills; on the Right bank of the River *Tagus*, or *Taio*, an Arch-Bishops See, the usual Residence of the Kings of *Portugal*, and a City of great Trade, having the Advantage of the Ebing and Flowing of the Sea, as being but Five Miles from it, held to contain Thirty two Parishes. Three hundred fifty Streets, Eleven thousand Houses, and One hundred sixty thousand Inhabitants; the Compas computed to be near Seven Miles accounting the Subburbs, and was once the greatest Emporium of Europe. *Santarim*, a place much in Request for the abundance of Olives, that grow about it; insomuch, that the Natives boast, but how truly, I know not, that they could make a River, as big as the *Tagus* of their Oyl: *Setuba*, an other Town in this Tract, is accommodated with one of the best Havens in the Kingdom, being no less than Thirty Miles long, and Three broad, abounding with Salt-Pits, and Wine, which bring a great Revenue into the Kings Coffers. *Alenteio*, extreamly abounds with Corn, insomuch, that it is held to be the Grainery of the Kingdom, and has in it the City of *Elvara*, the second to that of *Lisbon*, near which, the *Portuguez* won a considerable Victory against the *Spaniards* in 1663. And next this, *Elvas* claims Place, for the many Sieges it has held out against the *Spaniard*, and the plenty of Oyls the Neighbourhoods produce, *&c. Ourique* is the place, near to which was fought the Famous Battle, which occasioned the proclaiming the King of *Portugal* of the House of *Braganca*, *Portelegar*, is a Bishops See. *Algarve*, though little in extent, has the Title of a Kingdom, and was re-united to the Crown by the Marriage of *Alphonse* the Third, with *Beatrice* of *Castile*, abounding in Eggs, Almonds, Olives, Wines, Corn. Cattle, *&c.* And for the Chief Towns, they are *Tavila*, *Faro*, *Silves*, and *Lagos*.

The

The Natives of this Kingdom, are very frugal, yet [li]ve in much plenty, the Earth producing every [w]here abundance: Nor did their Navigation in for[m]er days, less conduce to their Support and Gran[de]ur; being held the first *Europeans* that publickly [tr]afficked into the remote parts of the World, to [bri]ng it to any considerable Perfection. The Peo[pl]e are generally straight Limbed, and well proporti[on]ed, very soft skinned, but somewhat inclined to [s]warthiness, by reason of the heat in those parts; [th]e Air is very healthy, and the Country for the most [pa]rt Hilly, though few of note.

The Roman Catholick Religion, is only publickl[y] professed. There are three Arch-Bishopricks, [vi]z: at *Lisbon*, *Braga*, and *Elvora*; and Ten Bisho[p]ricks. They have Parliaments as occasion requires [i]t, held at *Lisbon* and *Porto*, and Twenty seven pla[c]es have their Generalities; and the Revenues of [t]he Kingdom is held to be about Ten Millions of [L]ivers, not accounting their Collonies in the *East-Indies*: And although *Portugal* was seized on by the [K]ing of *Spain*, after the fatal Battle of *Alcazar* in [A]ffrick, and the Death of King *Henry*, who Succee[d]ed *Sabastian*, slain by the *Moors*; it revolted in the [y]ear, 1640. And is governed by a King of its own, [i]s a separate Kingdom from *Spain*, and thus much [f]or *Portugal*,

A Description of Italy, *In its Kingdoms and Dominions,* &c.

*I*Taly is a very Fruitful Country, and held for its Pleasantness to be the Mistriss of all Countries, as it once was Empress of the World, and is incompassed with the *Adriatick*, *Jonian*, and *Tyrrian* Seas: Except, towards *France* and *Germany*, from which it is parted by the *Alps*, which renders it in a manner

ner a *Penjusula*, but more peculiarly, it has on the East the lower part of the *Adriatick*, and the *Jonian* Sea, deviding it from *Greece*; on the West, it has the River *Varus*, and some part of the *Alps*, parting it from *France*; on the North, a part of the *Alps* divid's it from *Germany*, and on the other parts, the *Adriatique* Sea devides it from *Dalmatia*, being held by the Antients to be in form like an Oak-Leaf.

This Country branched out into sundry principalities and Provinces, is scituate in a most Fruitful and temperate Air, under the fifth climate of the North temperate Zone, which is totally taken up; so that the Longest day is 15 hours, and three fifth parts of an hour, Northward and Southward, not much above 14 hours, and the parts mentioned; and is reckoned in length, from *Augusta Prætoria*, now called *Aost*, unto *Otranto* the most Easternly part of *Naples* 1020 miles, and in bredth from the River *Varo*, which parts it from that Province to the Mouth of the River *Arsa* in *Friuli*; where it is the broadest 410 miles, and where the narrowest, which is about *Otranto*, exceeds not 23. so that the whole compass by Sea, reckoning windings and turnings, is held to be 3448 miles, but reckoned in a straight line upon the coast, it falls much short as not above 2550.

As for the first Inhabiters of this Country, they remaine doubtful, for as soon as Historians make any considerable mention of it, we find it Inhabited by divers Nations, held to be Greek Colonies, who transported themselves at sundry times; the people of the Sea Coast being said to come thither under *Janus*, Anno Mundi, 1925. After them *Saturn* out of *Creet*; then *Evander* or *Oenotrus* out of *Arcadia*, and then *Æneas* with his *Trojans*, with many others; but after the Romans grew powerful, they brought the whole Country into subjection, and held it in spite of the frequent Invasions of *Phyrus*

Ha-

Hanibal, the *Gauls*, *Cimbri*, and others, till the time of *Honorius* the Emperor, at what time the *Goths*, *Vandals*, *Herulies*, *Huns*, and other Barbarous Nations, passing the *Alps*, rent it from the Empire, and devided it amongst themselves establishing many Kingdoms and Principalities; and when these were in a manner subdued by the Valour and Conduct of *Narses*, *Bellarius*, and other Imperial Generals. *Albonius* King of the *Lumbards*, seized upon the greatest part of it calling it *Longobardia*, vulgarly *Lumbardy*; but they a considerable time after were brought under by *Pepin* King of *France*, called in by the Bishop of *Rome*, who reduced their Kingdom to a straight compass; after which the seat of the Roman Empire was fixed in *Germany*, and *Italy*, parcell'd out amongst sundry Princes, and the usual Division is into six parts viz. *Lumbardy*, the Land of the Church, *Napels*, *Tuscany*, *Genoa*, the Signory of *Venice*; but more particularly into five greater and six lesser; as for the first, the Kingdom of *Naples*, the *Papacy*, the Signory of *Venice*, the Dukedom of *Florence*, and the Dukedom of *Millain*, the lesser are the Dukedoms of *Mantoua*, *Urbine*, *Modena*, *Parma*, with the States of *Genoa* and *Luca*; and of these in their Order.

The Kingdom of Naples Described, &c.

AS for the Kingdom of *Naples* it is Governed at this day by a Vice-Roy, under the King of *Spain*; and is scituate in the most pleasant part of *Italy*, devided from the Territories of the Church, by the River *Axofenus*, being on the other parts Inviornd with the Seas; making many commodious Havens, and contains the Provinces of *Lavaro*, *Calabria* Inferior and Superior, *Otranto*, *Apulia*, *Puglia*, *Abruzzo*.

In.

In *Lavaro* is founded the City of *Naples*, from whence the Kingdom takes its Name, and many others of lesser note; but that which is most noted, is the Mountain *Vesuvius* lately called *Somma*, being exceeding high, and casting Flames out at the top of it, in a dreadful manner; though all the borders or parts of it are otherways very pleasant and fruitful, abounding in Vines, Flower-Gardens, Olive-Yards and rich Pastures; many of the Houses of the Gentry, and Country Villages; the City it self being seated at the foot of the Mountain, and other Hills that branch from it, extending from the South-West to the North-East, in a manner Triangular; and so Fruitful is the Country in Corn, that the Importation of Bread is forbidden upon great penalties.

As for the Buildings, they are of free Stone; many of them four Stories in height, and the Tops flat, the Windows are generally covered with fine Linnen or Tiffany in stead of Glass, which gives an equal Light and keeps out the heat of the Sun: Nor consists the City of *Naples* of any more than three considerable broad Streets, called *La Vicaria*, *La Lapuan*, and *La Toletano*; the rest being inconsiderable Lanes, and places of less note; having 8 Gates towards the Sea, and as many towards the Land; strongly walled and defended with three Castles. The Women here, are very beautiful, and through the abundance of Silks found in these parts, the meanest Citizens Wives go clad in it; the people are very thrifty and industruous, especially about their Gardens, from whence they derive a great part of their Food, in Fruits, Herbs, Roots, &c. as living very spare and temperate, though the Country abounds in plenty. The Estates of the Kingdom of *Naples*, as we may properly call them, under the *Spanish* Vice-Roy, are held to be 14 Princes, 25 Dukes, 30 Marquesses, 54 Earls, and 400 Barons

and

and Gentlemen; having 4 publick Houses, called the *Segii*, in which they meet to consult Affairs of Importance; as also places are appointed for the meeting of Merchants in the way of Trade.

Calabria is another Province of the Kingdom of *Naples*, bounded with the *Jonian* and *Tyrrenean* Seas, and with the River *Jano*, said to be 500 miles in compass, divided into the higher and lower *Calabria*: The chief Cities of the former being *Consentia* and *Salernum*, the chief resort of Italian Physitians, pleasantly scituated and well inhabited; the Buildings agreeing with those of *Naples*, though not in the General so sumptuous, and all the Neighbouring Countries are full of Villages, and very Fruitful; and in the latter *Calabria*, *Cuterzary*, is seated as principal, being a strong City well Walled, and Fortified; and formerly this Country was called *Magna Græcia*, from the many Greek Collonies that seated themselves in it.

Otranto is on three parts bound with the Sea, and on the other with *Puglia*, having *Tarentum* and *Brundusum* for its chief places; formerly boasting it self one of the best Havens in *Europe*; but for some years past choaked up, or much obstructed by shoales of Sand carry'd in by the Sea; so that a Ship cannot without some difficulty enter, by which means the places are much reduced: Here are found likewise the Towns of *Otranto* and *Gallipolis*, very plentious in Oyls, Wines, and Manufacturies of Silks, and other matters of value; there are found great store of Corn, Mellions, Citron, Saffron, &c. and what is one thing observable, no Partridges pass the Limits of this Country.

Apulia another Province of *Naples*, extends it self from the confines of *Brundusium*, to the River *Fortore*, and is properly devided into two Provinces, and has for its principal City that of *Manfredo*; Scituate beneath the Hill of St. *Angello*, accommodated

dated with many stately Buildings, and is the Seat of the Arch-Bishop of *Siponto*; and that which adds more to its advantage, is that it has a capacious Harbour, capable of receiving Ships and Galleys of great burthen, and is defended with a very strong Castle, the Country all about it being very Fruitful.

Puglia is bounded with the Rivers *Tronto* and *Fortore*, and has for its chief Cities *Barlet*, which has a good Haven belonging to it, and held to be one of the 4 strong holds of *Italy*; and *Cannæ* the Country though somewhat Hilly, or Mountainous; abounds with Cattle, Saffron, and many other Commodities incident to *Italy*.

Abruzzo is in like manner a part of the Kingdom of *Naples*, having for its chiefest Cities or Towns *Aquino*, giving Birth of *Thomas Aquinas*, and *Sulmo* Famous for the Birth of *Ovid* the Poet, both pleasantly seated and well inhabited.

The Papacy Described, &c.

AS for the Papacy, commonly called the Estate of the Pope, Inherent to the See of *Rome*; it consists of two Natures or Jurisdictions, as Spiritual and Temporal principalities, as touching the latter of which it has under its Jurisdiction many large Terretories lying between the River *Fiore* and *Cajerta*, between *Preneste* and the *Truentian* Straights, the Dukedom of *Urbin* excepted, containing the Provinces of *Romandiola*, *Murchia*, *Spolletto*, and that usually called St. *Peters* Patrimony is accounted Spiritual.

The first of these extends to the Venetian Terretories on the West, and to Rubicon on the East, a little River so called from the Redness of the Waters, over which in the flourishing time of the Romans; the Consuls were forbidden to come armed homewards, least the fear of any designed might bring

a

terror upon the City of *Rome.* As for the chief Cities in this part, they are *Bononia*, the prime University of *Italy*, and where the Civil Law is very much studyed: This City is Round of form Built with Brick and Free-stone, commodiously scituate, and has towards the Streets, Arched Cloysters to secure such as pass them from Rain, &c. Here is likewise found the City *Ferrara*, scituate on the banks of the River *Po*, and fortified on all other parts, with a strong Wall in which the former Dukes held the lately Pallace of *Beluedevere*, so named from its pleasant scituation; as also *Ravenna* of great antiquity, renowned in Antient History; accommodated about two miles distant with a famous Port or Haven. This Province or Country, produces Corn, Wine, Oyl, some Drugs, plenty of Cattle, and especially good Horses.

Marchia extendeth from *Puglia* to *Otranto* between the *Appenine* and the Sea, commodiously divided into little rising Hills, and fertile Plaines, by which means it is very Fruitful, greatly abounding with Corn, Wine, and Oyl: Its principal Empori is *Ancona*, by reason of the commodiousness of its Haven, and is a fair City incompassed with three Mountains, and hath the form of a half Moon, the Streets are narrow and paved with Flint; the Haven is Triangular, where are curious Walks, and a place called *Loggia*, where the Merchants that resort thither for Trade, do meet and is very healthy: the other considerable Cities are *Firmo*, and *Ascoli*, and in this Province stands *Loretto*, so Famous for our Ladies Miracles.

Spolletto, anciently *Umbria*, has for its chief Cities *Spolletto*, from whence it takes its name *Onietto*, scituate on a high Rock and *Asis*, where St. *Francis* was born: and though this Province is not large, yet it abounds with Wine, Corn, Oyl, Saffron, Cattle, Figs, &c.

St. *Peters* Patrimony, so called, and accounted the Spiritual Jurisdiction, contains all the ancient *Latium*, or *Campaigna di Roma*, and the chief City is *Rome*, formerly the Capital of the most considerable Empire in the World, Mistriss of the fairest part of the Universe, and said thro' the excess of her many Conquests to extend by Degrees, from 2 Miles in compass to 50, and had on her Walls 740 Towers, spreading over, or taking in her circumference 7 Mountains or Hills, viz. *Pallatinus, Capitolinus, Univalis, Aventinus, Esquilius, Cælius,* and *Querinalis*; and is scituate on the banks of the Famous River *Tiber*; though at this day it is not accounted above 1 Miles in Circuit, however containing many stately Structures and Monuments of its ancient Greatness: But what renders it most Eminent is the Popes Pallace on the *Vatican* Hill, the Famous Church Dedicated to St. *Peter*, one of the goodliest Structures in the World, accounted 520 Feet in Length, and 385 in Bredth, adorned with Paintings, Tombs, and other choice Pieces of Antiquity, almost Innumerable; the *Vatican* Library, and many Monuments of the Roman Emperors; and not far from this City is *Pont Mill*, where *Constantine* the great was shewed the Cross in the Clouds, with this Motto, viz. *In hoc vincis*, in this you shall overcome; which made him take the Insign of the Cross for his Banner; and accordingly prevailing over his Enemies he not only Imbraced the Christian Religion himself, but commanded it should be observed throughout his Empire: And indeed in *Rome* centers the Plenty and Glory of *Italy*, the Inhabitants being accounted two Hundred Thousand, most Clergy-men.

Seignorie or *Common-wealth of* Venice *Described,* &c.

[N]Orth of the *Alps* from *Roman-di-ola*, are the Italian Provinces, appertaining to the State of [Ven]ice, bounded on the South with the Territories [of F]errara, and the rest of *Roman-di-ola*; on the [We]st with the Dukedom of *Millain*; on the North [wit]h the main Body of the *Alps*; and on the East [wit]h the *Adriatick Sea*, and the River *Arsia* which, [divide]s them from *Liburnia*: besides it commands a [grea]t part of *Greece*, especially by the late success[ful] Acquisitions and Victories, as well as divers [Islan]ds in the Sea, and has all along been the Bulwark [of C]hristendom against the *Turks*.

[A]s for the chief City upon which the rest de[pend]ed, it gives a Name to the People, and is wonder[full]y situate, or seated at the bottom of the *Adri*[atic]k *Sea*, or *Gulf of Venice*, upon 72 Islands, five [mile]s distant from the main Land, defended from [the] rage of Sea and Storms by a prodigeous work; [bein]g a bank of (some say 60 other) 35 miles in [leng]th; open in 7 places for passage, with Boats and [Gal]lys, &c. of small burthen, of which they have [com]monly 1300, but for great Vessels the only pas[sage] is at *Malamacco*, and Castle *Lido*, strongly forti[fied] and yet this City is Computed no more than [8 m]iles in circuit; having for its better conveni[ency] 4000 bridges, one of which is very famous, pas[sing] over the Great Chanel; and the rest, pass wa[ters] of lesser note, which in divers places refresh [this] Maritime City.

[T]he Arsinal is the most beautiful, biggest, and best [finish]ed in *Europe*; being about 2 miles in circuit. [It] has a Magazine of all sorts of Arms, Engines and [Am]munition for Sea or Land Service, amongst which

C are

are 1000 Coats of plate Garnished with Gold, and covered with Velvet; but what is most admirable is the Church of St. *Mark*, their Titular Saint; wrought with Mosaick work, supported with Pillars of Marble and Porphery; adorn'd with Images, Tombs, &c. that for the abundance of Jewels, Pearls, Gold, and Silver, that cover and adorn them, and their Altars it may be thought that the whole Treasury of the State might be Imployed to that purpose; and besides there are found 200 Pallaces built of Marble, and adorned with Collumnes, Statues, Pictures, and other things of great Value; that for their grandure, they are capable of entertaining any Prince; They have likewise 73 rich Hospitals; 56 Tribunals, or Courts of Justice; 67 parish Churches, 26 Monasteries of Nuns 54 Convents of Friars, 18 Chappels and 6 Free-Schools; and so powerful once they were that they held War with all the Prince of *Europe*, &c *England* excepted, for the space of seven years, and wanted neither men nor money; and if we consider what Wars they have had for near 200 years (at times) with the *Turks*; we must needs proceed to wonder how they should support themselves under that expence of Treasure, and loss of men; but their Income is mostly by Navigation, and the fruitfulness of their Islands; so that according to a Modern account, it has amounted in the Treasury, (not reckoning the Effects of particular men,) to five millions and 320000 Duckets yearly: as for the City it is Governed by a Duke, and the Sennate; and so consequently all the Countries and Cities under its Jurisdiction, many of which we shall have occasion to mention hereafter, and therefore purposely omit them in this description: only by the way take notice, that the Terretories of this Signorie, are divided into Land and Sea; and in *Lombardy, Marca, Trevigiana, Friuli* and *Istri*, part of *Dalmatia, Sclavonia, Albania*, and the *Morea*;

and

nd in their Jurisdiction are the famous Cities of *Padua*, *Brescia*, *Bergamo*, *Vicenza* and others ; as or their Islands the principal are *Corfu*, *Cephalonia*, *Zant*, *Ithaca*, and others lately regained.

The Discription of the Dukedom of Florence, or Tuscany.

THis Dukedom now under the Grand-Duke of *Tuscany*, is divided from St. *Peter's* Patrimony, on the East, by the River *Pisco*, on the West by the River *Macra*, from the Common-wealth of *Genoa*; on the North from *Romaniola*, and *Marca Anconitana*, by the *Apennine* Hills; and on the South, has for its boundard the *Tyrrean* and *Tuscan* Seas.

This Country formerly had its name from the City of *Florence*, Scituate nigh the confluence of the River *Arno*, round in form and strongly fortified with a Wall, &c. and 8 Forts, whereof the greatest lyes towards the South; the buildings are very stately, erected with Free-stone and Marble, flat on the roofs, except the Pallaces which are adorned with Towers and Pinacles; the Pavements of the Streets being likewise for the most part broad Free-stone, a River running through the chief of them, which greatly cools and refreshes the City in the heat of Summer; and over it is a stately Bridge almost in the middle of the City, and towards the North East it is Encompassed with pleasant Hills, gently rising and planted with choice Fruits, and sheltered from storms by the *Apennine* Mountains that lye behind them; nor does the South side want the like advantage, whilest the West Exposes it to the Flowry Valleys of *Arno*; and without the Wall are the Garden houses and Pallaces of the Nobility and Gentry, which likewise scatter over all the pleasant

sant Fields; insomuch that it is accounted the Glory of *Italy*, frequently stiled its Garden, and takes its name from the Flowry Plains, and Gardens that inclose, or expend themselves about it. The next City of note is *Pisa*, through which the River *Arno* runs, from East to West, its Scituation being in a plain; and towards the North-west by North is a Gate, and a fair Cathederal Church, most curiously wrought and Paved with Marble; and here the Duke of *Florence* or *Tuscany* has a Pallace, seated on the bank of the River *Sienna*; another City is scituate on a rising Hill, indifferently ascending above the Valleys; the streets of which, a thing unusual, are paved with Brick, wherefore no Carts nor Coaches are allowed to pass through them, but the burthens are carry'd by men Mules and Asses; and has in it several stately Towers and Fountains, the Women of this place being likewise reckoned the fairest of all *Italy*. *Massa* is a Town most noted for the Quarries of Marble in its neighbourhood.

In this Dukedom is the famous *Legorne*, so much traded to by Merchants of most Nations in *Europe*; opening to the Sea a spacious Port or Haven, and is a Mart or Emporis for all the principal commodities of *Italy*, and many that are brought over-land out of remote Countries; and here our Merchants have frequently settled a Factory, the people being generally fair dealers, and wonderfully obliging to strangers; so that the Custom of this place is the greatest part of the Dukes Revenues, being very considerable.

As for this City it is seated in a fruitful Plain, with commodious Avenews, being somewhat long in form from North to South, and is defended with two Towers that stand inward to the Sea, for the guard of the Haven, that for great Ships lying farther into the Sea, than that for Gallies and lesser Vessels, which is sheltered by a Wall drawn almost
round

ound it; and here it is the *English* Merchants trading to *Italy* have their Lading.

The Dukedom of Milain Described, &c.

THE Dutchy of *Milaine*, is very pleasantly seated, in the Country of *Lumbardy*, amongst fruitful Plains, and little rising Hills; and held the most desirable Place of these Countrys. Its chief City is *Milain*, Anciently *Mediolanum*, which though so often ruined, as having been taken no less than Twenty times, and besiged Forty, has still rise out of its Ashes, more fair and splendid than it first, being now accounted the greatest City of *Lombardy*; seated in a large Plain, and incompassed with Rivers, strongly guarded with a spacious and well fortified Castle, and other extraordinary Fortifications. As for the Building, it is very stately and magnificent; but the most remarkable are Castles or Cittadels, the Hospital or *Lazarette*; the Cathedral or Dome: besides there are 36 Monastries, 10 Convents of Fryers of sundry Orders, 96 Parochial, and 11 Collegate Churches, most of which are beautified and adorned with Images, Paintings, Sculptures; there is moreover, a Cabinet of exceeding Rarieties, not to be paralelled, as report goes, in any place. The City in circuit is accounted Ten miles, very populous, imagined to contain 300000 Souls; the Inhabitants mostly Rich, as very much Trading in Merchandice, especially Silks, Gloves, Ribbons, &c. from whence our Millinary Ware-men derive the Denomination of their Trade; the City being much Traded to from *France*, *Spain*, and all parts of *Italy*.

As for other places of note in this Jurisdiction, they are principally *Pavia*, *Papia*, made a University by *Charles* the IV. guarded by a strong Castle, and has in it a fair Cathedral Church, supposed the richest

richest of Revenue in *Italy*, viz. 300000 Crowns per. Ann. And near this place, King *Francis* the first of *France*, was overthrown in a great Battle, and taken Prisoner by *Lanoy* the Duke of *Burbon* and others, commanding for *Charles* the V. *Alexandria* or *Aleſſandriu*, the strongest work in the whole Dutchey; *Cremona* seated on the Banks of the River *Poe*, accommodated with a good Trade, stately muildings, large Streets, and pleasant Gardens, noted for its Tower and Cathedral Church. And here it was that *Vitellus* his Souldiers were defeated by those of *Veſpatian*, and the Town fired by them.

The Lakes found here are *Lago Magiore*, in length 56 miles, and 6 in breadth, having in it 2 Islands called the *Boremeans*, fruitful and pleasant, even to a wonder, *Lago Delcoma*, and *Lugani Lacus*, and the Rivers are *Olgio Adde Lambro, Teſine*, &c. As for the Hills they are of no remark.

The Ancient Inhabitants of this Country were the *Inſubres*, Conquered by the *Romans*, then by the *Gauls*, and next by the *Lombards*, but now the Country is under the protection of the King of *Spain*, who appoints a Governour to reside in *Millain*, where St. *Ambroſe* once was Bishop.

The Dutchy of Modena deſcribed.

THIS Part, or Province of *Italy*, contains the City of *Modena*, and *Reggio*. with the adjoyning Territories: As for the Capital City of *Modena* it was known, and is so still in Roman History, by the Name of *Mutina*, famous for the first bloody battle between *Marcus Antonius*, and *Auguſtus Cæſar* and is at this day the Residence of the Duke, whose Pallace, though not appearing very large outwardly is nevertheleſs very Famous and Magnificent, by the rich Adornments within; his Cabin or Muſeum being

ing furnished with the choice of Natural Rarities, as Jewels, &c. to an extraordinary Value: And here *Otho* the Emperor slew himself, upon his Army being defeated by *Vitellus*.

As for the Country, though it is not large, it nevertheless is very fruitful, and abounds with great store of curious Fruits, Corn, Cattle, and other things fit mans for Subsistance, watered with many small Streams, and mostly plain, but that which renders it more Famous, is its being the Native Country of our present Queen *Mary*, Consort to his Most Sacred Majesty, King *James* the Second.

The People of this Dukedom are said to be better natur'd than most of *Italy*; quick in their Resolution, easie to be pacified when wronged, and Friendly in their Entertainment of Strangers.

A Description of the Dukedom or Principality of Parma.

THIS Country hath on the North *Mantua*, on the South the *Appennine Hills*, on the West *Milan*, and on the East the Country of *Modena*. The chief City is *Parma*, seated on the River *Pirma*, in a Fruitful Plain, being about 4 miles in compass; adorned with many Rich and Stately Structures, well Peopled, and much frequented by Gentry, greatly Addicted to Learning, Arts and Arms; the adjoyning Plains produce excellent Pasturage, which feed abundance of Sheep, of whose Milk is made the *Parmasan* Cheese, so much in esteem in all Countries; and here the Duke's Pallace is seated, where he holds a Court in great State: as for the Churches they are beautified, and rarely imbellished with Pictures and Images.

Piacenza or *Placentia* is the second City, famous for the Resistance it made against *Hannibal*, and h's

Bro-

Brother *Asdrubal*, upon their cutting their way through the *Alps*, and Invading *Italy*; and now as much esteeemed for the Fairs and Marts kept here, to which the Merchants and others resort from the Neighbouring Country to make their Exchanges: The Principal River is *Trebia*, where the *Romans* in a Fatal Battle were overthrown by the *Carthagenians*, and 40000 of them computed to be slain; and near to *Placentia* are many Salt-pits and Mines of Iron.

A description of the Dukedom of Mantoua.

THE Dukedom of *Mantoua* is a very fair Country, very plentiful in Corn, Wine, Cattle, and rich Pastures, and Fruits of sundry Kinds: As for the chief City that gives it the Name, it is Seated in a Lake of 20 Miles compass, by Nature very strong and fencible, there being no Land access to it but by Cause-ways, and in it stands the Dukes Pallace, very fair and stately, though he has another Pallace for Pleasure and Delight exceeding this, at *Marmirolla*, five Miles from this City; As for *Mantoua* it is in a manner round, save that the Lake on the North-East sides, enters it like a half Moon: The Buildings are partly of Brick, and partly of Free Stone, and the Streets large and clean: In the midst is a large Market-place, where all manner of Strangers are admitted to vend their Ware, though the greatest Traffick is in the hands of the *Jews*, who grow Rich by the Impoverishment of the Citizens, and is in compass 4 Miles, having 8 Gates, and strengthened by a good Wall. This City is of antient standing, and contains about 50000 People, and has often been brought into Distress by the *Germans*, especially in the Year 1619. and 1630. As for the Dukes Revenue, it is counted

400000 Crowns *per Annum*, though many will
be credit it, seeing some few Years since, he made
over part of his Dutchy to the *French* King, for a
considerable Sum of Money; and here it is held
unlawful to wear a Sword, or any other Weapon
without Licence; and in this City the Famous *Vir-*
gil had his Birth, as by his *Ecclogus* appears, &c.
And to this Dukedom partly appertains the Dukedom
of *Montferrat*, in the South-East of *Piemont*, and other
Territories.

The Dukedom of Urbin described.

THE Dukedom of *Urbin* may be said to lie
within the Territories of the Church,
bounded on the North with the *Adriatick*,
the South with the Apennine Hills, on the West
with *Romagna*, or *Roma-di-ola*, and on the East with
Marca Aconitania, being in length Sixty, and in
breadth Thirty five Miles, and is accounted to contain Two hundred Castles, and Seven Principal
Towns, the chief is *Urbin* seated at the bottom of
the *Apennine* Hills, and built in the fashion of a Mi-
tre. The next to it *Pisauro*, containing an excellent Haven, for the Reception of considerable Vessels; and a Third is *Belforto*, more inward, and supposed to be in the middle of the Country: The
chief of the Castles are, the Rocks of St. *Leo*, and
Trivolo; and at *Urbin*, *Polidorus Virgil* was born,
who being a Collector of *Peter* Pence in *England* for
the Pope, wrote a History of the many remarkable Transactions of our Country, and is quoted by
most of our modern Historians

The Eſtate or Common Wealth of Genoa Deſcribed.

THE Eſtate of *Genoa*, formerly contained a large part of *Italy*, and were accounted the moſt expert in Navigation of all Europe, but of late, through the many Wars they have maintained againſt the *Venetians*, and other neighbouring Princes, their own Inteſtine Broils, and their neglect of Navigation and Traffick, they are greatly reduced, holding little more than *Liguria* and *Corſica*: The firſt of theſe has on the Eaſt the River *Varus*, on the Weſt parted from *Tuſcany* by the *Magura*, on the North the *Apennine* Hills, and on the South the *Ligurian* or *Tyrrenian* Seas. As for the City of *Genoa*, it is ſeated on the ſides of ſmall riſing Hills, tho' behind it are thoſe of greater height, lying open on the South ſide to the Sea, where it has a goodly Haven, in the form of a Creſant or half Moon, upon the Horn whereof, towards the Eaſt, is the Sea Bank *Lamola*, about 600 paces in length, keeping off the Waves that beat upon the City on the Eaſt ſide; and in the middle of this Bank is a Fort built to defend the Navy that may Anchor there, ſo that the circuit of this City is accounted Eight miles, and though the Streets are narrow, yet the Palaces of the *Dey*, and Houſes of the Senators, are very ſtately; nor are their Walls leſs ſtrengthned with Bull-warks, and other Fortifications. The Houſes in the High-ſtreets are Four Stories, and many Five, the Windows being Glazed, which is not uſual in *Italy*, many of them built of Marble, but all of Freeſtone: The Streets paved with Flint, and the Suburbs full of Gardens and Houſes of the Nobility and Gentry. As for the People, they are Maſters of other Cities, as *Noli,*
Sar-

Sarazena, and *Savon,* being noble minded and generous in all their Actions, formerly much inclined to War and search of Adventures; insomuch that they assisted, with a great Fleet in the Holy War, and taking of *Jerusalem* by the Christian Army, and aided *Phillip* the French King with 10000 Men, against *Edward* the Third of *England,* where in one Battle they were most of them slain. They Aided likewise the *Spaniards* in 1588 to Invade *England,* with several great Carracts and Galleys; which were either lost upon the Coast, or cast away in their Flight homeward, which loss they have never since fully recovered; yet they lately made a stout Defence against the Naval Power of *France,* which could effect no more, than beating down some part of their City, by Bombing it at a distance, as being well assured they had no Fleet capable of Engaging.

The Country abounds in all the Plenties of *Italy,* and here only the Women have the greatest Freedom, without the Jelosie or Suspition of their Husbands of any *Italians*; and as a further Honour to this place, it gave Birth to *Christopher Columbus,* the first Discoverer of the New World or Country of *America.*

The State of Lucca Described.

THe State of *Lucca* is held to be scituate within the Dukedom of *Tuscany* or *Florence,* comprehending the Town and Terretory of *Lucca.*

As for *Lucca,* it is seated in a fruitful Plain, strongly fortified with a good Wall, and incompassed with pleasant Trees, so that at a distance it seems to stand in a Wood, and the Plain wherein it is seated, is invironed with Mountains or large Hills, except towards *Pistola,* where it opens to the Sea, and is three miles in compass; as for the Streets, they

they are narrow and paved with broad Freestone, and in it are many Palaces, and Merchants Houses, curiously built of Free-stone, according to other Building in *Italy*, and was formerly a place of great Trade for Silks, Stuffs, Carpets, Cloth of Gold, and the like; there being a great concourse of Merchants, call'd *Luccois* Merchants, that were wont to meet there at several Fairs or Marts, held for that purpose, but of late the Trade is declined: however the Inhabitants inrich themselves by their Manufacture, which they send to other places of greater Trade. And here there is a strict Law, that no Person shall wear any Weapon, no not a Knife, unless it be blunted; the People being generally very courteous to Strangers. And thus much for what may be properly call'd *Italy*, which taken in general, is one of the most fruitful and pleasant Countrys of the World, of which *Europe* being call'd the Head, this is accounted the Face. But for brevity sake I must desist any further Comment, and proceed to other parts adjoyning.

The Dukedom of Lorrain *Described.*

THIS Country is Invironed with a part of *Belgium*, *Alsatia*, the Country of *Burgundy* and *Campaign*, and is about 180 Miles in compass, exceeding Fruitful in Corn, Wine, store of Cattle, but especially Horses of an Excellent Breed; the Rivers and Lakes abounding with Fish, and the Soil with rich Mines: The chief Town is *Nancy*, seated upon the River *Meuse*, and in it the Ducal Pallace, much resorted to for Wines, Brandies, and other Commodities; the Buildings are very stately and commodious, most of them of Stone, and well fortified with a Wall of great Strength: The next to this are St. *Nicholas*, and

Vancolem very strong and well Garisoned by the *French* into whose hands the Country fell, in the Reign of King *Lewis* the 13. though the present Duke of *Lorain* now warring in *Hungary*, is on all hands concluded to be the rightful Prince. As for the manners and Customs of the people they are a mixture of *Germany* and *France*, as being seated between those Countries, &c.

The Dukedom of Savoy, *and Country of* Peimont *Described,* &c.

AS for *Savoy*, it is a very Mountainous Country bounded by the *Dauphenet*, *Bress*, *Switzerland*, *Peimont* and the *Alps*; the Antient Inhabitants were the *Allobroges*, who submitted to *Hanibal*, when he entered *Italy* with his *Carthagenians* to War against the *Romans*; at what time *Bruncius* and his Brother being at variance about the Succession to the Kingdom, he reconciled them; afterward it was made a *Roman* Province, and was called from one of the Kings that then Reigned being a Favorite to *Augustus Cæsar*, *Alpes Cottia*; but in the declining of the *Roman* Empire, it became a part of the Kingdom of *Burgundy*, and passed with other rights of the Empire to *Germany*; but now is independent under a Duke, who is soveraign Lord of the Country.

The Chief Towns of *Savoy* are *Chambiers*, Scituate in a pleasant Valley amongst Mountains, and is graced with a Ducal Pallace and many stately buildings of the Nobles, who are for the most part very Gentile, Active and Airy, though the Country people on the contrary are very Imbicil and Slugish. *Tarantaise*, an Arch-Episcopal See, Scituate amongst Mountains as the former, full of pleasant building:

ings: *Aquabelle, Mauridune* another Arch-Episcopal See.

Under the power and Jurisdiction of the *Savonian* Duke, it is *Peimont* unless a small part of it claimed by the Duke of *Mantoua*, seated at the Foot of the Mountains, and bounded on the East with *Milain*, on the West with *Savoy*, on the North with *Switzer-land*, and on the South with the *Mediterranean*; being more fertile than the other; containing 52 Earldoms, and 15 Marquesats, besides Barronies and Lordships; and here dwell the progeny of the *Albigenses*, who about the year 1100 stood, for the Liberty and Doctrine of the Church of their Predecessors and about the year 1250, were near all destroyed and ruined by the Popes and *French* Kings; when the remainder prefering their Concience before their Country, retired up into the Mountains, and by their Industry and Indefatigable Husbandry, made the very Rocks bring forth Grass and Herbage for themselves and their Cattle, *&c.* and here they worshiped God, according to the Worship of the reformed Churches; greatly increasing in number, as being followed with blessings, untill the latter end of the Reign of *Francis* the first, at what time happened the Massacre of *Merinianum*, or *Mariguan Gallis* and *Chabriers*, and in the year 1662 and 1663, they were again persecuted by the *Savoiard*, and since that in the year 1684 we had a Mellancholy account of their treatment: and although there are many good Towns under the Government of *Savoy*; yet the Duke chiefly resides at the City *Turin* Scituate on the River *Po* and is the seat of an Arch-Bishop and a University, where *Erasmus* took his degree, and for Scituation is accounted one of the plesantest in *Europe*.

The

The Seignory of Geneva, and the Alps Described.

GENEVA is within the Limits of the Dukedom of *Savoy*, the whole Seignory not exceeding Eight Leagues in compass, Scituate on the Lake *Lemanus*, and devided into two parts by the River *Rosne*. The City strongly walled and fortified, as being the head of a Free state; containing a flourishing University, Governed by a Common Council, or 200 of the chief Burghers, four of which are called. Sindiques: As for the Church Government it is composed of Lay-men, Elders, and Ministers founded by *John Calvin* 1541. and although this City has been beseiged by the Duke of *Savoy*, and others who have undertaken to reduce it, yet it has manfully defended it self against all Invasions; and as for the revenue it is reckoned 60000 Crowns *per annum*. The building is generally of Free-stone, and the North side of the City lies close to the South side of the Lake, where is a little Haven for Gallies, built to keep free passage on the Lake, defended by a strong Fort; a River Issuing from the Lake runs through the lower part of the City, and is passed by two commodious Bridges. And although it is a Receptacle for all manner of Religions, and people that fly from Persecution, yet such is the Law, that even a Malefactor is Condemned there for a Crime committed in his own Country, if proved against him, and Adultry punishable with death; Fornication the first time with 9 days fasting or living with Bread and Water in Prison; the second time with Whipping, and the third with banishment; notwithstanding which and although the Women be more reserved here than in any

any other place, thofe Affairs go forward in private.

This Signory abounds with all manner of Fruits, great ftore of Fifh; and is much Traded to efpecially by the *Italian* Merchants for Velvets, Taffatas, Mufquet Barrels, and Calevers, &c.

The *Alps* are the greateft Ridge of Mountains in *Europe*, parting *Germany*, *France*, and *Italy*, and in fome places require five days to afcend them. There being five paffages through them into *Italy*, viz, 3 out of *France* and 2 out of *Germany*. The 1 from *France* is through *Provence*, clofe upon the *Tyrrenian* Seas, through *Liguria*, being the Eafieft; the 2 through the Hill *Geneara*, into the Marquefat of *Zaluzzes*, and fo into *Lumbardy* : The third is over the Mount *Cenis*, and through the Country of *Turin*. As for thofe out of *Germany*, the firft is through the Country of the *Griffons*, by the Province of *Valtoline*; the laft through the County of *Tirol*, near to the Towns of *Jufpurk* and *Trent*; and as for thefe Mountains, they are in many parts very fruitful; divers Villages and Towns, being Scituate on them, though moftly barren, and in many places the Snow and Froft continues all the year, without the Suns having power to diffolve it, by reafon the affent is fo near the cold Region; and through part of them *Hanibal* cut, diffolving, or loofening the Rocks with Fire and Vinegar, when he broke unexpectedly into *Italy* and defeated the *Roman* Army; and indeed in fome places they are dreadfull even to look on.

The

The Description of the County of Rousillon and Catalonia.

Rousillon by the French Included between the branches of the Pyreenean Mountains, if we begin at Mount Cavo, the one extending to Colibre and C. de Creux a Promontary, that is the furthest point East of Cattalonia; as for the other it passes into Salsas, and as for the places of note, they are Perpignan, Papirianum, and Perpinianum built out of the ruins of Ruscinum, by Guinard Earl of Roussillon, situate upon the banks of the River Thelis or Thes, in a pleasant fruitful plain, &c. A rich and flourishing Emporie, and a strong hold against the French, till the year 1644; and of such esteem was this little Country in former times, that it was pawned by John King of Aragon in 1462, to Lewis the 11th. of France for 300000 Crowns, and restored to Ferdinand the Catholick, by Charles the Eight, that he might not be diverted from the Conquest of Naples, and abounds with plenty, &c.

Catalonia, or as the French call it, Castalogne, joyns to the Country of Roussillon, is accounted 170 Italian Miles in length, and in breadth 130, and held to contain the Dukedom of Cardona, 3 Marquesates, 11 Earldoms, divers Barronies and Lordships, and 45 Cities or walled Towns, and 600000 Inhabitants; amongst which (in the time of Boteru) were 10000 French Shepherds and Husbandmen. As for the Country, some Authors inform us, that it is generally Hilly, and full of Woods, yielding but small store of Corn, Wine, and Fruits; though others speak more favourably of it, and affirm, it affords plenty of Corn, Wine, and Oyl, though indeed it is mostly inriched by its Maritime situation.

The

The chief Town is *Bracelonia* seated upon the *Mediterranian* Sea, between the Rivers *Besons* and *Rubricat* or *Lobrecat*, and is a rich noted Port much Traded to: The buildings are very stately, and contain a Bishops See; an Academy, and sundry other advantages of Gardens and pleasant places that render it delightful and well Inhabited.

A Description of Belgium, or the Neitherland Provinces, &c.

THE Tract now called *Belgium* or the *Neitherlands*, is bounded on the East with *Westphalia*, *Gulick*, *Cleve*, *Triers*, and the Provinces of the higher *Germany*, on the West with the main Ocean, which divides it from *Brittain*, &c. on the North with the River *Ems*, which parts it from East *Friezland*, and on the South with *Picardy* and *Campaign*, two *French* Provinces, and upon the South-East with the Dukedom of *Lorain*; and as for the Country in its present Estate, it is divided into 17 Provinces, viz. The Dukedoms of *Limburg*, *Luxenburg*, *Gelderland*, *Brabant*, the Marquisate of the Holy Empire, the Earldoms of *Flanders*, *Artois*, *Hainault*, *Namurre*, *Zutphan*, *Holland*, *Zealand*. the Barronies of West *Friezland*, *Utrecht*, *Overyssel*, *Machlyn*, and *Groyning*, or *Groningen*, and of these in their Order.

Limburg.

THE Dukedom of *Limburg* is pleasantly scituate, and a very fruitful Province; having the Famous City of *Mastreich*, so lately renowned for its Sieges, as its Capitol, though the

the Bishoprick of *Leige* is its appendent, in which is the City of *Leige*, the Bishop Regents usual Residence, the See at present vacant by the Death of the late Bishop, and hath under it 52 Barronies, and in it a University, where at one time (if the Story may be credited) Studied 9 Sons of Kings, the Sons of 24 Dukes, and 29 Earls; it being commodiously and healthfully scituate on the River *Meuse*; the Buildings very fair and spacious, and is accommodated with divers Monasteries and Abbies, the whole Bishoprick containing 24 walled Towns, and 1800 Villages; as also the Eastern part, properly termed a part of the Dutchy of *Limburg*, contains 5 walled Towns, and 22 Villages, where *Limburg* (that gives the Province Name) is pleasantly scituate on the River *Wesa* or *Wesel*, or *Wesar*; and from this Fertile Country, abounding with whatever is necessary for the Support of Humane Life, is found that Stone so much used in publick, called *Lapis Calaminaris*.

Luxemburg.

Luxemburg is another Province of the *Low Countries*, having *Limburg* for its boundard on the North, *Lorain* on the South, the Bishoprick of *Triers* on the East, and the River *Meuse* on the West, and is accounted in circumference 240 Miles, containing 23 walled Towns, and 1169 Villages of the former, of which *Luxemburg* scituate on the River *Asnaius*, *Danvillees* and *Bostonake* are chief: The upper part of this Dukedom is generally Inhabited by *Germans*, but the *French* possess most of the lower part, and indeed they speak either Languages in most of the Villages, and in manners participate of both Nations; and bordering

ing upon this Dukedom is the Famous Forreſt of *Ardena*, formerly accounted the greateſt in *Europe*, as being 500 Miles in compaſs, confiſting moſtly of Cheſt-nut Trees, but now burnt, and otherways deſtroyed to the circumference of 90 Miles, and near it are found the *Spaw Baths*, ſo much frequented by divers Nations for the reſtoring them to Health, by removing ſundry Malladies and Diſeaſes; and in this Region are held to be 7 Earldoms, and many other petty Governments. The Soil is naturally Fruitful and Pleaſant by Scituation.

Brabant.

BRabant has for its boundard on the South-Eaſt and North, the River *Meuſe*, on the Weſt the *Schald*, or the *Sclade*; in length it is accounted 70 Miles, and in breadth 60, containing 26 walled Towns, and 700 Villages; the principal of the former being *Lovaine*, a City 6 miles in compaſs, incloſing beſide the ſtately Building, pleaſant Hills, Valleys, Meadows, Fragrant Gardens, and is a noted Univerſity, conſiſting of 20 ſtately Colledges. The next of note is *Bruxelles*, or *Bruſſels*, the uſual ſeat of the Governor, for the King of *Spain*, pleaſantly ſeated and Inviorned with Gardens and little riſeing Hills; and near it is the City of *Bergeaupzone*, a garriſoned place, ſtrongly fortified; and here is found likewiſe, the Town of *Breda*, ſurpriſed by the Prince of *Orange*, and taken from the *Spaniards* by a ſmall number of Gentlemen, who came upon it in the night time, in a Boat covered with Turfs, and deſperately ſetting upon the Garriſon poſſeſſed themſelves of it; and yet more famous for the Treaty between his Late Majeſty of *England*, and his Subjects, whereupon enſued his happy Reſtauration; and in this Province is contained the Marqueſate

of

of the Empire, whose chief Town or City is *Antwerp*, 7 Miles in compass, once a famous Empori, or the Scale of ...ope, by reason of its Scituation on the River ——— having two Marts yearly, and for the more safe Resort of Strangers, qualified with extraordinary Priviledges, and here the *Portugals* exposed their *East India* Goods to Sale, and dispersed them through *Europe*, but of late the *Hollanders* growing powerful at Sea, and great Traffickers, have removed the Scale for the most part to *Amsterdam*.

Flanders.

THIS Province which amongst the vulgar passes current for the 10, is divided into *Galicam, Imperialem,* and *Tutonicam,* the latter being separated from the two first by the River *Ley,* where is found the City of *Gaunt,* the Birth Place of *John* Duke of *Lancaster,* Son to *Edward* the Third of *England,* from thence called *John* of *Gaunt*; ·d is so large within the Walls, that there is large tures, and Corn Fields, besides many Gardens, nd other pleasant places, and is Commodiously seated upon the River *Schald,* which devides it in many parts; so that for the conveniency of the Inhabitants there are 98 Bridges: The next to this are *Bru-is* and *Ypres,* walled and well fortified, and within the Jurisdiction of the Province, are the famous Sea Ports, or Frontier Towns of *Dunkirk,* taken from the *Spainards* by the Valour of the *English,* and since delivered to the *French*: *Scluse,* which has a spacious Haven, capable of containing 500 Sail of Ships; and to these we must add *Newport* and *Ostend.*

Imperial Flanders, so called for Distinctions sake, is levided from *Brabant,* by the River *Dender,* and in t are found the Towns of *Alost* and *Dendermond,* scituate very pleasantly upon the Banks of that River

with

with *Hulst*, a confiderable Town, indifferently fortified, the Country is generaly fruitful, and the people very thrifty and sparing, &c.

Gallicam, or *Gallica Flanders*, taking its Denomination from its dependency on the *French*, or the nearness to that Country, has for its chief Town, *Lifle* or *Lile*, a Town of great Trade, and much Refort, where fundry Merchants have Ware-Houfes, and fome petty Factories; the next to it in Dignity is *Doway*, much noted for its Univerfity, and the great Refort of moft Chriftian Nations thither to fee the curious Library, and other Rarities; and here likewife ftands *Tornay*, taken from the *French* by King *Henry* the Eighth of *England*, and ranfomed by the Inhabitants at 100000 Ducats, there are moreover 32 walled Towns of lefler note, and 1178 Villages, within the Jurifdiction of this Province, adorned with ftately buildings, and pleafant Gardens, replenifhed with Fountains, and pleafant Streams; and is in all parts very Fruitful, as lying low, and not any where incumbred with Mountains, from which indeed the Provinces are generally free, &c.

Artois is a very pleafant Province, and was once intirely *French*; but now (as the reft I have mentioned) under the Government of the King of *Spain*, quitted by *Henry* the Second of *France*, to *Philip* the Second of *Spain*, in the League of *Chambray*; and is faid to contain 854 Villages, and 12 Towns of note; the chief being *Arras*, from whence our Cloath of *Arras* comes, and *Lilliers*. The Principal Frontier Towns that oppofes *Piccardie* are *Hedinfort*, *Ayre*, *Pernes*, and St. *Omers*, moft of them very ftrong and fencible.

Hainault is confiderably fpacious, as being Sixty Miles in length, and Fourty Eight in breadth, in which are computed 950 Villages, and 24 confiderable Towns, as *Monts* Famous for the overthrow of the *French* Army, under the command of the Duke of of *Luxembnrg*, by the *Dutch* and *Germans*, under the command of the Prince of *Orange*, &c. routed near this Town 1676. *Valenciens* very commodiously seated, so that it cannot be besieged but by a considerable Army, divided into three parts: *Conde* and *Bavais*, Towns of considerable strength, the latter supposed to be built upon the ruins of the antient *Belgium*, the Province in general is very pleasant and fruitful.

Namurre is very commodiously scituate, and yields the Inhabitants great Advantages from the Iron Mines, and Marble Quars; as also those of Free Stone, and what is indeed a wonder in nature, *viz.* The Stone Cole which is extinguished by Oyl, but burns the brighter for having Water cast upon it; and here are found the City *Namurre*, giving name to the Province as also *Charlemont*, *Valen-court*, or *Bornies*, with about 182 Villages, accommodated with rich Pastures, pleasant Gardens, with store of Fruits and Cattle.

Machlyn, though it is reckoned to be scituate within the circuit of the Province of *Brabant*; yet has in it 19 Villages, with several Castles and Places of strength, as its dependences being a strong Town, seated in the midst of the Waters of the River *Dole*, so that upon drawing up the Sluces, the Country about it may be drowned; and was of such esteem before the Wars with *Spain*, that it was the seat of a Parliament; but now is somewhat impaired by a fire that happened some years since, by the blowing up of a Magazine of 800 Barrils of Gun-powder. These are those properly called the *Spanish* Provinces and *Netherlands*, which were formerly free Estates, and most of them Independent, governed by their proper Princes and Magistrates; but under a claim of right by Title, and the more prevailing Power of the Sword, wearied by War, they were reduced by the *Spanish* Kings part, of whose Dominions they are at

this

this day accounted: However, the 7 confederated Eftates, commonly called the United Provinces, *viz.* Zealand, Holland, Utretch, Guelderland, Zutphen, Groningen, Over-Yssel, and some part of *Brabant*, and *Flanders*, have yet those Priviledges the former enjoyed, making for their better defence against the Incroachments of their powerful Neighbours, a strict League and Union in the year 1581. which has ever since inviolably continued, called now the Estates of the *Low-Countries*.

A Defcription, particularly of the Low-Countries.

Zealand or *Sealand*, is a Country standing upon 7 Islands Northward in the Sea, commodiously scituate for Shipping, and Harbours, so that it may in a manner be questioned, whether the Inhabitants live on the Water or on the Land, and though it consists of 7 Islands only at present, it formerly was 15 whereof 8 have been swallowed up by the Waves, with their Towns and Cities, so that we may well alude.

Invenies sub Aquis, & ad-huc auftendere nauta, Inclinata solent, cum manibus opida verfis, &c.

The Waters hide them, and the Sailers show,
The Ruined Walls, and Steeples as they Row.

The chief Towns of this Province, are *Middleburg*, Famous for Traffick, and the Staple for *French* and *Spanish* Wines; *Flushing*, a strong and fortified Sea Town. All the Islands are fertile, much abounding with Pastures, Corn, and plenty of Cattle, yielding a great deal of *Madder*, for dying, Wooll, &c.

Hol-

HOLLAND, (the chief of the Provinces, under the Denomination of which the rest are vulgarly called, and is the most powerful in Shipping, and Navigation,) comprehends the Famous City of *Amsterdam*, by which the River *Tay* flows like a large Sea, and is one of the chief Empories of *Europe*, *Rotterdam*, *Leyden* an University, *Doort*, *Delph*, *Harlem*, and other places of note, as the *Hague*, &c. the which, though but an Inland Village, is much honoured by the Concourse, resorting thither, and the frequent assembling of the Estates; and this, more than any other part, abounds with Woods, esteemed though but small, to contian 400 Villages, and 20 walled Towns in its Jurisdiction.

UTRECHT, another of these Provinces has five considerable Towns in it, of which *Utrecht*, *Mont-fort*, and *Rhenen*, are the principal; as also 70 Villages, many of them very fair and pleasant, all well watered, and accommodated with Gardens, Pasturages, and other things necessary for the use of Man; the Province was anciently called *Antonia*, but since took its Name from a Ferry that was kept there, for the Transportation of Passengers, &c.

OVER-YSSEL, another of the Provinces, is memorable for the City of *Daventree*, won by *Robert* Earl of *Leicester*, an English Peer, in the time of Queen *Elizabeth*, from the Spaniard, a delivered to the States, and has besides 11 good Towns of which *Campene*, *Swall*, and *Daventree* are the chief 101 Villages, and abounds with good Pastures, Meddows, Corn and Cattle, producing yearly an extraordinary quantity of *Butter* and *Cheese*, and the rather Fruitful, as being well watered by the River *Yssel*, from which it appears to take its name.

ZUTPHEN, though it claims the Jurisdiction of a Province, yet it is no more than a Town in *Guelderland*, free, and independent, before which (to the great Grief of all good Men) the Famous and Learned Sir *Philip Sidney*, received the Mortal wound

wound of which he dyed, though the Town was notwithstanding won by his Conduct and Valour, being a very antient Earldom.

GUELDERLAND is a Dukedom of considerable note, abounding with Plenty of all sorts of Provisions, and many curious Manufactures, and is held to contain 24 Towns, and 300 Villages. The chief of the Towns being *Nimegen*, seated on a branch of the River *Rhine*, and much noted for the Treaty held there, *Ruremond* and *Arnheim*, and is recounted in Historians to take its name from *Geluba*, once a famous Town Scituate in the Province, but now altogether ruined or reduced to a strait compass.

GROINING or GRONINGEN, is a Barrony of West *Friezland*, so large that under its Jurisdiction it has 154 Towns and Villages, the principal being *Old Haven* and *Keikerk*, and boasts of great Plenty and much Riches.

FRIEZLAND contains 11 chief Towns, the most considerable being *Harlingem*, *Lewarden*, and *Zwichen*, with about 345 Villages, Incompassed with Excellent Pasture grounds, abounding in Herds of Cattle, of a more then ordinary bigness, and is in a manner, every where refresh'd with pleasant Streams; and not far from it is the Island of *Scelinck*, on the Coast whereof the Fishing trade is continually maintained; and there are found Dog-Fish in abundance.

The Air in these, and the other Provinces, is at this day very temperate; so that, although the Winters last long, yet are they not excessive; and as for the Summer it is gentle and mild, resembling the Spring, in the more Southern Countries; as for the People they are generally corpulent, well proportioned, and great Artists, being quick of Invention, and very curious Artificers. The Women are for the most part tolerably handsome and constant House-wifes much in subjection to their Husbands and very careful in the management of such Affairs as they understand: They are (both Men and Women) frequently great drinkers; nor do they come behind hand, especially those of the 7 Provinces last mentioned, in eating; and as for their Warfare they are better Soldiers, and more fortunate by Sea then Land, for indeed Navigation is in a manner their greatest business; many of those, we properly call the *Dutch*, being born on Shipboard, and there brought up; their Parents having no Land, Houses or Tenements, but live on board for the most part, and are seldom in Lodgings which is all they take care for, rejecting any settlement; and thus much in brief for the 17 Provinces, or Lower *Germany*, from whence I proceed to the Higher, &c.

Germany, *properly so call'd, Described in its Province and Principalities.*

GERMANY, in which at this day the *Roman* Empire has its Establishment, is bounded on the East with *Prussia*, *Poland* and *Hungary*, on the West with *Belgium* and *France*, on the North with *Denmark*, and the Main Sea called the *German Ocean*, and on the South with the *Alps*, and is Scituate in the Northern Temperate Zone, under the 7 and 11 Climates having 17 hours and a half in the longest day Northward, and 14 and a half Southward; the compass of this spacious Country, being accounted 2600 *English* miles, held to be effectually the largest in *Europe*, and in most Parts is exceeding Fruitful, the Air wholsom; and consequently the Natives (were they more temperate) would be exceeding healthful; however the Inhabitants for honesty of conversation and firmness to their Governors, are much to be applauded

plauded; Valiant they are, and very deliberate in their Actions; the Women are corpulent and tolerably handsome great breeders, and very fruitful; though for the Vulgar sort they are generally poor, notwithstanding they are curious in invention, and performance of Arts; and the World is beholding (if we may rightly so term it) to this Nation for the Invention of Printing and Gun-powder.

GERMANY is exceeding fertile, many parts of it abounding with Corn, Wine, Cattle, Minerals, as Tin, Copper, Silver, and some Gold, Quicksilver, Linnen Cloath, Allom, and many other valuable Commodities, and is properly divided into the upper and lower *Germany*. The first of these more bordering upon the *Alps*, may be reckoned to contain *Austria, Bavaria, Suevia, Helvetia, Switzer land* and *Alsatia*; and of these in their order, &c.

The Upper Germany Described.

AUSTRIA, a Hereditary Province of the Empire, or Arch-Dukedom of the House of *Austria*, Antiently *Pannonia* Superiour, is accounted the most fertile of the Provinces, in Corn, Wine, Fish, Cattle, &c. And has for its Metropolis, the famous City of *Vienna*, called by the *Dutch Wien*; more noted for the great overthrow, the *Turks* received before it, in the year 1683. after it had sustained a Siege of near 3 months; and is commodiously Scituate upon the dividing of the River *Danube*, antiently called *Ister*, adorned with a great number of stately Buildings, and has not only frequently baffled the *Ottoman* power, by putting a stop to their further incroachment into Christendom, but is usually the *Imperial* Residence, being strongly defended with a Wall, and several Towers: and under the Jurisdiction of this Arch-Dukedom are

the

the Provinces of *Styria*, or *Steir-Mark*, *Carinthia*, *Tyrolis* and *Carniola*. The first Scituate on the Spurs of the *Alps*, yet confiderably fruitful, and has for its chief Towns *Gretis*, *Hall* and *Marpurg*, with many pleafant Villages. The fecond is confiderably large, as containing many good Towns and Villages: Thofe of note being *Spital*, *Veit*, and *Vellach*, with good Paftures, and fruitful Plantations of Gardens, Orchards, &c.

The Third borders, or is rather Scituate on a part of the *Alps*, very montainous, and but indifferently Fruitful, yeilding more in Mines then in other Commodities; yet contains the noted Towns of *Infpurch*, *Tyrol* and *Trent*, fo much known by the Council that was held there, in the year 1546. Seated on the banks of the River *Odefis*: The Country is in a manner fquare; as being 72 Miles, without any confiderable difference, every way.

The Fourth is larger than any of the former as being 150 miles in length, and 45 in breadth, Invironed with *Sclavonia* on the Eaft, *Italy* on the Weft, *Iftria* on the South, and *Carinthia* on the North; a Country, it is very fruitful, and has in it many good Towns the principal being *Efling* and *New Marcht*; Scituate on the Banks of the River *Save*.

BAVARIA is a large Country, and has for it's Boundards *Styria* and *Auftria* on the Eaft, *Leike* on the Weft, the *Danube* and part of *Franconia* on the North, and *Carinthia* together with *Tyrol* on the South; and has for its principal City *Munich*, upon the River *Affer*, being the Dukes principal Seat; *Ingolftadt* on the *Danube*, comprehending an Univerfity *Ratisbon*, *Paflaw*, *Donow*, *Saltzburg*, and others; and is watered with the Rivers *Danube* and *Saltzech* as principal ftreams, and with Rivers of leffer note; and fo opulent is it, that Travellers affirm.

firm 34 Cities and 46 confiderable Walled Towns, are found within its circumference, and is fruitful in every thing except Wine, with which it is fupplyed out of other Parts.

SUEVIA called by the *Dutch Schwaben*, is bounded Eaftward on *Bavaria*, Weftward on the *Danube*, Northward on *Franconia*, and Southward on *Tyrol* and *Retia*, or the Country of *Griffens*; and has for its Principal Towns *Ulm* or *Elmus*, *Lindair*, a free City Seated in a *Peninfula*, made by the Lake *Acronius*, *Aufpurg*, *Rauenfpurg*, *Wherlingen* and *Norlingen*; moft built with Free-ftone, with Houfes of an extraordinary height, as four and five Stories, and many ftately Pallaces, Churches, *&c.* The Country is generally well peopled and with thofe of a good Complexion, tall and well fet; the women Ruddy and Fair, and the Plains abound with rich Paftures, Cattle and Corn; for Hills there are none of confiderable note; and the principal River that paffes through it, is the *Danube*, receiving other Rivers into its ftream; and although *Aufpurg* is accounted a City of this Province; yet in it felf and dependencies, it is a Marquizat.

HELVETIA, now more vulgarly known by the name of *Switzerland*, is a very Mountainous Country, as being pofited amongft the *Alps*, for the moft part, or fpurs of that mountain, accounted the higheft habitable Region in *Europe*, bounded on the Eaft with *Tyrol*, on the North with *Lorain*, on the Weft with *France*, and on the South with *Italy*; and is at this day cantoned or divided into 13 Divifions or Jurifdictions, under a United Confederacy and League, the better to oppofe the Invafion of any powerful Neighbours; and thefe have for their Capitals confiderable diftinct Cities and Countries, from which they hold their Regulation; as *Zurich, Berne, Lucerne, Glaris, Prenij, Zugh, Friburg, Bafil, Schaffhanfen, Apenfel, Soloturn, Vandenew* and *Swits*; befides sides in the Confederacy is comprehended, the City and Marquesat of *Baden*, and although they are divided in Matters of Religion, 5 being of the Reformed Church, and the rest Roman-Catholicks, yet that makes no Separation in the common Interest, but against any opposer, they mutually joyn their Forces.

As for the length of these Countries thus United, it is accounted 240 miles and the breadth 180 miles, and from these Mountains Issue the Famous Rivers *Po*, and *Rhone* or *Rosne*, with others of lesser note, which pass through many Famous Kingdoms and Provinces; and indeed the Plains that are found amongst the Mountainous places, are exceeding Fruitful, and produce many Cattle, and the men are accounted the best Soldiers in *Europe*; and for as much as their Country is poor, they much addict themselves to the Sword; serving for pay any Prince that will entertain them; whereby it appears, that no less than one Million of them have fallen in sundry Battles within One hundred years past.

ALSATIA is bounded on the East with the *Rhine*, on the West with *Lorain*, on the North with the *Palatinate*, and on the South *Helvetia*; having for its Metropolis the famous City of *Strasburg*, on the *Rhine*; lately taken, or surprized by the *French*, who undertook the Quarrel of the Bishop that layed claim to that Dignity; though indeed it has been held a free City: As for the Building, it is very stately, mostly of Free-stone, and contains several fair Churches, Senate-Houses and Stores; the Streets, though not very wide, are in most parts refreshed by the Streams of Water that pass through them, and all the Country about it abounds with fruitful Fields, Vineyards, Cattle, Gardens, and every thing that may be termed pleasant and delightful, and has in the circuit a considerable number of

D. 4   Towns

Towns and Villages, and was reckoned, as is said, amongst the free Imperial Cities.

To these in this division of the Empire, we may add *Rhetia*, or the Country of the *Grisons*, bounded on the West with *Switzerland*, on the East with *Tyrol* on the South with *Milain*, and on the North with *Suevia*, lying half in *Italy* and half in *Germany*; so that the People for the most part are Familiar with either Language, and is a Region well peopleed and pleasantly Scituate, only somewhat Mountainous. The chief Towns are *Coyra*, not far from the *Rhine*, *Musocco* and *Bormia*; and in these parts the Reformed and *Romish* Religion are indifferently Practiced; and thus much of the upper or higher *Germany*.

The Lower Germany Described, in its Provinces, Free-Towns, &c.

THAT which we properly term the lower *Germany*, may be conveniently divided into *Franconia*, and the appendant Territories, the three Electorates of the *Palatinate*, *Brandenburgh* and *Saxony*; with its dependencies, *Pomerania*, *Medenburgh*, *Brunswick*, *Luneburg*, *Hassia*, *East Friezland*, *Westphalia*, *Cleveland*, *Wetteraw* or *Vetravia*, &c. and of these in their order.

FRANCONIA, supposed by some to be the first Seat of the *Franks* or *French*, has for its boundards, on the East *Saxony* and *Bohemia*, on the West *Elsas*, on the North *Hassia*, and on the South *Bavaria*; and contains many fair Cities within its circle or circumference, as *Bamber*, *Weirtzburg*, and *Metz* or *Mentz*, the Seat of a Bishop, and moreover has in it the Pallace of the chief Electoral Bishop; and as for the City, it is commodiously seated upon pleasant riseing Hills, incompassed with a Valley and spacious Pleins

Plains, yielding great abundance of Corn, Fruits and Pastures; being Antiently the Seat of a King, called the King of *Mentz*: And in the Province are the free Cities of *Noremburg, Rotenburgh*, and *Francfort*, at the latter of which the Electors of the Empire meet, as occasion serves, for the Election of the Emperor; all three pleasantly Seated, either by the nature of the Soil, or the industry of the Inhabitants, well fortified and of great concourse; there being two of the most noted Fairs in *Europe*, held twice a year, and in one of it's streets on the East side, the *Jews* are permitted to Trade and Inhabit.

The Kingdom of *Bohemia*, is an Antient and Famous Kingdom; containing the Dukedom of *Silesia*, the Marquesates of *Lusatia* and *Moravia*; accounted in circuit 550 *English* Miles, being cast in a manner round or circular, Walled with Mountains or large Hills, and was once held to contain 78 Cities, Castles and Walled Towns, and 32000 Villages and stately Buildings of the Nobility.

As for the Soil of this Kingdom, it is generally Fruitful producing great increase of Corn and Wine, and in many parts there are Mines of Iron, Lead, Tin, Copper, Gold, Silver, and some Quicksilver: As for the Natives, they are of a chearful Countenance, modest behaviour, and strong of Body; the Women very fair and comly, tall of personage and broad Shouldered. As for the King of *Bohemia*, which now rests in the house of *Austria*, he is one of the Electors of the Emperor, and has precedency in the casting voice; and is great Cup-bearer on the Coronation day.

The chief Cities of this Kingdom are *Prague*, seated on the River *Mulda*, consisting of three parts, by reason of the division the River makes, though joined by Bridges, and has in it many stately Buildings of Free-stone, though in the generality, the

D 5 Houses

Houses are Timber built, and the Walls of Clay or Loam; *Egra*, a place very commodious, and much traded to, watered with a pleasant Stream, and accommodated with curious Gardens and Orchards, *Budweis* and others.

SILESIA is a Part or Province of the Kingdom of *Bohemia*, extending in length 240 Miles, and in breadth 80 Miles, divided almost in equal parts by the River *Oder*, into which many lesser Rivers discharge themselves, and so well water the Country, that it is exceeding fruitful almost every where, though the Air is much colder than with us at all times, and what the Soil wants, the Inhabitants by their industry make out; and in it is scituate the famous City of *Breslaw*, or *Preslaw*, accounted for stately Building, and Commodiousness, one of the chief Cities belonging to the Emperor. There are moreover the Cities of *Jadendorf*, and *Glogaw*, with a great number of pleasant Villages.

LUSATIA, or *Lusutia*, is divided into the Higher and Lower Countries, and though but small, yet exceeding Populous, so that Historians affirm, that this little Province has sent 20000 Armed Men into the Field, and is in most parts Fruitful, as being watered by the River *Nise* or *Nisso*, and other Streams, and has as chief Cities *Trabel* and *Groliz*, with many walled Towns, and a great number of Villages, though several have been destroyed, by the Incursions of the *Turks* and *Tartars*, and the Intestine Wars.

Moravia is a very pleasant Country, affording store of Wine, Corn, and curious Fruits, with some Myrrh, and Frankincense, the Shrubs and Trees growing naturally wild, as well as in Gardens by Improvement; the Country being very Wooddy and Mountainous, and is a Marquisate of the Empire, the chief Towns being *Almutz*, an University, and *Brinne*, the Seat of the Marquess; the Country receiving its name (as most conjecture) from the River *Moravia* that
runs

runs through it; and although the Territories are not large, the People are nevertheless divided in Language, between the *Teutonick*, *Bohemian*, and *Sclavonian*.

The Electorate of the *Palatinate*, or the Country under that Denomination, contains the Upper and Lower *Palatinates*, and extends for the most part along the *Rhine* 96, and is in breadth 72 Miles, said to be the fruitfullest of all others, affording abundance of *Rhenish* Wines, pressed from the Grapes that grow in great plenty on the Banks of that famous River, from whence the Wine takes its Name; and in any vacancy of the Empire, the Prince Elector of these *Palatinates* has a far larger Jurisdiction, which terminates not till the Coronation of the Emperor, where he takes his place as *Arch-Sewer*, and in the Upper of these *Palatinates* is scituate, the City of *Newburg*, *Amburg*, and *Castel*; and in the Lower *Heidelburg*, the Seat of the *Palsgrave* of the *Rhine*, incompassed with high Hills, on the North-East, and South *Frankendale*, *Openheim* and *Crutznach*; and on the East-side of this Country are *Lauden*, and *Winheim*, and on the West *Weifers* and *Newstadt*.

The Electorate of *Saxony* has for its Eastern boundard *Lusatia*, for its Western *Hassia*, for its Northen *Brunswick*, and on the South *Bohemia* and *Franconia*; and contains the Countries commonly called *Turingia*, *Misnia*, *Voitland*, and the proper *Saxony*; as for the first of these, it comprehends the Principalities of *Mansfieldt* and *Anhalt*, the Prince of it being a *Lantgrave*; and although the Country exceeds not 12 *German* Miles, either way, yet the Soil is exceeding Fruitful, and so abounds that its Fruitfulness supplies other Places of greater extent; and being divided into 12 Counties, is held to contain 44 Cities, walled Towns, and strong Castles; and about 2000 Villages, and great Houses of Noble Men; as for the Duke of *Saxonies* chief Seat it is *Ersdorf*, though there are

are other famous Places within his Jurisdiction, as *Dresden*, seated on the River *Albis*, in a pleasant Plain, passing between two Mountains: *Leipzich*, a Famous University, especially for the study of Physick, and Philosophy; built mostly with free-stone, and pleasantly invironed with Corn-Fields: *Wintenburg*, the place where *Faustus* studied *Necromancy*, with many others; and this by some is held to be the Country that gave Birth to those *Saxons* that invaded *England*, and brought it under Subjection.

The Electorate of *Brandenburg* (though no more properly held than a Marquisate, notwithstanding the Elector is stiled a Duke.) is a very spacious Country, bounded on the East with *Saxony*; on the West with *Poland*, on the South with *Lusatia*, and on the North with *Pomerania*; accounted 500 Miles in Circumference, containing fifty considerable Cities, and 64 walled Towns, besides a great number of Villages: This Elector being held the most potent of the Empire, as it has been evident by his contending with the *Sweeds*, *Danes*, and others.

The chief Cities are *Brandenburg*, curiously scituate, and adorned with many stately Buildings, and rare pieces of Antiquity: *Berlin*, the place of usual Residence, and where the Duke has a Magnificent Pallace, seated on the River *Spree*: *Oderam* and *Havelburg*, the See or Seat of a Bishop, though the Reformed Religion is that which is maintained and supported by the Prince: And this Marquisate is divided into the New and Old, Water'd by the *Oder* and *Albis*, and the Elector is great Chamberlain of the Empire, all the Country being exceeding Fruitful, and naturally bringing forth abundance of Corn, Pasturages, and some Wines.

POMERANIA is on the East bounded by the River *Vistula*, on the North with the *Baltique* Ocean, on the West with *Medenburg*, and on the South with *Brandenburg*; and here is found the famous *Stetin*, which

which with a very small Garrison, held a Siege of 3 Months, against the whole Power of the Elector of *Brandenburg*: *Wolgast*, *Gripswald*, *Wallin*, and *New-trepen*, with many other places of strength, commodiously seated on the banks of Rivers, or the Sea-Coast; and although this Province is not large, it nevertheless yields great store of Corn, Cattle, &c. and lies very advantageous for Sea Traffick, and to it appertain the Islands of *Volinia*, *Wisedonian*, and *Rugia*.

MEDENBURG is scituate on the West part of *Pomerania*, and is the more Fruitful of the two, as having many Populous Cities and Towns within its Jurisdiction, the chief being *Steremberg*, from whence the Late Governour of *Vienna* derives his Title, *Malchaw*, *Wosmar* and *Rostock*, the latter of these a University, and is watered with pleasant Streams, &c.

LUNBURG, and *Brunswick*, have for their Northern boundard *Denmark*, for their Southern *Saxony*, and *Hassia*, and East and West *Brandenburg*, and *West-Phalen*, being properly two Dukedoms, pleasantly scituate; as for the chief Cities, they are *Brunswick*, a free City of the Empire; from this place the true Mum is brought over, and is a strong fortified Garrison, no ways in Subjection to the Emperor; *Halbertstadt*, or *Herbertstadt*, a Bishops See; *Wolf-bitten*, the Residence of the Duke, where he has a stately Pallace: And *Lunburg* the Seat of the *Lunburg* Duke, a very pleasant City, commodiously seated for Trade and Pleasure: The Country about it producing store of Fruits, and Corn, and the Pastures breeding up a great number of Cattle.

HASSIA, is governed by a *Lant-Grave*, and lies East-ward of *Saxony*, South-ward of *Franconia*, West-ward, and North-ward of *West-Phalen*, being a Mountaineous Country, though in many Parts, there are fertile Plains, which yield great store of Corn, and Fruits: nor do the Mountains that rise by degrees fail

fail, especially about the skirts of them, to bring forth considerable encrease, and as for this Country, at present it is divided into two Families, the one of *Cassel*, and the other of *Darmstat*, being of the Younger House: As for the chief places that appertain to the *Lantgraves*, they are *Cassel*, or *Castel*, on the River *Fuld*, *Marpurg* on the River *Lohn*; an University founded Anno 1426, by *Lewis* Bishop of *Munster*, and near it is a stately and well fortified Castle, seated on a Hill, high and steep, so that it is accounted impregnable, if well defended; and is the chief Place of Residence in time of War, or Danger, giving a prospect of the whole Country. *Darmstadt*, is another chief Town, guarded by a strong Castle, and is the Inheritance or Seat of the Younger House of the *Lantgraves*; and part of this Country belongs to the Abbey of *Fulda*, accounted one of the greatest Revenues in *Europe*; and was founded by St. Boniface an *English*-man, insomuch, that the Abbot is accounted a Prince of the Empire; and takes Place, as Chancellor to the Empress, stiling himself Primate of *Gallia*.

EAST FRIESLAND, has on the West, the River *Ems*; on the North, the Ocean; on the West, the *Weser*; and on the South, *West-Phalia*; and though it is a Country of no large extent, yet it is in many parts very Fruitful; and is divided by the River *Ems* only, from the Provinces of the *United Netherlands*; and has *Embden*, the utmost Borders of the Empire for its chief City, pleasantly scituate, and contains many stately buildings, though in general they are built of Brick; and the next to this is *Oldenburg*, considerable for its Trade, and is of it self an Earldom.

WEST-PHALIA, has for its boundaries on the East, *Brunswick*; on the North, the Ocean; on the South, *Hassia*; on the West, *Belgium*; being a Country full of Woods and Forrests, which yields them

them notwithstanding great Commodities, by reason of the abundance of Wild Hogs found therein; said to take their beginning from one Farrow, which a Sow, straying from a Farm-House, cast in these Woods; and of the Legs of these Hogs, taken in great numbers, are our *West-Phalia Hams* so much in Esteem. &c. And although this Country is properly *West-Phalia*; yet the Northern part, changes its name to that of *Bremen*; and is governed by a Bishop, who is Lord of this Tract; notwithstanding, the Duke of *Saxony* claims a part, and other parts are held to belong to the Bishopricks of *Cullen*, *Munster*, and *Triers*: The chief Cities are *Asdrop*, *Clappenburg*, and *Exenburg*.

As for the chief Towns under the Bishop of *Munster*, they are *Munster*, scituate on the bank of the River *Ems*, *Warendrop*, and others, and have a pleasant Country, all about their Neighbourhood, very Fertile, and abounding with store of Corn and Cattle, plain for the most part, there being few or no considerable Hills in this Tract.

CULLEN, or the Bishoprick of *Collen*, though not large, is nevertheless a very Fruitful Country, and greatly to be desired, whose Arch-Bishop is Chancellor of *Italy*, and held to be the second chief Elector of the Empire; and has in his Jurisdiction, besides the City of *Cullen* as chief, those of *Lintz*, *Ernance*, and *Bonna*, much noted for the Arch-Bishops Pallace, held to be one of the most stately in the Empire.

TRIERS is a Bishoprick of note, and contains many fair Cities and Towns, as *Triers*, from whence it takes its name, *Coblents*, *Boport*, and *Engirs*, in chief; and is pleasantly watered with the *Moselle*, which renders the Country in its passage, very Fruitful, the Bishop whereof is accounted the third Spiritual Elector of the Empire.

CLEAVE,

CLEVELAND, is accounted a Dutchy, and borders upon *Gelderland*, a small Country, yet as the rest in this Tract of Land, by reason of its commodious Scituation, very Fruitful, containing the Regiments or Territories of *Guliak*, *Cleve*, and *Berge*: As for the Dutchy of *Gulick*, it contains the City of *Akan* in chief, and some other Towns of note, with sundry pleasant Villages, and claims the honour of the Emperors Presence, soon after his Election, as taking here a Silver Crown, and performing some other customary Ceremonies.

As for the chief Cities of the Dutchy of *Cleveland*, they are *Cleve*, *Wesel*, *Emmerick*, *Calkar*, and others, with their Villages and Dependancies; and those of the Dutchy of *Berge*, or *Mont*, are *Mursourg*, *Dusledorp*, *Huttingen*, very commodiously scituate, and the whole Country watered with pleasant Streams, so that the Soyl yields naturally an extraordinary increase to the Husbandmen.

VETERAVIA is another Country of this Tract, accounted a Province of the Empire, lying to the South-West of *Hassia*, somewhat larger than those lately mentioned, as comprehending the Countrys of *Nassaw*, *Hannaw*, and *Friburg* a Free City; as for *Nassaw* it contains many considerable Towns, and is Famous for the Princes of that House, who in defence of the *Netherlands*, so long opposed the Power of *Spain*; and from which House, the Illustrious Prince of *Orange* is descended; this Country yields abundance of Corn, and many Vines, yet producing no great store of Wine; and in them, besides the Towns I have mentioned, are found the Towns of *Dellinbourg*, *Windeck*, *Hebron*, and *Catzenelbogen*, which latter has been accounted an Earldom.

As for the Nobility of *Germany*, the Title descends to all the Sons, which makes them numerous, though the Younger Houses want for the most part

Estates

Estates to support them; and thus much briefly of the Empire, and its dependencies.

Sweedland *Described, in its Countryes and Provinces,* &c.

SWEEDEN, or *Sweedland*, is a Famous Northern Country, renowned for its many great Enterprizes, and Undertakings; and is bounded on the West with the *Dofrin* Hills, dividing it from *Norway*; and on the North with the Frozen Ocean; on the South with *Denmark*, *Leifland*, and the *Baltick* Sea, taking, as many hold, its Name from *Sueci*, *Suetheans*, or *Suethedie*; and is in length from *Stockholm* to the Borders of *Lapland* 1000 *Italian* Miles, and about 600 in breadth, reaching in a manner, from the first Parallel of the Twelfth Clime, where the Pole is elevated 38 Degrees, and 26 Minutes, as far as to the 71 degrees of Latitude, by which account, the longest day in the Southern point, exceeds not 18 Hours, though in the extreamest Northern parts, they have scarcely any Night for Two Months; and this Kingdom, though posited in an extream cold Region, is notwithstanding kept so warm by the Mists that arise from the Islands, that much of the Rigor other Countries in the same Latitude suffer is abated, and is a Monarchy, one of the Antientest in the Northern Parts of the World (if their report be true who boast the immediate Succession, from above 100 Kings; and that the first amongst them was the Son of *Japhet*, one of the Sons of *Noah*.)

As for the Kings of *Sweedland*, they stile themselves Kings of *Sweeds*, *Vandals*, *Goths*; great Princes of *Finland*, Dukes of *Estonia* and *Carolia*; Lords of *Ingria*, and bear three Royal Crowns for their Arms; and the present King of this Country is
Charles

Charles the 11. of the Family of the *Palatine* of *Deuxponts*; as for the Soil (by the industry of the people) it is render'd exceeding fertile, and the Air very healthful; unless in places where the *Moorish* damps arise from *Fenns*, by the neglect of not opening the Water course; so that the Inhabitants generally live to an extream old Age: And as for the Country it abounds with Corn, Cattle, Fruits and Minerals as Silver, Copper, Lead: There are found considerable quantities of Furs, and other Commodities, and is divided into, or distinguished by the Provinces of *Lapland, Gothland, Finland*, and *Sweeden*.

LAPLAND or LAPPIA is the most Northern Part of *Scandia*, and is divided into the Eastern and Western parts: The first containing *Biarmia* and *Corolia*, which properly appertains to *Russia*, or the Jurisdiction of the Czars of *Muscovy*, and the latter comprehending *Lappia* and *Serisinia*, under the Government of the King of *Sweeden*; and the people in many parts, especially the most extream are Heathen Idolaters, or such as pay Adoration to Creatures; especially such as they first see in the Morning, and are held to deal in Magick and Witchcraft, and to sell Winds to Saylors that Navigate those Seas; however they are miserably poor, as living in the most barren part of the Country, and pay their acknowledgement or Tribute only in Furs of Foxes, Martins &c. which tolerably abound in those parts; and they dwell for the most part in Cotts, where they are by reason of their Temperance very Healthful; some of them living to 140 years.

Next to the before mentioned Division is *Finland*, between the *Finland* Bay and the *Baltick* Ocean of considerable Extent, and is full of pleasant Pastures, yielding very much Corn and Fruits, and is properly a Dutchy which some of the *Sweedish difh* Kings were wont to affign, for the fecurity of their Brothers Portions; and has for its chief Cities *Albo*; a Bifhops See, *Viburg* or *Viborch*, a Fortrefs of confiderable Strength; *Narve*, *Rangia* and *Caftle-Helm*, and near a place called *Razeburg*; in this Country is a Province in which the *Needle-touch* by a Load-ftone keeps continually turning.

GOTHLAND held to be the Birth-place of the antient *Goths*, is accounted one of the moft fertil Provinces appertaining to this Monarchy, participating both of Ifland and Continent; as being divided into both the Iflands, lying in the *Baltick* Sea, being the biggeft in thefe parts, containing five or fix commodious Ports; and on fome of the Rocks appear yet divers Infcriptions (by way of Monuments) in the Antient *Gothifh* Characters, one Ifle being 18 miles in length, and 5 in breadth; and as for what is of this Province, on the main Land, it is pofited in the hithermoft part of *Scandia* bordering on *Denmark*, where is Seated the noted City of *Norkoping*, commodioufly on the Sea, the place from when abundance of Copper is brought: *Lodwvifa* a place much traded to, *Colmar*, fortified with a very ftrong Caftle, *Waldburg* and others, and is in all parts very fruitful; fo that it is called by many of the *Sweeds Goodland*, inftead of *Gothland*.

SWEDLAND properly fo called, though contributing its name in general to the reft of the Provinces is fertil in many parts; but it holds not throughout by reafon of the many Rocks and barren Hills, and the chief City is *Stockholm*, or *Holmia*, defended with a Caftle Royal on a Sea Port, at the Mouth of the Lake *Meler*, which fome of the Sweedifh Kings defigned to cut into the *Werner*, or *Lake*, thereby to have joyned the *Baltick* and the *Ocean*, fruftrating thereby the Paffage of the *Sound*, but it proved a Work of fo much Difficulty,

that

that it was laid aside; and this Lake is held to receive Twenty Four Rivers, and disburthens it self with such noise and fury, that it is by some called *Devils Mouth*: But as for the Kings Ships, and Vessels of great Burthen, they generally lye at *Elsenore*, defended by a strong Castle, and so shelter'd from the Wind, that they may lye without Anchors. *Upsal* contains the Metropolitan Church, where the Kings are usually Crowned, and formerly held their Court; and is a University of this Kingdom, and the most remarkable *Mart*; *Carlstat* upon the *Wenner*, abounds with Brass and Copper: *Strongnes* is a Bishops See.

There are yet two other Provinces, or Divisions of this Kingdom; viz. *Livonia*, by the *Germans* called *Liefland* and *Ingria*, vulgarly *Ingermanland*; the first deliver'd by the *Poles* upon treaty, and the last taken from the *Muscovites*, and are both of them indifferently fruitful, and have in them many considerable Villages and some Towns of note.

The Commodities of these Countries, in general are Copper, Brass, Lead, Ox-hides, Tallow, Furs, Goat-skins, Elks-skins, the Skins of Deer; Honey, Allom, Corn; and in many places there are Silver Mines, but of no considerable advantage. The men are Active, Naturally strong, indifferent good Seamen, and resolute Soldiers; Industrious, Ingenious, and very courteous to strangers; and had the Christian Faith first planted amongst them, by *Ausgarius* Arch-Bishop of *Bremen*; and in matters of Judicature, or deciding Controversies, each respective Territory has its Viscount, every Province its Lans-men, or Consul, and every Town it's Lay-man or Consul; and there lyeth an Appeal from the Consul to the Laymen, and from the Lay-men to the Viscount, and from him to the King, in whose only power it is absolutely to determine the matter. As for the Women they are generally
well

well featured, proper in person, very modest and courteous, loving to their Husbands, and affable to strangers.

A Description of Denmark, in its Countries, Provinces, &c.

DENMARK, *Quasi*, *Danes-Mark*, comprehending it's intire Circuit or Territories, is bounded on the East with the *Baltick* Sea, and a part of *Sweedland*, on the West with the Main Ocean on the North East, with another part of *Sweedland*, full North with the Frozen Ocean, and on the South with *Germany*; lying partly on the North temperate Zone, and partly within the Artick Circle; extending from the middle Parallel of the tenth Clime, or 55 degrees of Latitude, where it joyneth to *Germany*, and 71 where the Frozen Ocean bounds it; the longest day in the most Southern parts, being 17 hours and a quarter; but for 2 Months and 3 Weeks they have no Night at all in the extream North, and is commonly distinguished in these parts, comprehending the Appendances.

The Dukedom of *Holstein*, containing *Wagerland*, *Dithmarsh*, *Stormaria* and *Holstein*. The Kingdom of *Denmark* containing the two *Juitlands*, and the *Hemodes* or *Baltick* Islands, and the Kingdom of *Norway* (now in subjection to the *Danes*) with the Islands in the North Sea, &c. that properly belong to it; and of these in their order.

The *Cimbrick Chersonese*, in which the two *Juitlands*, and the Dukedom of *Holstein* are contained, is in length 120 miles, and in breadth 80, and accounted to have within that Tract of Land; being in a manner a *Peninsula*, 20 Royal Castles and Pallaces; 28 Cities of note; 4 Bishop Sees, and a
con-

considerable number of Villages; in many places very Fruitful, and affording sundry curious Havens; and on the South East is *Wagerland*, and has for its chief Towns *Hamburg* on the *Elbe*. *Lubeck* seated on the confluence of the *Trave* and *Billew*, near the fall of that River into the *Baltick* Sea; much traded to by sundry Merchants, where they find great store of the Commodities of those Countries which are accounted the most fertile.

Dithmarsh spreads the West side of the *Chersonesus*, Scituate between the River *Albis* and *Endera*, giving Title to the Eldest Son of the King of *Denmark*, and has *Meldrop* and *Marnes* for its principal Towns; and although by reason of the many Marishes and Moorish grounds, the soil in many places is not commodious for Tillage, yet nevertheless it feeds great store of Cattle.

STORMARIA or *STORMARSH* lying between the River *Elbe*, and the Rivers *Billew* and *Store*, and has for its chief Towns *Crampe* on the Bank of a little River of the same name, falling into the *Store*, and is well fortified and reckoned one of the Keys of the Kingdom; nor less noted for the great resistance it made against *Walestein* the Imperial General; who's powerful Army it resisted 13 Months, and at last brought him to good terms of Composition. *Tychenburgh* on the Banks of the River *Elbe*; *Bredenburg*, *Jetzebo*, *Gulickstadt* and others.

South *Juitland*, or the Dukedom of *Sleswick*, is that part of the *Chersonesus* that lyes next to *Holstein*; having for its chief Towns, *Fleusburg* on the *Baltick* shoar Scituate amongst high Mountains: *Sleswick* on the River *Slea*; from which the Dukedom of *Sleswick* has its name, *Goterp* and *Londen* a Haven Town upon the Banks of the River *Ender*.

North *Juitland* is the most Northern part of the *Chersonesus* and has for it's chief Towns *Halne*, *Rin-*

copen,

copen, Arhaufen and *Nicopen*; the foil very Fruitful, and much abounding with Wheat, Barly, Rice; ſtore of Cattle, producing Butter and Cheeſe in great abundance; and able Horſes for War, or any other ſervice, here are alſo found Rich Furs.

As for thoſe that are called the *Baltick* Iſlands, properly belonging to the King of *Denmark* though they are 35 in number diſperſed in the *Baltick* Sea, many of them are Inconſiderable, and ſome not Inhabited; the chief are *Zeland, Fionia,* or *Funen; Arſen* or *Aria, Langland, Laland, Falſter, Mone, Heuen* or *Wern,* Iſland and *Bornholme*; of which only the firſt is very conſiderable, as having in it 13 Cities, the chief of which is *Copenhagen* the Reſidence of the *Daniſh* Kings; where the Regal Pallace, though not very ſtately, is ſeated; and is a City of conſiderable Trade, though the Buildings are generally mean, as Erected of Loam and Timber; there is a Market conſtantly kept, and is the only Univerſity within the Government; it is defended with a ſtrong Wall and a Caſtle, and thither are brought all ſorts of Commodities the Kingdom affords.

SCANDIA that part which appertains to *Denmark*, is in the South of a *Peninſula,* divided into three Provinces; as *Scandia, Hallandia,* and *Bleſcida*; the firſt of theſe is 72 Miles in length and 48 in breadth, reckoned the moſt fruitful and pleaſant of all the Countries lying about it, as being on three parts bounded by Sea, and has for its principal Towns, *Lonpen* a ſpacious *Haven. Falskerbode, Elbogue* and *Elſinburg* one of the Keys of the Sound.

HALLANDIA is but a ſmall Tract of Land, yet yields much Fruits and Corn, many Cattle, and lying South of *Scania,* has *Halænego* for its principal Town, from which it ſeems to take its name; and is well watered with pleaſant Streams.

BLE-

BLESCIDA lies North of *Sweedland*, and though it has many fertile Plains, yet it is generally Mountainous or Craggy hilled, having for its chief Trading Town, *Malmogia* and *Colmar*, a strong Fortress bordering on *Sweedland*.

A *Discription of* Norway.

NORWAY, though under the King of *Denmark*, is however a Kingdom of it self, being bounded on the East with *Denmark*, on the West with the *Ocean*, on the North with *Lappia* or *Lapland*, and on the South with *Sweeden*; but lying so much in the extremities of cold, though it is a vast tract of Land, it is for the most part Rocky, Mountainous and Barren, not being furnished with stores of its one Production, fit for the support of these few People it contains, the greatest Commodity it affords being Stock-Fish, Ship Masts, Deal Boards, Tackle for Shipping, Pitch, Tann'd Leather, Train Oyl, Furrs, and Tallow. As for the Towns or Villages, they are very thinn, and the Houses for a great part are made of Dirt and Hurdles, covered with Thatch, and windowed with Lattice; and the whole Country is divided into 5 Præfectures or Governments, according to the Number of the Royal Castles, built for the defence of the Country, known by the Names of *Bohus*, *Ager-Huis*, *Agger-Huse*, *Trundheim*, and *Ward-Huis*. The chief Towns in these several Jurisdictions, are *Anslo* or *Astoia*, on a Bay opposite to *Juitland*, an Episcopal See, *Bergen*, an Episcopal Sea, and the ordinary Residence of the Governour for the King of *Denmark*; *Marstrand* seated in a half Island amongst Rocks &c. *Trandtheim*, Antiently *Nichrosia* an Arch-Bishops See who is Metropolitan lican of *Norway*; and *Ward-huis* seated in the Island of *Ward*; and although the Country (abounding with horrid Woods, and desolate Mountains) is naturally Poor, yet at certain Seasons little Beasts, about the bigness of Field Mice, over-spread like *Locusts* the Fertile Parts of the Field, *&c.* and consume every thing that's green or pleasant in their way, and then gathering together they die in heaps, thereby occasioning a Pestilential Noisomness, that much afflicts the Inhabitants with Diseases; and these they call *Lemmers*, affirming them to be dropt out of the Clouds in Tempestuous Weather: Nor do the Whales, that appear on that Coast in great number, less disturb their Fishing Trade, by the indangering the sinking of their Boats and small Vessels; which monstrous Creatures they have lately found the Art of chasing away, by throwing Oyl of *Castor* into the Sea, at the Scent whereof they fly: And though the People are miserable Poor, they nevertheless hate dishonesty, and greatly delight in Plain Dealing.

A Description of Russia, comprehending the Dukedom of Muscovy.

THIS large Tract of Land is bounded on the West with *Livonia* and *Finland*; on the East with *Tartary*; on the North by the *Frozen Ocean*, and part of *Lapland*; on the South with *Lithuania*, *Crim Tartary*, and the *Euxine Sea*; and is accounted in its greatest length from East to West 3300 Miles, and in breadth 3065, being subject to the Czar of *Muscovy*, or great Duke, who notwithstanding stiles himself Emperor of *Russia*, or *Russland*, which is part in *Europe*, and part in *Asia*, divided by the River *Tanais*, the boundary of two parts of the World.

E

The chief City is *Mosco*, the Seat of the great Duke, and the Patriarch, and of most of the Nobility, being very large, though not stately; there are besides this of note, *Rascovia*, and *Novograd*, Archepiscopal Sees, *Vologda*, *Smolensko*, and *Pleſcovia*, held to be the only walled Town in *Muſcovy*, *Uſtium*, *Moſayce*, *St. Nicholas*, *Sugana*, *Gragapolis*, and the chief *Maritime* Port is *Arch-Angel*, ſeated in the proper *Ruſſia*, whither our Merchants Trade, and the *Ruſſia* Company have a Factory, the Country yielding ſtore of Furrs, as Sables, White Fox, Martins, Black Fox, Honey, Wax, Cattle, Tallow, Red Deer-skins, Hides, Hemp, Flax, Tar, Brimſtone, Salt Petre, Train Oyl, Tongues, and the like; and the Soil towards the Southern Parts is exceeding Fruitful, producing abundance of Corn, and rich Paſtures, with Fruits of various Kinds, watered by the River *Volga*, that paſſes from thence through a part of *Tartary*; but to the Extream North, which lies in upward of 76 Degrees, the Weather is ſo Cold, that little but Rocks, Woods, Mountains, and Ice are found there, containing a Viciſſitude of Light and Darkneſs; for the Day, if we have a reſpect to the Twy-light, laſts ſix Months, and a great part of the other ſix they ſee not the Sun, but have the Country covered with Snows and during Froſts, the Sea being never free from Rocks and Mountains of Ice, over great Arms of which the Inhabitants paſs with Wagons, Sleads, and other Carriages: Nor are there found any Inhabitants in thoſe deſolate Parts during the Winter Seaſon, but in that little Summer they have, the Shepherds and Fiſhermen, ſet up Hutts or Tents, though in the Woods on this Coaſt, are the talleſt Trees in *Europe*.

The

The Inhabitants of this Country are Thick, not tall, but rather square, habiting themselves in Furrs, course Cloth, and Feeding to excess, given greatly to Drinking, though it be strictly forbid, and are generally False and Perfidious, not regarding their Words, but studying to Over-reach, or Cozen all they can, insomuch that being in other Countries, they strive to dissemble their own, the better to be Credited: The Women are tolerably handsome, well Limbed and Proportioned, and have a strange Custom amongst them, not to think their Husbands either Love or Regard them, unless they once or twice a day Cudgel their Sides. Their Religion in most things agrees with that of the *Greek* Church, not making any acknowledgment to the Pope, or See of *Rome*, but have a Patriarch of their own, to whom all their Ecclesiasticks submit: And as for the Government it is absolute, the Czar, who is by the People in extraordinary Esteem and Veneration, having in his Hands the Power of Life and Death, disposing at his Pleasure both of the Body and Goods of his Subjects, and is seldom out of War with the *Tartars*, a Roving People that border upon the most Fruitful part of his Country; and though the Armies of the *Muscovites* are generally numerous, yet are they composed for the most part of stragling People, and seldom answer in vapour the least that may be expected from them, as has not only in times past, but lately been manifest, and the reason is, because they go poor, and unfurnished into the Field.

A Description of Poland, &c.

POLAND is a very considerable Kingdom bounded on the East with the River *Boristhenes*, on the West with the *Vistula*; on the South with *Hungary*; and on the North with the Baltic Sea; and is for the most part plain and level, tho in some places there are little rising Hills, abounding with Woods, and is properly divided into the Provinces of *Livonia, Lithuania, Volhinia, Samogitia, Prussia, Massovia, Podalia, Russia Nigri, Podlassia,* and *Poland*; and the chief Cities are, *Guesna,* an Archiepiscopal See, *Posnavia, Cadissia, Siradia, Vladislavia, Cracovia,* and *Caminiec*; the latter in the Possession of the *Turks,* who hold it as their Frontier in those parts; and in *Cracovia* is a famous University.

The Buildings in this Kingdom, and the Provinces that compose it, are for the most part of Timber and Loam; the Land full of Forrests, with many Rivers, yielding notwithstanding abundance of Corn, but is defective in Wine; Honey and Wax, are likewise found in great store, with Fruit of divers Kinds, and a great Number of Cattle and wild Beasts; there are also Salt-pits, and in some places Mines of Brimstone, Copper and Iron. The *Polanders* are generally Tall, well Proportioned Courteous, and Pleasant of Behaviour; their Garments are rich, and of divers Colours, being much conceited of their own worth, and loving to be Praised, or rather Flattered: As for *Lithuania,* one of the Provinces of this Kingdom, though it is a very large one, yet it is so full of Fenns, and pestered by the over-flowing of Rivers, that it is not currantly passable, but when the Frosts are great at what time they have no hindrance, neither by

Rivers nor Fenns, and their greatest Wealth consists in Cattle, Honey, Wax and Furrs: As for the Language generally spoken, it is the *Sclavonian*; and in the North Extremities, where Villages and Towns are very scarce, the People dwell in Hutts of Straw and Loam, with Holes at the top of them to let in the Light, and give vent to the Smoak, living in miserable Poverty, as do (for the major part) the Peasants or inferiour People, being in a manner Slaves to the great ones, whose Tenants they are, though the Richer Sort are very Profuse and Expensive, rather Prodigal than Liberal, Impatient of Injuries, Delicious in Diet, and costly in Attire, often shaving their Heads, except one Lock, which they preserve with great care, being generally good Soldiers, and much Glory if they can kill a Turk in Battle, and bring off his Head, in Token of which, they wear Feathers in their Caps.

Theft in these Parts is very rare, especially to be committed by a Native *Polander*, and all Crimes are severely punished: As for the Religion they Profess, in Relation to the Government, it is that of the *Romish* Church, though the Reformed way of Worship is allowed and tolerated; and the King is of late Elective; the Women are tolerably Fair and well Proportioned, very Witty and Ingenious, great admirers, and observers, of their Husbands, and very neat in their Houses. A Peasant in this Country (unless in time of great Danger or Invasion) is not suffered to bear Arms; and when the Gospel is Read in the Churches, the Gentry and Nobility draw their Swords, in token that they are ready to defend it with their Lives. As for the Circumference of this Kingdom, and the Provinces appertaining to it, some Account it 2600 Miles, and is Scituate under the 8 and 12 Climates: So that the longest Day Southward, is 16 Hours,

E 3 and

and Northward 18; bordering upon it are the huge *Carpathian* Mountains, where sundry Rivers have their Springs, that Water the Provinces, and pass through many Countries.

A Description of the Kingdom of Hungary, &c.

HUNGARY, one of the Fruitfullest Countries of *Europe*, before Wasted and Destroyed by a Tedious War, is bounded on the East with *Transilvania* and *Wallachia*, on the West *Stiria*, *Austria*, and *Moravia*, on the North with the *Carpathian* Mountains, on the South with *Sclavonia*, and some part of *Dacia*; accounted in Length 300 *English* Miles, and 109 in Breadth, lying in the North Temperate *Zone*, between the middle Parallels of the 7 and 9 Climates, so that the longest Day in the South is 5 Hours and a half, and 16 in the North, and was Anciently called *Pannonia*.

The People of this Country are strong of Body, boisterous of Behaviour, and have no great regard to Liberal Arts, or Mechanick Occupations, as giving themselves mostly to War, and taking it for the greatest Affront Imaginable to be esteemed a Coward, which they find no other way to obliterate, but by killing a Turk, after which they have the Liberty of wearing a Feather, as a Trophee of their Exploit; and though they are extreamly Covetous, they are no ways willing to Labour, but rather desire to live upon the Spoil: As for the Females they have no claim to any Inheritance, so that the Male Line failing, the Estate goes to the common Treasury; nor have the Daughters any other Portion given them, than a Wedding Garment, and are for the most part obliged

bliged to lie on hard Quilts, till such time as they are Married. As for their Cities and Towns, they are fortified for War, as having for upward of two Hundred Years been Imbroiled with the *Turks, Transilvanians*, and other Neighbouring Nations; the chief of which are, *Presburg, Buda, Belgrade, Gran, New-haufel, Great Warradine, Alba Regalis, Raab, Commora, Temefwar, Gyula, Agria, Effeck, Peft*, &c. which have ftrugled with various Fortunes and Succefs, though at prefent moft of the ftrong Holds of this Kingdom, through the late good fuccefs are in the *Imperialifts* hands; the Kingdom being Hereditary to the Houfe of *Auftria*, of which *Joseph* the Emperor's Son, and Arch-duke of *Auftria*, is now Crowned King.

The Soil, though for the moft part Untilled, is notwithftanding wonderful Fruitful, yielding Corn where they Till it, thrice in a Year, and in fome places the Paftures are fo rank for want of Feeding, that it rifes the height of a Man; it abounds likewife with Fruits of all Kinds, efpecially abundance of Rich Vines, of whofe Grapes rich Wine is made, and Deer, Goats, Hares, Conies, and wild Foul are here in great Plenty, though none be forbidden to take them; there are likewife Mines of Silver, and in fome places Gold is found; and in time of Peace the Cattle fo multiply, that they are obliged to fend great ftore of them into divers parts of *Europe*, to prevent their over-running the Country.

The Religion Eftablifhed in the Kingdom of *Hungary*, is that of the *Romifh Communion*, though at prefent the Reformed Worfhip is Tollerated. The chief Rivers are the *Danube*, the *Gran*, the *Waag*, and the *Nitrea*; though many other Water this Fruitful Country; but for Mountains there are none confiderable, the Country being generally plain, unlefs a few pleafant rifing Hills, many of them

them Crowned with Vines; and here is the Famous Bridg of *Esseck*, 7 Miles in Length: passing over 3 Rivers, and divers Marshes, though lately it has been much ruined and destroyed.

The Description of Sclavonia.

SCLAVONIA is a considerable Country, bordering on *Hungary*, which bounds it on the North; as the *Adriatick* Sea does on the South; *Carniola, Histria,* and the Seignory of *Venice* on the West; and *Servia, Epirus,* and *Macedonia* on the East; accounted in Length 480 Miles, and in Breadth 325, of *Italian* Measure, Scituate in the North Temperate *Zone*, between the Middle Parallels of the 6 and 7 Climates; so that the longest Day exceeds not 15 Hours and a half.

This Country contains many small Provinces or Divisions, as *Windishland, Croatia, Bosnia, Dalmatia, Contado-Di zara,* and the *Sclavonian* Islands; and the chief Cities or Towns are, *Zatha, Zacaocz, Windisgretz, Sagona, Ragusa,* scituate on the *Adriatick*, being a place of great Traffick, *Sebenicum* or *Sicum, Zara* or *Jadera, Scodra* or *Scutary,* before which the *Turks* lost 100000 Men, *Lissa, Gradiska, Buman, Novigrad,* and *Sisseg,* or *Sisseck,* with others of lesser Note, scatter'd throughout the Provinces, which are partly in the Hands of the *Turks,* and partly in the Possession of the *Imperialists* and *Venetians.*

These Countries for the most part afford abundance of good Pasture, abound in Fruits, and are rich in Corn, yielding some Mines, and great store of Cattle, watered in many places by the *Danube, Saw, Drave,* and other Rivers of note; and as for the People they are hardy, and inured either to War or Labour; and though they give themselves

not

not much to Till the Ground, becaufe the Turks and *Venetians* for the moft part, reap the Benefit of their Labours, yet they want nothing that is neceffary for the fupport of Humane Life; forafmuch as the Cattle and Sheep bring forth their Young twice in the Year; and although Corn be but barely caft on the Ground, without Tillage, it will bring forth Increafe.

As for the People, though they are ftubborn, and much addicted to Pride, yet are they put to many fervile Labours, by their more proud Conquerors, who Lord it over them as if they were no other than their Drudges; for which reafon the Word *Slave*, is derived from thefe *Sclaves*, through the unmerciful Ufage they found at the hands of the *Venetians*, when they were firft brought into Subjection by the Seigniory of *Venice*: As for their Religious Worfhip, it is in moft parts according to that of the *Greek* Church, whofe Patriarch they acknowledg Supream in Ecclefiaftical Matters; and here they permit their Women very rarely to marry, till they are 24 years of Age, nor the Men till 30. And at this time, the *Venetians* have 3000 *Sclavonian* Horfe-men Inrolled amongft their Militia, and have at all times drained this People to affift in their Wars againft the *Turks* and neighbouring *Chriftians*: And as for the Native *Sclaves*, their Garb is half Sleeved Gowns, of violet Cloth, and a Bonnet of the fame, much like to that of the *Scots*, fhaving their Heads all but a Lock of Hair o. their Crown, after the Fafhion of the *Turks*; the Women likewife cut their Hair indifferent fhort, and if fo it be not naturally Black, they ufe Art to render it of that Colour.

A Description of Dacia, *in its sundry Principalities and Provinces,* &c.

DACIA, properly so held in the time of the flourishing *Roman* Empire, is bounded on the North with *Podolia,* and some other part of the Realm of *Poland* ; on the South with part of *Thrace* and *Macedonia* ; on the East with the rest of *Thrace* ; and on the West with *Hungary* and *Sclavonia* ; held at present to comprehend the Principalities of *Transilvania, Moldavia, Wallachia, Rascia, Servia,* and *Bulgaria* ; extending from the 7 to the 10 Clime, so that in the most Southern parts, the days are 15 hours 3 quarters at the longest, and 17 in the most Northern.

TRANSILVANIA the first Division of *Dacia,* takes its name from its lying behind the great *Hungarian* Woods, and is in time of Peace an exceeding Fruitful Country ; abounding in Fruits, Corn, Cattle, Fish, Salt-pits, Stone-quarries, Mines of Gold and Silver, Quicksilver, and other Metals ; and in the Woods are found many wild Bulls, and wild Cattle ; and the Pastures breed many fair Horses, the best for War in all those parts ; and in the Frontiers they have Seven Towers to guard the approach from *Hungary,* which gives the *Dutch* occasion to call it *Seven-Burg* ; though the chief Towns are *Clusenburg, Carolstadt, Harmanstadt,* and many others, and are Governed by a Prince of their own, who has a long time been Tributary to the *Turks* ; but since their late bad success, put himself and his Country under the Protection of the Emperor.

MOLDAVIA Quasi Matavia, said so to be called from its nearness to the Fenns of *Mæotis,* is a Country abounding with Woods, yet very plenteous in Wine

Wine, Corn and Pastures, producing great store of Cattle though thinly peopled, by which means it is but slenderly Tilled; however they have out of this small Province, supplyed the great and populous City of *Constantinople*, with store of Provisions; so that together with what they send to *Poland*, the tenth Peny, by way of Custom, amounts to 150000 Crowns yearly; though the Gentry and Clergy are excused from paying any thing of this nature; *Constantinople* receiving from hence every year 500 Ship Loads of Provision only.

The chief Towns are *Occazima* the Seat of the *Vaivod* or Prince *Cotiim* a strong Fortress *Biohgrade* and *Bender*, and has in it two Arch-Bishops Sees; the people in Religious matters following the Traditions of the *Greek* Church.

WALACHIA is another Province of *Dacia*, held to derive its name from *Flaccus*, a noble *Roman*, who was Governor of it in the time of *Trajan* the Emperor; so that the people at this day speak a kind of a corrupt *Latin* or *Italian*; and this Country is in length 400 miles, in breadth 120, being for the most part plain and full of Pastures, flourishing Medows which feed a great many Cattle, and bring up excellent Horses for War and Service of any kind; here are found likewise Salt-pits and Iron Mines; Mines of Gold and Silver, the which for fear it should entice the *Turks* to seize their Country, they keep for the most part concealed; they also in sundry places have store of Vines, yielding plenty of Wine; and have for their chief Towns *Galatza* on the Influx of the River *Pruth*, into the *Danube*; *Frescortum*, *Prailaba*, and *Zorza*; and is watered with the Rivers *Danube*, *Teln*, *Alluta*, *Fulmina*, *Stertius* and *Herasius*; and is as the former, Governed by a *Vaivod*, and dependant in Religious matters on the *Greek* Church;

the

the Ecclesiastical Affairs being Governed by an Arch-Bishop and two Bishops, and pays at this day Tribute to the *Turks*.

RASCIA, another Province of *Dacia*, has in it the Towns of *Bodon, Zarnovia, Covin, Novebard, Severire, Colambes* and *Columbella*; but continually lying in the way of War; the *Turks* and *Tartars*, by their often marching through it, have by the Waste and Plunder they made, so impoverished the Inhabitants, that the Towns and Villages are extreamly thin; and although the Soil is in many parts capable of producing Corn and Fruits, yet wanting men to Till it, it produces nothing material; nor are those that Inhabit it any ways incouraged to Manure the Fields, as knowing others will reap the Fruits of their Labour.

SERVIA is a Country by Nature more Fruitful, and was Antiently very Rich and Flourishing, till the *Turks* made themselves masters of it, by the fatal overthrow of *Lazarus* the Despot, on the plains of *Cossovia*, and was well stored with Mines of Gold and Silver, especially near the Town of *Zorbenick*; but now they are either Exhausted, or thrown in, so that little advantage accrues by them; and the people indeed are degenerated from their former manners and behaviour, as being Rude, Gluttonous, and much given to Wine.

Their principal Towns are *Nissa, Vidina, Cratovia, Zorbenic* and *Semunder*, and the Province is commodiously watered by the Rivers *Colubra, Lem, Ibra* and *Moravia*, with some others, very pleasant and plentiful in many places.

BULGARIA was Antiently a Kingdom, and called by the *Romans Missa Inferior*, as *Servia* was *Missa Superior*; and is a Country very Mountainous and full of rugged Hills, steep Rocks, and fearful Water-falls, taking its name from the *Bulgars* a *Scythian* people, who in the year 566 seized upon it, driving out the Antient Inhabitants; and is divided from Thrace by the great Mountain *Hæmus*, whose Spurs and Branches in a manner over-run it; yet the Kings hereof have been accounted very powerful; insomuch that they have worsted in sundry Battles, the *Latin* and *Greek* Emperors of *Constantinople*: and received the Christian Faith, towards the end of the Reign of *Justinian* the Second.

The places of most note are *Mesembria*, *Divogatia*, *Axium*, *Nicopolis*, *Marcionopolis*, and are watered by the *Danube*; which in part of this Country takes the name of *Ister*, and is now Tributary to the *Turks*; who for the most part imploy the Natives in their Wars, as being very Valiant and Daring.

A Description of Greece, *in its Kingdoms and Provinces, as Antiently it stood*, &c.

GREECE as we now must take it, is bounded on the East with the *Propontick*, *Hellespont*, and *Ægean* Seas; on the West with the *Adriatick*; and on the North with the Mount *Hæmus*, parting it from *Servia* and *Bulgaria*, and some part of *Illyricum*; and on the South with the *Ionian Sea*; being in a manner a *Peninsula*, or rather a half Island, commodiously Scituate for Navigation, and has had divers notable Revolutions, being now intirely in the possession of the *Turks*, unless what the *Venetians* have preserved, or wrested from them; and as this large Country properly stands at present, I think it highly necessary, for the better conveniency of describing it, to divide it into respective Provinces and Countries, &c.

1. *Peloponesus*. 2. *Achaia*. 3. *Epirus*. 4. *Albania*. 5. *Macedonia*. 6. *Thrace*, and as for the Islands of the *Ionian*, *Ægean* and *Propontick* Seas;

together

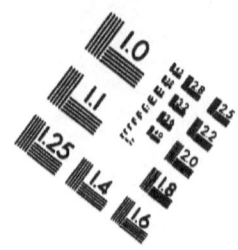

**IMAGE EVALUATION
TEST TARGET (MT-3)**

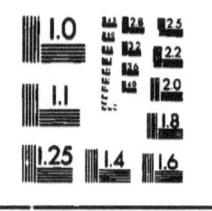

Photographic
Sciences
Corporation

23 WEST MAIN STREET
WEBSTER, N.Y. 14580
(716) 872-4503

together with the famous *Creet*, I shall leave them to a particular description of all the Islands of note, &c.

Peloponesus is in a manner inclosed by the Sea, only where by a small *Isthmus* it is joyned to the *European* Continent, of no more than six miles in breadth; which the *Grecians* and *Venetians* formerly fortified with a great Wall and five Castles, Antiently called *Hexamillium*; but in the Wars with *Amurath* the second *Turkish* Emperor they were overthrown; and this Country is accounted 600 miles in circuit, and though it has passed under divers names, it is now called the *Morea*, and held to be the most pleasant Country of *Greece*, abounding in fruitfulness, and all things necessary for the support of Human Life; adorned with many goodly Plains and pleasant rising Hills, furnished on every side with sundry commodious Ports and Havens; and though for the bigness of it no Country has suffered more in the ruin of so many stately Cities, yet it remains at this day, the most populous and best Inhabited of all the *Grecian* Continent; and near the middle of it, in *Laconia* is the Mount *Taygetus*, the top whereof gives a prospect over the whole Country, which is properly divided into 7 Provinces, viz. *Achaia-Propria*, *Elis*, *Messene*, *Arcadia*, *Laconia*, *Argolis* and *Corinthia*.

Achaia-Propria has on the East for its boundard *Argolis* and *Corinth*; on the West the *Ionian* Sea; on the North the Gulf of *Lepanto*; on the South *Elis*; so named from the *Achæi* once Inhabiting it; the *Adjuncta Propria* being added to difference it from *Achaia* in the main Land or Continent of *Greece*.

In this part the considerable places are *Chiarenza* Antiently *Dyme*, Scituate in the most Western point of it, on or near the *Promontory*, *Araxum*, *Ægria*, once the chief City of this Tract, now called *Xilocastro*, *Chaminisa*, Antiently *Olneus*, *Patreæ*; a pleasant pleafant Town Scituate oppofit to the Mouth of the Gulf *Lepanto*; being a place of confiderable Trade, and moft note on the Bay of *Corinth*, from whence it is called *Golfo-di-Patras* and here the *Englifh* had once a Conful for the eftablifhment of Trade, called the Conful of the *Morea*, and is memorable for the death of St *Andrew*, the Apoftle, who there fuffer'd Martyrdom; and next to thefe are *Pellene*, *Hellice*, *Buris*, the latter two much ruined or rather funk in the Sea by a Tempeft, about the time of the Battle of *Leuctres*; *Tritæa* and *Phera*; but the chief Town which feparated from the reft, we may term a Province is *Sicyon*, Scituate in the moft Eaftern part, and gives name to the Country of *Sicyonia* abounding in Olives, Wine, and Iron Mines; the Inhabitants whereof count themfelves the Antienteft of *Greece*, and have been Governed by a Succeffion of 26 Kings, before they fell into other Methods of Government.

The Country of *Elis*, is bounded on the Eaft with *Arcadia*, on the Weft with the *Ionian Sea*, on the North with *Achaia-Propria*, and on the South *Meffenia*; and has for its chief City *Elis*, giving name to the Province, and was founded as fome Hiftorians have it, by *Elifha* Son of *Javan*, and Grandchild of *Japhet*; and near unto it runs the River *Alpheus*: In this Tract is found *Olympia*, near to which once ftood the Statue of *Jupiter Olympicus* 60 Cubits in heighth, and every way proportionable, compofed of Gold and Ivory, by *Phidias*; and here were held the *Olympic* Games, Inftituted by *Hercules*.

MESSENIA is feated in the moft Southern part of the *Peninfula*, and takes its name from the City of *Meffene* Scituate on *Sinus Meffenaicus* now called *Golfo-di-Corone*, lately taken and poffeffed by the *Venetians*; in this Tract ftood *Pylos* the chief City of King *Neftor*, but now called *Navarino*, a fmall Village.

Village of little note *Metron* or *Methone*, is commodionſly ſeated in a half Iſland, and has on the South ſide a capacious Bay about 3 miles over, fit for the reception of great Veſſels. *Corone* the City that gives name to the *Golfo-di-Corone*, &c. *Cypariſſi* now called *Arcudia*, from which the Bay adjoyning takes its name; and although this Province abounding with Corn, Cattle and Fruits, was taken by the *Turks* in the year 1500, yet in this laſt War it is moſtly recovered by the *Venetians*.

ARCADIA is bounded on the Eaſt with *Laconia*, on the Weſt with *Elis* and *Meſſene*, on the North with *Achaia-Propria*; and on the South with the Sea; and is ſaid to take its name from *Arcas* the Son of *Jupiter* and *Califto*, called before that *Pelaſgia*, and has for its chief City *Mantinia*; near unto which the *Thebans* in a mortal Battle, overthrew the *Spartans* and *Athenians*; and then *Epaminondas* that famous Leader received his Mortal wound. This Province is exceeding fertil, abounding in Cattle and rich Paſtures, Fruits of ſundry kinds, and divers Minerals; inſomuch that for its pleaſantneſs, many curious fancies have been Fabled upon it; and in this Country Sir *Philip Sidney* layed the Scene of his famous work.

LACONIA has on the Eaſt and South the Sea, on the Weſt *Arcadia*, and on the North *Argolis*, Antiently called *Lelegia*; and was once reckoned to contain 100 Cities, though now it comes very ſhort of that number: The chief are *Leuctres*, *Amycle*, *Thulana*, near to which *Hercules* is ſaid to kill the *Hydra*; *Salaſſia*, *Epidaurus* ſeated on the Bay of *Malvaſia*, a Town well Built and Fortified; and *Sparta* ſo called from *Spartus* a Prince of *Argos*; as for this part it is wonderful fruitful, and lies very commodious for Traffick and Navigation, greatly abounding in all the Commodities common to *Greece*; being pleaſantly watered with the River

Eurotas

Eurotas, and other Streams of leſſer note; having many fair Promontories, Bays, and Havens.

ARGOLIS is bounded on the South with *Laconia*, on the Weſt with *Corinthia* and *Achaia-Propria*, and on the Eaſt and North with the Sea; taking its name from the City *Argos*, its Metropolis, once the Head of a famous Kingdom; and in this City King *Pyrrhus* the great *Grecian* Conqueror, after he had Victoriouſly forced his entrance, was ſlain with a Tile thrown at him by an old Woman, from the top of a Houſe; and beſides this, it has *Trœzan*, *Tyrinthia*, *Nemea*, and ſome others; and grew in times paſt from a ſmall Province, to a powerful Kingdom; being once the chiefeſt of *Greece* in ſtrength giving Birth to many renowned perſons, and the moſt famed for the breed of Horſes.

CORINTHIA, though but a little Region, is yet nevertheleſs exceeding pleaſant and fruitful, lying towards the *Iſthmus* or neck of Land that joyns the reſt of *Greece* to *Peloponcſus*, between *Argolis* and *Achaia Propria*; containing only the Territories of *Corinth*, and the chief Towns are *Cincrea*, *Corinth*, memorable for the Epiſtles Saint *Paul* wrote to the Inhabitants; commodiouſly Scituate for the command of all *Greece*, but that the Inhabitants give themſelves more to Merchandiſe than War; and although it has been a long time in the hands of the *Turks*, it was the laſt year taken by the *Venetians*; and is Seated on the bottom of the neck or *Iſthmus*, the *Ionian* Sea being on the Weſt, and the *Ægean* on the Eaſt, waſhing its walls; and makeing on each ſide a Capacious Haven, and was formerly exceedingly Fortified but of latter times the Security the *Turks* ſuppoſed themſelves in, on that part of their Empire, made them little mind keeping it from running to decay.

And

And thus much may briefly suffice, as for that part of *Greece* called *Peloponesus*.

As for the other *Achaia*, it is properly divided into *Attica*, *Megaris*, *Bætia*, *Phocis*, *Ætolia*, *Doris*, *Locris*; and the chief City accounted amongst these is *Athens*, once the head of a famous Common-wealth, and sometime a Kingdom; and is Seated very advantagiously, making a Port into the Sea, and was once the Mistriss of Arts and Arms; and in St. *Pauls* time, who wrote his first and second Epistle from hence to the *Thessalonians* a very flourishing City, but by the Wars and Misfortunes it has sustained, is now only noted, for what it has been, more than for what it is.

MEGARIS is but a small Region, yet very pleasant and much abounding in Corn and Fruits, and has for its chief City *Magaria*.

BÆTIA is much larger than the former, and was once all the Dominion or Kingdom of *Thebes*, that famous City, so much noted to be built by *Cadmus* the *Phænician*, being the Metropolis: and in this Tract are found likewise *Aulis* and *Platea*, and is watered with divers pleasant streams.

PHOCIS is memorable for the Mountain *Parnassus*, and was much noted for the Temple of *Apollo* at the foot of it, but now that stately Structure where the *Delphic* Oracle gave Answers is ruined, and scarcely any part of it remaining.

ÆTOLIA is another considerable part of this Tract, divided by the River *Pindus* from *Epirus*; once a country of great note, and full of Towns and places of strength, but now retains at present few of note except *Chalcis* and *Thermum*; however the whole Country is pleasant, abounding in Pastures, watered with many Rivers, yielding some Mines, and great store of Cattle.

LOCRIS though it is but a small Region, yet lies Commodiously on the Sea Coast, and has for its chief Town *Lepanto*; in sight of which was fought the famous Battle or Sea fight, between the *Turks*, *Venetians*, and confederate Christians; in which 29000 of the *Turks* were killed, 4000 taken Prisoners, 140 Gallies Burnt, Taken, and Sunk, and 1200 Christian Slaves rescued, in the year 1571. and as for the Trade here, it consists in Leather, Oyl, Tobacco, Furrs, Wheat, Barly, Rice, &c. And is again in the Possession or under the Power of the *Venetians*.

DORIS is a small Province bounding upon, or rather appertaining to *Locris*, and has for its chief Town or City, *Amphissa*, bordering upon the Mountain *Parnassus*; here is also found *Guidas*, where the stately Temple of *Venus* stood, and where St. *Paul* continued a long time: And as for this Tract it is very Pleasant and Fruitful, watered with small Rivers, but none of note.

Epirus, was once a Famous Kingdom, of which *Pyrrhus* (who Invaded the *Romans* in *Italy*) was King, but more memorable for being under the Regency of the great *Scanderbeg*, who with a handful of Men stood out against the whole Power of the *Turkish* Empire, in the Reigns of *Amurath* the Second, and *Mahomet* the great, defeating and destroying Prodigious Armies of the Infidels; and has for its chief Cities *Croija*, *Petrela*, *Petra*, *Alba*, and *Stelusia*; the Country is very Fruitful, tho' somewhat Mountainous, and was once accounted next to *Macedon*, the most powerful in *Greece*, and at this day greatly abounds in Cattle, rich Pastures and Corn.

ALBANIA is bounded with *Macedon*, *Sclavonia*, *Epirus*, and the *Adriatick* Sea, and has for its chief Cities *Durazzo*, and *Albinopolis*, memorable for its Breed of Horses, which the *Turks* use mostly in their

their Wars, and the Courage of its Inhabitants, whose Country being but Indifferently Fruitful, and too strait for the Inhabitants, they like the *Swiss*, rather choose the Exercise of Arms, than Husbandry.

MACEDON, once Famous for being Head of the *Greek* Empire, is bounded with *Missa Superior*, *Migdonia*, *Epirus*, and *Achaia*, and is a very Rich and Flourishing Country, though the Turks greatly oppress the Native *Greeks*, and make them labour that they may reap the greatest Profit, and abounds not only with Cattle, Corn, and some Wine, but in it are found Mines of Gold, and other Metals; and of this Country *Alexander* the Great was King, who not only Conquered the greatest part of *Asia*, but brought all *Greece* into Subjection, founding here the third Empire of the World: And as for the chief Cities, they are *Ædassa*, *Andrastus*, *Eriba*, *Scidra*, and *Philippus*, or *Philipopolis*, Built by *Philip* the Father of *Alexander*; and to the People of this City it was, that St. *Paul* Wrote his Epistle.

THESSALY was once likewise a Kingdom, lying on the South of *Macedon*, abounding with Pleasant Valleys and Hills, and amongst the latter are found that of *Olympus*, so famed for Transcending the Clouds, *Othris*, *Pelion*, and *Ossa*, so often struck with Thunder, and Fabled to be laid one upon the other, when the Giants went about to Storm the Skies. The Country indeed is very Fruitful in many Parts, and produces an Excellent Breed of Horses, the Natives being held first to Invent the Art of Breaking and Backing them; and here *Achilles* Reigned, who was Slain at the Siege of *Troy*: The chief Towns of this Country are *Lamia*, *Tricca*, *Pharsalia*, on whose large Plains *Cæsar* and *Pompey* fought for the Empire of the World; as also

Phi-

Philippi, in whose Fields *Augustus Cæsar* and *Marcus Antonius*, overthrew *Brutus* and *Cassius*.

MIGDONIA is a small Country, and accounted by most a part of *Thrace*, and famous for nothing more than the Hill *Athos*, held to be the highest in the World, as being 3 days Journey in Ascent, and 75 Miles in Circuit; so that its shadow reaches (upon the declining of the Sun) 40 Miles: nor are there wanting in this Country Cities and Towns of considerable Note, as *Thessalonica*, commonly called *Salonica* (to whose Inhabitants two of St. *Pauls* Epistles are directed) *Appollonia*, *Nicladia*, and others.

THRACE, properly so called, though now *Romania*, as it lies at present circumscribed is within these Boundaries, viz. on the East the *Euxine*, or black Sea, the *Propontis* and *Hellespont*; on the West with *Macedon*; on the South with the *Ægean* Sea, and part of *Macedon*, and on the North with the large Hill *Hæmus*; and is a large and goodly Province, accounted 20 Days Journey in Length, and 6 in Breadth, and in Relation to the Heavens reacheth unto 44 Degrees North Latitude, so that the longest Day in Summer is about 15 Hours, and 3 Quarters; and in this Country is Scituate the great City of *Constantinople*, so Named by *Constantine* the Great, and made by him the Capital of the *Roman* Empire, and is now the like to the *Turkish* Empire, and the chief Residence of the *Grand Seigniour*; Built in a Triangular manner, the one Angle thrusting into the Main Land, and the other two bordering upon the Sea; *Adrianople*, Built by *Adrian* the Emperor, and *Trajanopolis*, Founded by the Emperor *Trajan*; with others of lesser Note.

This Country as to the Soil, is very Fruitful, but by Reason of the sharp cold Air coming off the Seas, they ripen not kindly, nor do the Inhabitants trouble themselves much with Husbandry, as knowing they labour but for others; however in their Gardens towards the Sea, they are very curious, so that much Wine is produced from the Grapes that grow there, which is properly called *Greek Wine*, and mostly sent into other Countries, the *Turks* by their Law being forbidden to Drink it: They have large Plains likewise where Corn grows indifferently Plentiful, but more Pulse which is amongst them in great use. The Natives of this Country, as indeed of all *Greece*, are much declined from what they formerly were, in Learning, Arts, and Arms, as being no better than Slaves to the Imperious Turks, who Lord it over them, whereby they are discouraged and dulled, even to a kind of Stupidity; nor does the Eloquence of their Original Language continue pure amongst them, but is mostly corrupted, insomuch that they in few parts perfectly understand the Antient *Greek*.

The Commodities found in the Principal Trading Towns of this, and other Sea Provinces, are Grograms, Carpets, Silks, Drugs, Leather, Chamlets; and indeed the chief Commodities of *Europe* and *Asia*, which Pay great Customs to the *Grand Seigniour*. And thus much for the main Land of *Europe*, whose Islands we shall hereafter consider, with those of the other Three Parts of the World, when we come to treat of the Respective Seas in which they are posited, and therefore, for Orders Sake, Omit them here, and proceed to *Asia*.

A

A Geographical and Historical Description OF ASIA:

In its Kingdoms and Provinces, &c.

Of Asia in General.

ASIA held to be larger than *Europe* and *Africa*, is bounded on the West with the *Mediterranean* and *Ægean* Seas, the *Hellespont*, *Propontis*, and the *Thracian Bosphorus*, the *Euxine* Sea, *Palus Mæotis*, the Rivers *Tanais* and *Duina*, a Line in that case being drawn from the first to the second River, as its boundard to *Europe*; on the North it is bounded with the main *Scythian Ocean*, on the East by the Streights of *Annian*, the *Indian Ocean*, and *Mare del Zur*,

Zur, on the South, with the *Mediterranian*, or so much of it, as is called the *Carpathian* Sea, bathing the Shoars of *Anatolia*; and the Main Southern Ocean, passing along the Coasts of *India*, *Arabia*, and *Persia*; and on the South-East, with the *Arabian* Bay, or *Red Sea*, parting it from *Africa*, and is indeed washed on all sides with the Sea, but where a narrow *Istmus* joyns it to *Africa*, and the space of ground between the *Tanais* and *Diuna*, where it is joyned to *Europe*.

This large Tract of Land, is held by some, to take its Name from *Asia*, the Daughter of *Oceanus*, and *Thetis* the Wife of *Japetus*, and Mother of *Prometheus*, and others, from *Asius*, Son of *Atis*, a King of *Lydia*; but Originals of this kind, being generally uncertain, it will be convenient to wave them, and proceed to what is more Material, *viz.* In Antient times *Asia* was divided into the Greater and Lesser; but by modern Writers, it is divided into five parts, according to the Divisions it is settled in; as First, that which Borders upon *Europe*, is alotted the Great Duke of *Muscovy*; the Second, the Great *Cham* of *Tartary*; the Third, the *Turk*; the Fourth, the King of *Persia*; and the Fifth, held by the Great *Mogul*, and others, known by the Name of the East *India*; not accounting the petty Princes, who have independent Provinces, nor what remains in the Hands or Possession of the *Europeans* in sundry Parts, &c. To which five we may properly add *China*, a large Country, very populous, and powerful, accounted one of the Fruitfullest in *Asia*.

This part of the World, may rightly be held or termed, the Noblest of all other, as conjectured, on all hands, once to contain the Earthly Paradise: Here the Law was given, and here our blessed Saviour, wrought the stupendious, and amazing work of our Redemption: Hence sprung the Noble Sciences, that the *Greeks* learned of the *Hebrews*, and

flou-

flourished under the Monarchie of the *Medes, Persians* and *Assyrians*: And is divided into two Parts, or Divisions, as *Asia Major*, and *Asia Minor*, the latter called *Anatolia*; the whole Country scituate East and West, from 52 to 169 Degrees of Longitude; and North and South, from 82 Degrees of Latitude, to the very Æquator or Æquinoctial Line; some few Islands only lying beyond that Circle, which occasions the longest Summers Day in the most Southern part, to exceed little above 12 Hours, though in the most Northern Parts, for near the space of Four Months, they have no Night at all.

As for the Commodities, this great part of the World abounds with in general, they are Gold, Silver, all sorts of Minerals, Jewels, Pearls, Spices, Odours, Ivory, Drugs of sundry kinds, Silks, Dyes, Sweet-woods, Perfumes, &c. But to come nearer to the Description of the Countries, for Orders sake, it is convenient to begin with *Asia Minor*, or *Anatolia*.

Asia Minor, *or* Anatolia, *described, in its Kingdoms, and Provinces*, &c.

ASIA MINOR, or *Anatolia*, is bounded on the East, with the River *Euphrates*; on the West, with the *Thracian Bosphorus, Propontis, Hellespont*, and the *Ægean* Sea, parted by them from *Europe*; on the North with *Pontus Euxinus*, or the *Black Sea*; on the South by the *Rhodian, Lydian,* and *Pamphilian* Seas, and several parts of the *Mediterranean*; extending from 51 to 72 degrees, of Longitude; and from 36 to 45 degrees of Latitude, and is accounted in length, from the *Hellespont* to the *Euphrates* 630 Miles, and in breadth from *Trabezond*, a City so called to *Sinus Issicus* in *Cilicia*, &c. and is under the middle Parallel of the Fourth, to

F   the

the Sixth Clime, by reason of which, the longest Day in the Summer Southward, is but 14 Hours and a half, and differs not above an Hour in the extreamest North, which is longer, insomuch that the Air is very Temperate, and the Soil very fit for any sort of Grain or Fruit; but that Husbandry is neglected by reason of its being under the Turkish Yoak, though the Rich Pasture of its own accord breeds great store of Cattle, and an excellent Race of Horses; and here stood the Famous City of *Troy*, so much renowned for its sustaining Ten Years Siege, against the whole Power of *Greece*: nor did this Country formerly boast of less than 4000 Cities and Towns, but at this day most of them are found to be Ruined by War and Earth quakes.

As for the Division of this part of *Asia*, it is properly divided into *Bythinia, Pontus, Paphlagonia, Galatia, Cappadocia, Armenia minor, Phrygia minor, Phrygia major*, the greater and the lesser *Missia, Æolis*, and *Ionia, Lydia, Caria, Lycia, Lycaonia, Pisidia, Pamphilia*; and what in the time it appertained to the *Roman* and *Greek* Empires, were under the Province of the *Rhodes*; and of these in their Order.

BITHYNIA, is a very pleasant Province of *Asia minor*, formerly called *Bebrycia*, and afterwards *Migdonia*, taking the present Name from one *Bithynius*, who was King thereof when a Kingdom, though some will have this Name derived from *Thyni* a People of *Thrace*, who Subdued and Possessed it. The Country is naturally Rich on that part bordering upon the *Bosphorus*, opposite to *Constantinople*, which is Scituate on the *European* Shoar, full of little rising Hills, and grassy Plains, and was once the Delight of such as sailed those Seas, or Streights; but the *Turks* (who affect neither Art nor Sumptuousness in their Retirements or Recreation) have neither

ther

ther Improved, nor kept up the pleasant Gardens and Pallaces they found in it.

The Principal Towns of *Bithynia*, are *Scutari*, facing *Constantinople*, *Chalcedon*, memorable for the Fourth General Council there Assembled, for the Suppression of the *Nestorian* Hereticks, *Nicomede*, so named from *Nicomedes* once King of *Bithynia*, *Libussa*, memorable for the Death and Sepulchre of the Famous *Hannibal*, the *Carthaginian* General, who fell by Poison, *Prusa*, once a considerable City, and the Residence of the *Turkish* Kings, till *Mahomet* the First removed to *Adrianople*: *Nice*, or *Nicæa*, Scituate on the Fenns of the River *Ascanius*, Famous for nothing more, than the first General Council held there under *Constantine* the Great, *Anno* 314. to Settle the Peace of the Church, greatly disturbed and put out of Order by the *Arian* Heresie, where there Assembled no more than 318 Bishops, yet in such Esteem for Learning and Piety, that to this Day, it is highly approved by all good Men; and here after the taking of *Constantinople* by the Latin Princes, the *Greek* Emperor held his Residence; and the Rivers of this Province are *Phillis*, *Ascamius*, *Sangaris*, or *Sangri*, but for Hills or Mountains none of note appear.

PONTUS, or *Metapontus* is a Bordering Province on *Bithynia*, has for its chief Cities *Flaviopolis*, *Claudiopolis*, *Juliopolis*, *Diospolis*, *Heraclea*, *Amastris*, *Phillium*, and others formerly very famous, but of later Times not of much note; and in that Part called the Eastern *Pontus*, is *Sinope*, pleasantly seated on a long Promontory, shooting into the Main, and memoralble for the Sepulchre of King *Mithridates*, who held a Forty Years War against the *Romans*; *Themisciyra*, now called *Fanogoria*; *Amasia*, the Birth Place of *Strabo* the Geographer; *Cabira*, afterward called *Diopolis*, noted for the overthrow *Lucullus* gave King *Mithridates* near it, when to retard the Pursuit of his Enemies, he was obliged to scatter his Treasure in the way, and thereby escaped their Hands, with the greatest part of his Forces: As for the Rivers in these Parts, or any other Division of *Pontus*, they are not (except *Thermodon*, on whose Banks the *Amazonians* formerly Inhabited) of any considerable note.

PAPHLAGONIA, though a Country of little compass, yet once was the chief Seat of a Powerful People, but ruined by *Cyrus* for their Assisting the *Lydians* against him, and the Principal Cities were *Gangra*, now memorable for nothing more than the Council held there in the Year 339. *Conica*, or *Goniata*, *Pompeiopolis*, *Germanopolis*, *Xoana*, and *Andrapa*; and from this Country the *Venetians* had their Original, as sprung from a People called *Heneti*, anciently Inhabiting a part of it; and, as the rest, the Soil is very Fruitful in places where it is Manured: The Inhabitants are a mixture of *Greeks* and *Turks*, with some *Christians* and *Jews* amongst them, but not very many; nor have they any considerable Traffick at Sea, which renders the Province poor.

GALATIA, deriving its Name from the *Gauls*, when they over-ran these Parts, who called it *Gaul-Asia*, and corruptly *Galatia*; it was likewise called *Gallo-Græcia*, from the mixture of *Galls* and *Grecians*; and here to this day the Ancient Language of the *Galls* is much spoken, or at least mixed with that of the *Greek*.

This Country (above what we have mentioned) is very plentiful in Fruits, and other things necessary for the Support of Man-kind; and in this part only is the *Amethist* (that great Preservative against Drunkenness) found; and here the People of Old had the Vanity to throw Written Papers into the Funeral Fires of their Friends, as conceiting they would read them in the other World, and thereby

know

know the Sorrow they made for their Departure; and were so much given to Sacrifices, that it is Noted by *Athenæus*, how a Rich *Galatian* for the space of a Year, Feasted the whole Province with the Flesh of such Beasts, as were ordained for Sacrifices. To perswade them from which, and confirm them in a more Glorious Religion, St *Paul* Wrote his Epistle to this People: As for Rivers of note, there are none that rise in this Country, however it is supplyed with refreshing Streams, from *Halys* and *Sangarius*.

The chief Cities are *Ancyrana*, now called *Angauri*, *Olenus*, *Agriama*, *Tavium*, or *Tanium*, *Androssia*, *Fabarena*, *Thermæ*, and *Talachbacara*; there are likewise sundry lesser Towns and Villages, but of no Note.

CAPPADOCIA, is on the East of *Galatia*, and is a Country abounding with Wine, and sundry kinds of curious Fruits, many Mines of Brass, Iron, Silver, and other Minerals in the Mountains, and other Parts, as also store of Allom, and Alabaster; moreover the Chrystal, Jasper, and Onyx Stone; it affords a great number of Cattle, but more especially a great many Horses, insomuch that they are sent into most parts of *Asia*; and as a boundard of this Country is the Famous *Ante-Taurus*, a ridg or chain of Mountains, bending towards the North, and in it were Born most of the noted Ring-leaders of those Sects of Hereticks, that so much opposed the Church in its Infancy, insomuch that it grew into a custom, to call a wicked Man a *Cappadocian*; and has for its Principal Cities and Towns *Erzirium*, upon the Borders of the great *Armenia*, where the *Turkish* Army usually Wintered in their return from the *Persian* Expeditions, and is the Seat of a Bassa. *Mazaca* once the Residence of St. *Basil*: *Sebastia*, so named in Honour of *Augustus*, whom the *Greeks* called *Sabastus*; *Trepesus* or *Trepesond*, once the Seat of an Empire, but now under the power of the Turks, where the *Amazons* were said to Inhabit, at the time *Troy* was razed by the Greeks, and till displaced by *Alexander* the Great.

ARMENIA MINOR, though somewhat mountainous, is however a very fertile Country; and is held by some to be that *Ararat*, upon whose Hills *Noah*'s Ark rested after the Deluge; and so consequently first to have been peopled after that Universal Calamity, and is only parted from *Armenia Major* by the famous River *Euphrates*, and is so inclosed in most parts, with that and the Mountains *Taurus* and *Ante-Taurus*, that it is difficult to be entred, though in other places it is delightful, and well watered by pleasant Streams issuing out of the Mountains; the chief being *Melas*, which falls into *Euphrates*, and is so called from the blackness of the Waters.

This Country was once a part of *Cappadocia*, till the *Armenians* wrested it by force, and planted their Colonies here, from whom it took the present name; and has for its chief Cities *Nicopolis*, *Suur*, antiently *Melitene*, *Oromandus*, built by *Pompey* the Great, in token of his Victory over *Tigranes* the *Syrian* King, under whom was both the *Armenia*'s, *Garnace*, *Caucusum*, and *Arbyssus*, whither St. *Chrysistom* was Banished by the means of the Empress *Eudoxia*, who took part with the Hereticks: and these Countries had the Blessing to be converted to the Christian Faith, by St. *Paul* and St. *Peter*, as appears by the Epistle of the first to the *Galatians*, and of the last to the Strangers scattered or dispersed in *Pontus*, *Galatia*, *Cappadocia*, *Asia*, and *Bithynia*, &c. And what remains is more properly called *Asia*, though circumscribed in *Anatolia*, or *Asia Minor*, viz.

Asia Propria, was formerly held to be the most rich and flourishing part of this *Peninsula*, as *Tully* affirms,

affirms, when he certifies that the Roman Tributes from other parts were but sufficient to defray the charges of keeping them; but *Asia* says he, is so Fertile and Rich, that for the fruitfulness of the Fields, variety of Fruits, largeness of Pastures, and quantity of Commodities, which were brought from thence, it abundantly excelled all other Countries; and it properly includes *Phrygia Minor*, *Phrygia Major*, *Mysia*, *Æolis*, *Ionia*, *Lydia* and *Cario*.

Phrygia Minor, so called, as many hold it, from the River *Phryx*, descending from the greater *Phrygia*, is a very fruitful Country, mostly Champaign and watered with sundry noted Rivers, as *Scamander*, *Xanthus*, *Simois*, and others so much renowned by *Homer*. In this Country, upon the Banks of *Scamander*, stood the famous City of *Troy*, whose goodly Ruins, appear in some sort, to this day; and from the Inhabitants of which City most Nations labour to fetch their Original. Near to it stands *Troas* or *New Troy*, begun by *Alexander* the Great, and finished by *Lysimachus*, one of his Captains, who yet named it *Troas Alexandri*, in honour of his Master. Here are found likewise the Ports of *Lyrnessus* and *Sigeum*, with many other things, upon which the Poets especially have been large, who keep them alive even in their Ruins; for indeed little else remains at this day; for as *Ovid* has it,

Jam seges est ubi Troja fuit, resecandaq; falce,
Luxuriat Phrygio sanguine pinguis humus.
Corn ripe for Sciths, grows where *Troy* once stood,
And the Soils fatted with the Phrygian Blood.

PHRYGIA MAJOR, joyns to the former, and is a very fruitful Country, abounding with some Corn, Wine, and some Olive-Yards well watered, by the River *Sangarius* and *Marsyas*; the former taking

taking its Spring in this Country, discharges it self into the *Euxine* Sea. And the Towns are *Gordian*, once the Residence of *Gordius*, who of a Husbandman being made King, hung up the Furniture of his Waggons and Ploughs in the Temple of *Apollo*, tied in such a Knot, that an old Prophecy run, *That he who could unty it should be Monarch of the World*; which *Alexander* the Great, upon his coming thither, trying to do and failing therein, cut it in sunder with his Sword, shewing thereby, what Policy could not do, Force should effect. *Colosse*, where the *Colossians*, to whom St. *Paul* wrote one of his Epistles dwelt: *Miedeum*, once the Seat of *Midas*; *Pesinus* where the Statue of *Cibele* was held in great Veneration, and being from thence shipped for *Rome*, the Ship by no means could be brought to pass up the *Tiber*, till a Vestal Virgin, who had been accused of Inconcinency, to clear her Innocence, by tying her Girdle to it (if you will believe the Story) drew it up the River; and the reason why the Romans so coveted it was, that the Empire of the World had been promised to those that could get it into their possession.

MYSIA is a Country lying, as it were, between the *Phrygia's*, supposed antiently to be a *Phrygian* Nation, being much the same for Fertility: And here is found the *Asian Olympus*, a vast Mountain, but Inferior to that of the same name in *Greece*, and has for Rivers of note *Cacus* and *Æsopus*; on the Banks of the former stands the once famous City of *Pergamus*, but now of little note. There is likewise the River *Granicus*, having its Fountain in *Mysia Major*, and falling into the *Propontis*, on the Banks of which *Alexander* gained the first Victory against *Darius* the Persian King; who upon his first coming into *Asia*, had made so little account of him, that he sent Order to his Lieutenant in *Anatolia* to take him alive, and after having whipped
him

him with Rods, to send him bound to his Presence. And this *Mysia* is divided into the lesser and greater; and here stands the Tower of *Abydos*, over against *Sestos* in *Thrace*, memorable for the Story of *Hero and Leander*; with many other things more remarkable; as the Inhabitants slaying themselves, to prevent falling into the hands of *Philip* the Father of *Perseus* King of *Macedon*, its being betrayed to the *Turks* by the Daughter of the Governour, upon her falling in Love with *Abderachmen*, a *Turkish* Officer; upon her Dreaming she fell into a miry place, and he coming by took her up and wiped her clean, &c. *Cyzicus*, famous for its Port, Marble Towns and stately Buildings, &c. And in *Mysia Major* are found *Apollonia*, *Daima*, *Trajanspolis*, *Alydda*, and others.

ÆOLIS and IONIA Are generally conjunct, as Countreys much depending on each other, indifferently Fruitful, and contain sundry good Harbours. The principal places in the first are *Pitane*, *Ararnea*, *Elæa*, *Myrina*, now *Sebastopolis*, *Cene* the chief in this part; *Cumæa* the Birth-place of one of the *Sybils*, and *Phocia*; and the People are held by *Josephus* to descend from *Elisha* the Son of *Javan*, but by the many Conquests that have been made of this and other Countreys, whereby the People have been either destroyed or carried away, and others planted in their steads, such Originals must needs be uncertain.

IONIA, Has for its principal Cities *Mias* on an Arm of the Sea, which *Artaxerxes* assigned to *Themistocles* the noble *Athenian*, when the ingrateful City of *Athens* had banished him after the glorious Conquests he had Atchieved in their behalf. *Erythra*, memorable for the Habitation of one of the *Sybils*; *Lebedus*, *Clazomene* and others, especially *Smyrna*, a fair Haven City, on a Bay named from it the *Bay of Smyrna*, and is not only famous for comprehending bending one of the Seven Churches of *Asia*, written to by St. *John*, but is at present a place of great Traffick, where the English have a Factory, and most *Europeans* trade for Chamlets, Grograns, and other Stuffs, Drugs, with many such like Commodities: The Grand *Signior* having there a Custom-House which brings in a vast Revenue; and in old times there stood a goodly Temple, dedicated to *Homer* the Greek Poet, as supposed to be the place of his Birth. In this Tract is likewise found the City of *Ephesus*, so renowned for the Temple of *Diana*, accounted one of the Seven Wonders of the World, and was in its Splendour 425 feet in length, and in breadth 220, supported with 127 Pillars of polish'd Marble, curiously wrought, and was indeed a very goodly Structure, and so it had need, for after it was modelled by *Ctesiphon*, a most expert Architect, it was 200 years in Building, though Burnt in one day by *Eraftrotus*, on purpose, as he alledged to get him a Name, though of Infamy.

LYDIA once a famous Kingdom till ruined by the *Persians*, under the leading of *Cyrus*; took its name, as many Historians will have it, from *Lud* the Son of *Sem*; the People of which Country are said to be the first Coiners of Monies, and Inventers of sundry Games; and here is the Mountain *Tomalus* covered naturally with Vines and *Sipylus*; and which are very fruitful Valleys; and yield the best Saffron of *Asia*: the Rivers of note are *Hermus*, which taking its source in *Phrygia Major*, passes by the Skirts of *Lydia*, pleasantly watering the Pastures, &c. and falls into a fair Bay of the *Ægean* Sea, opening towards the Island of *Clazomene*; likewise *Pactolus Castros*, and the *Meander*; the which though upon a direct line not exceeding 60 miles is nevertheless in measuring the winding, accounted 600 which greatly letters the Country; in which are found Mines of Gold and Silver, and some

Stone

Stone of considerable value; and has for it's chief City *Sardis*, seated on the River *Pactalus*. *Philadelphia* near to the bank of the River *Caistrus*: *Thyatyra*, *Laodicea* and others; nothing more renowned than to be of the number of the 7 Churches, to which St. *John* wrote his *Apocalypse*; and of this Country *Croesus* the Rich was King, who was deceived by the Oracle, in these words, viz.

CROESUS Halyn penetrans magnam subvertit opum vim.

Thus Englished:
When *Croesus* over *Halys* goes
A mighty Nation he o'erthrows.

Which he Interpreting according to his own hopes, crossed the River, and was vanquished and taken Prisoner by *Cyrus*; overthrowing indeed his own People, and was the last King of *Lydia*.

Caria is on the North of *Lydia*, in which is the Hill *Latmus*, where *Endimion* retired for the better privacy in the study of Astrology, and there finding out the course of the Moon and her changes, gave occasion to the Fable of his being beloved by her and her kissing him, &c. and the River *Sabmacis* which enfeebles any Person that enters into it or drinks of the water; and has for its chief Cities, &c. *Miletus*, *Mindus*, *Heraclea* and *Latmum*, *Borgilia* or *Borgilos*, *Milusa*, *Primassus*, and others; and in the Southwest of this Province, thrusting it self into the Sea like a Promontory, stands the little Country of *Doris*; so called from *Dores* a *Greek* people that first Inhabited it; and has for its chief Cities *Cnidus*, *Cressa*, formerly a noted Haven Town; *Halicarnassus*, where Queen *Arthemisia* in Memory of King *Mausolus* her Husband, raised at vast expence a Monument, accounted one of the 7 Wonders of

the

the World; from which all great Structures of that kind are called *Mausoles*.

As for the people of *Caria*, their names or denominations, is conjectured to be derived from *Cares* the Son of *Pharoneus* King of *Argos*; though *Bochartus* rather alludes it to the *Phœnician* word *Car*, signifying a Sheep or Ram, because they were formerly dealers in Flocks, with which their Country abounded, and is indeed full of rich Pastures.

LYCIA lyes on the West of *Caria*; said to take its name from *Lycius*, Son to *Pandion* King of *Athens*; and is a Country inclosed in a manner with Sea and Mountains; the principal Mountain being *Taurus*, the biggest in *Asia*; which begins in this Province, and extends to the Eastern Sea; one of its branches in this Country is the *Chimæra*, casting out Flames like Mount *Ætna*; which gave occasion to the Fablers of former times, to render it dreadful, by likening it to a Monstrous Beast, with a Head like a Lyon, a Belly like a Goat, and a Tail like a Serpent; though some to justifie this Fiction, will have it to be infested at the bottom by Serpents, grazed in the middle by Goats, and containing nearer to the top, dens of Lions, altogether framing the Monster, said to be destroyed by *Bellerophon*; which indeed tended to nothing more than that he first caused the Mountain to be Inhabited; and this Country in former days was so opulent, that 60 Cities of note were found in it, but now most of them Ruined; the chief in it being *Ara*, *Phaselis*, *Myra*, *Solima*, *Rhodia*, *Pataras*, *Mylias*, and *Podelia*; and so powerful were the *Lycians* in the time of *Cyrus* the *Persian*, that they were not without great difficulty brought under, but from thence forward followed the Fortune of the Conquerors, as the *Greeks*, *Romans* and *Turks*, &c.

LY

LYCAONIA is a Country so named from the *Lycaones*, a people of *Lycia*; or from the *Lycaonians* a people, the Inhabitants of *Lyconia* a Town in *Phrygia Major*; and has for its chief Cities *Iconium*, once the chief Residence of the *Caramanian* Kings, who so stoutly opposed in its beginning the Growth of the *Ottoman* Empire; *Lystra*, the birth place of *Timothy* the Evangelist; and here it was that the superstitious people would have done divine Sacrifice to *Paul* and *Barnabas*; *Darbe, Laranda, Paralais, Adopissus, Gemna* and *Caratha*; but as for the Inhabitants, they are not found in History to be of any considerable note; nor does their Country much abound in Fruits or Corn, for want of Convenient streams to water it.

PISIDIA is on the South of *Lycaonia*, and is a small Country, yet furnished with great plenty of all things necessary for Human subsistance; where the Plains extend themselves, though in some parts it is much Incumbered with Barren Mountains; and has in it the Towns or Cities of *Antioch, Seleucia, Lysinnia, Selge, Sagalassa, Cremna, Termessus, Olbanassa* and *Plutanessus*; the Antient Inhabitants being said to descend from the *Solimi*, a people on the Borders of *Lycia*; and were formerly daring and valiant, as appeared in their opposing *Cyrus*, and did more wonders than any of their more powerful Neighbours; but now being in subjection to the *Turks*, who hold them as Vassals or Slaves, they have lost much of their Courage and Industry.

PAMPHYLIA has *Pisidia* on the North, and is separated from it by the Mountain *Taurus*; and its hold to take its name from its being Inhabited by a mixture of Nations; which word in the Greek expresses no less, and is much over-run with the Spurs or Branches of *Taurus*; rendering it Barren in many places; yet on those Mountainous parts abundance of Goats are fed, whose Flesh serves for

Food

Food; Hair for making Chamlets, and Skins for Leather; yet that part which is the Sea coast, and runs 150 miles on the Mediterranean, is well-Inhabited, and enjoys sundry Towns of Note, as *Attalia, Perge, Side, Magidis, Aspendos, Oliba, Caracensium, Colobrassus, Cretopolis,* and *Menedemium,* and is watered with the Rivers *Cestrus, Cataractus,* and *Eurymedon;* and since they first planted this Country, they have been frequently brought under subjection by the *Pontois, Persians, Romans* and lastly by the *Turks,* who at present remain Lords of all the lesser *Asia,* and good part of the greater.

CILICIA has *Pamphylia* on the West, and is a very fruitful Country, especially on the Eastern part; and is said to take its name from *Cilice* the Brother of *Cadmus;* and though it is but meanly Inhabited, yet it is much traded to; and has in it many Towns of Note, as *Tarsus* the Birth place of St. *Paul, Anchiala, Epiphania, Adena, Mopsuestia, Nicopolis, Amavara, Scandelora,* and others watered with the River *Pyramus,* now called *Malmistra, Orismagdus, Calicadnus,* and the famous *Cydnus,* whose waters are so Cool, and withal so Rapid that they had like to have proved fatal to *Alexander* the Great, and did so to *Fredrick* the first *German* Emperor; for whilst he was bathing in the stream, he was carried away by the violence of the Current, and smothered in the waves. As for the chief Mountains they are *Amanus* and *Taurus* accounted the largest in the world.

ISAURICA is a distinct Province from the former seated on both sides of *Taurus,* which renders it altogether Mountainous, being East to *Pamphylia;* parted in the midst by the River *Calecadnus* on whose banks are many Vines and pleasant Pastures and has for its principal City and Towns *Seleucia, Isauria,* and *Claudiopolis;* and as for this and the

Province

Province of *Cilicia*, they were Anciently famous for Piracies; but *Pompey* breaking their power at Sea placed them in a more Inland Country, and especially on these Mountains in a strait compass, but they have since inlarged their borders.

And thus for *Anatolia* or *Asia Minor*, except such Islands as are reputed to appertain to it, which shall be treated of in another place; it being our design that nothing shall be omitted, though we are obliged to be brief, constrained to it by the narrowness of our compass; only note that it is wholly subject to the *Turks*.

The Kingdoms and Provinces of the greater Asia Described.

AS to the Boundards and Scituation of this Part of the World, it has been already laid down in general, wherefore now nothing remains, but to describe it in particular, &c. and to do this in order, we will begin with

The Kingdom of Syria.

THE Kingdom of *Syria*, as it Anciently was, is bounded on the North with *Cilicia*; on the South with other parts of *Asia minor*; on the East with the River *Euphrates*; and on the West with the *Mediterranean Sea*: And is Inhabited by divers sorts of People, Professing sundry Religions, as Christianity, Judaism, Mahometism, and in some places not altogether freed from Paganism; for upon the Borders next to *Armenia minor*, there dwell the *Cardi*, or *Cœrdes*, a People who pay Veneration

neration to the Devil, and the slender excuse they alledg for it is, to prevent his doing them Mischief, they being on the contrary assured, that God being in his Nature good, he will not injure them. And the whole Country is divided into 3 Provinces, viz. *Phænicia*, *Cœlo-Syria*, and *Syro-Phænicia*.

PHÆNICIA, is bounded on the East and South with *Palestine*; on the North with *Syria*, so properly called; on the West with the *Mediterranean Sea*; and has this Name given it by the *Greeks*, from the abundance of Palm Trees that are found growing therein, the Word signifying in that Language a Palm. As for the Country it self it is not great, for though in Length it reaches to the further side of Mount *Carmel*, and again to the River *Volanus* on the North, the Breadth however is so inconsiderable, that it rather seemeth a Sea-Coast, than a Country; nor did the *Phænicians* less improve the opportunity in former times, but were accounted the chief Navigators of the World. As for the Cities of note they are, *Acon*, seated in a Pleasant Plain of great Length, Besieged by the Western Christians in their Expedition for the regaining the Holy Land. *Sarepta*, the place where the Woman sustained *Elias*, or rather he her, by Miracle in the time of Famine. *Tyre* once a Famous Sea Town, but now little of it remains; *Sidon* a Pleasant Place, but wants of its former Largeness and Grandeur, being reduced to a narrow compass. As for the chief Mountains they are *Libanus* and *Carmel*; and as for Rivers there are few of note, the principal being *Adonis*, however the Country is Fruitful in Olives and Vines.

CŒLO-SYRIA is more compacted than the former, and is watered with the Rivers *Abana* and *Pharphar*, called in Scripture the Rivers of *Damascus*, and has in it the Mountains of *Asmadamus*, a ridg of Hills beginning at the East Point of *Anti Libanus*, and bending directly Southward, shuts up that part from the Land of *Israel*, and has for its chief Towns *Heliopolis*, so called from an Image of the Sun formerly Worshipped there; *Chalcis*, *Abila*, *Adida*, *Hippus*, or *Hypone*, *Capitolias*, *Gadara*, *Gerasa*, *Scythopolis*, *Philadelphia* and *Damascus*, the Head of this Province, once a Famous City, but now reduced to a small compass, however it is Scituate in a large Plain, Invironed with Hills, and watered by the River *Chrysorheas*, having about it many pleasant Gardens, Orchards and Fountains; and indeed the whole Country, where the Mountains interpose not, is a Terrestrial Paradice, which made the Impostor *Mahomet* refuse it for his Regal Seat, lest swallowed up in the Delights and Pleasures of that Country, he should forget his Business.

SYRO-PHÆNICIA is a third Province of this Kingdom, and has for its chief Cities and Towns *Aleppo*, a considerable Mart Town, though not bordering on the Sea, but standing within the Land, for hither the Merchants of *Egypt*, *Arabia* and *Persia*, come over Land with their Camels Laden with Silks, Cloth of Gold and Silver, Drugs, Spices, &c. *Biblis*, *Tripoli* a place taken and possessed by the Western Christians, in their Expedition to the Holy Land; and is a very considerable Sea-Port Town, Fortified with a strong Wall, and many Towns, and has many Store-houses for the Accommodation of Merchants; and that part of the Mountain *Libanus*, that stretches upon it like a Curtain, aboundeth with Fruit Trees, Vines, and Trees harbouring abundance of Silk Worms; but of this Country *Antiochia* is accounted the Metropolis, and not far from it is the River *Orontes*, which beginning in *Cœle-Syria*, ingulfs it self and riseth near *Apamea*, watering *Antiochia*, and passing thence 16.

Miles,

Miles, falls into the *Mediterranean* Sea, and from hence come the greatest part of our Tapistry Hangings.

The Building in this Country, and indeed in all *Syria*, is one high Roof, with a plain Top, Plaistered or Terrassed to walk on the Plat-form, and Arched Cloisters before the Doors. so that People may walk dry in the Streets, in all Weathers. As for Religion they are as the first, a mixture, &c.

A Description of the Land of PALESTINE.

PALESTINE is bounded with the Hills of *Hermon*; on the East parted by them from *Cœlo-Syria*, and *Arabia Deserta*; on the West with the *Mediterranean* Sea, and some part of *Phœnicia*; on the North with *Ante-Libanus*, and the remaining part of *Phœnicia*; on the South with *Arabia* the Stony, called *Palestine*, from the *Philistines*, a People that Inhabit it; but it is not conjectured they held any more than a part of it, but being very Powerful gave a general Name to this Country; as the *Asiaticks* usually call the Europeans *Franks*, from *France*, which is only a small part of it; however we will take it as formerly it stood, viz. its Division into *Galilea*, *Judea*, *Idumea*, and *Samaria*, accounted 200 Miles in Length, though not above 50 in Breadth, possessed by the Tribes of *Israel*, as the Land Promised to *Abraham*, &c.

GALILEA is accounted the most Northern Part of *Palestine*, being divided into the higher and lower, the first allotted to the Tribes of *Napthali*, *Asher*, and part of the Tribe of *Dan*, is a pleasant Country abounding with all manner of Fruits, and Exuberant, that for its Plenty this Conjunct with the rest, was called a Land flowing with Milk and Honey; the chief Cities being *Apheck*, whose Wall falling slew 27000 of *Benhadad*'s Soldiers. *Giscala*, the Birth-

Birth-place of *Jehu*, who Slew *Joram* his Master, and took upon him the Kingdom; here is likewise found *Capernaum*, where our Blessed Saviour healed the Centurions Servant, and Fed 3000 with 5 Loaves and 2 Fishes; not far from it *Ribla*, where Unfortunate King *Zedekiah*, after he had seen the slaughter of his Children, had his Eyes put out, and to these we may add *Genesareth, Hamath,* and *Ramath.*

As for the lower *Galilea*, it contained the Tribes of *Zebulon* and *Issachar*, and the first of these had for their chief Cities *Cana*, where our Bless'd Saviour wrought his first Miracle; *Bethsaida*, the Birth place of St. *Peter*, St. *Andrew*, and St. *Philip. Hippopolis, Tiberias* on the Sea Coast, and some other Towns of lesser note, as *Nazareth*, and *Bethulia*; here is likewise found the Mount *Tabor*, on which our Lord was Transfigured, as a manifestation of his Glory; as also the Brook *Kishon*, out of which flows the Famous River bearing that Name.

The principal places appertaining to the Tribe of *Issachar*, were *Tarichea*, on the side of the Lake, about Eight miles from *Tiberias*; and was so stoutly defended against *Vespatian*, that it cost him the Lives of 1200 men, before he made himself Master of it; *Chishon* a City of the Levites, *Rameth*, called also *Jarmouth*, another City of the Levites, where the Hills of *Gilboa* take their beginning, and pass Westward to the *Mediterranean*, and East to *Jezreel; En-haddad,* near which *Saul* being discomfited by the *Philistins*, flew himself in dispair. *Naim* on the Banks of the River *Kison*, where our blessed Saviour raised the Widows Son to Life; and on the Banks of the same River standeth *Haphraim* or *Aphraim, Endor,* the place where *Saul* consulted the Witch, about the raising *Samuel; Deborath,* one of the Cities of Refuge, *Arbela,* &c. And although these Tribes are held to be carried away by

Salmanasser,

Salmanasser, and the *Galileans* placed in their stead, yet they were strict Compliers with the Jewish Ceremonies and Customs, and so zealously affected that neither Threats nor Force could oblige them to offer Sacrifice to the Health of the *Roman* Emperors.

SAMARIA, The Country taking its name from the chief City, is bounded on the East with the River *Jordan*; on the West with the *Miditerranean* Sea; on the North with *Galilee*; and on the South with *Judea*: And gives in all parts a curious Prospect of pleasant Fields and Valleys, with little rising Hills, from whence issue refreshing Streams; and is every scattered over with Fountains, affording abundance of Grass, and consequently a great number of Cattle; and the People were for the most part *Assyrians*, sent thither by that Conquering King to supply the places of the Captive *Israelites*, and were Gentiles at first, till better instructed by the Lyons God sent amongst them, and afterward by the Priest, who returned with the Five Books of *Moses*, and taught them the manner of the God of the land, 2 *Kings* 17. However they frequently relapsed and forsook their living Strength, as may be seen in Holy Writ: and this Province upon its being first possessed by the Children of *Israel*, was allotted to the Tribe of *Ephraim*, and the two half Tribes of *Manasses*; the one seated on the *Mediterranean*, and the other beyond *Jordan*. In the half Tribe of *Manasses*, on the *Mediterranean*, the chief Cities were found to be *Bethsan*, *Tirza*, *Acrabata*, *Thebes*, *Ephra* or *Ophra*, *Aijalon*, *Bezek*, *Jezreel*, *Megiddo*, *Dora* or *Dor*, *Cæsarea*; and others, many of them memorable in Scripture upon sundry occasions.

The Tribe of *Ephraim* had for their chief Cities, or most considerable places, *Saron*, on the *Mediterranean*, *Lydda*, *Ajalon* or *Helon*, a City of the

Le-

Levites, *Thenath-Chares*, given to *Josuah*, *Adasa* or *Adarsa*, where *Judas Macchabeus* overthrew with 3000 men, the vast Army of *Nicanor*: *Jestori* or *Palethi*, giving name to the *Felothites*, that were of *David's* Guard: *Silo* situate on the top of a lofty Mountain, and the receptacle of the Ark, till taken by the *Philistines*; *Michmas*, *Najoth*, *Bethoron*, the City of the *Levites*, *Pirhathon*, *Simor*, and *Samaria*, the Metropolis of the Kingdom of *Israel*, founded by *Omri*, one of their Kings, on the top of the Mountain *Samron*, taking thence its name, overlooking the Sea-coast, and was very stately and magnificent, vying with *Jerusalem*, but much impaired by the Wars that have frequently happened, and at this day scarce to be found, or at least extreamly wanting of its former Glory; and in this compass mixed together in a manner the other Tribes mentioned were contained.

JUDEA, The Country of the more peculiar remnant of the *Jews*, containing the Tribe of *Juda*, but may be said to be divided between the *Philistines*, the Tribes of *Dan*, *Simeon*, and *Benjamin*: At first the *Philistines* commanded the Sea Coast from the South of *Phænicia*, to the North of *Idumea*, or from the City of *Gaza*, to the Castle of Pilgrims, taking both, except *Joppa*, into the Accompt, and but that and all the Northern Towns were the Israelites; and though the Philistines held no more then six of note, yet they were of such importance and so strongly fortified, that having the *Edomites* to back them, and some other Neighbours, who relished not the Jewish Nation, they perplexed and wearied them continually with Wars and Inroads, and became more troublesom, than the whole body of the *Canaanites*; which Towns were *Gath* or *Geth*, where the Giant *Goliah* slain by *David* was Born; *Accaron* on the South of *Gath*, a Town of great Wealth and Power; *Ashdod*, by the *Grecians* called

led *Azotos*, Memorable for the Temple of *Dagon*, whither the Ark of the Lord was carryed when taken by the *Philistines*; *Ascalon*, Scituate on the Coast of the *Mediterranean*, and first Founded by a Noble *Lydian*; *Gaza* more Inland, signifying in the *Persian* Language the Place of Treasure, where indeed *Cambyses* layed up the Tribute of those Countries; and *Majoma* the Port Town of *Gaza*: And in these they had their strong Holds, from which they so often vexed the *Israelites*.

The chief places possessed by the Tribe of *Dan* were *Joppa*, since called *Jaffa*, once a Famous Mart Town, and the Principal Haven of those parts, taken by the Christians in the Holy War; *Rama* or as the Moors call'd it *Romula*, built with Free-stone, and scituate upon rising Hills, in a Sandy Plain, where yet remain the Ruines of a Monastery and several Christian Churches. *Imnia*, the place where *Judas Macchabeus* Burnt the Syrian Fleet. *Ceder*, or *Cedron*; *Modini*, where the *Macchabees* were Buried; *Gibbethon*, *Cariathjarim*, *Beth-shemesh*, to which the Ark was brought by the Oxen, when dismiss'd by the *Philistines*; *Tisrah*, *Caspin*, *Lachis*, *Ajalon*, a City of the *Levites*, mentioned before in the Tribe of *Ephraim*, in the Borders whereof it is Scituate; which occasions Authors to disagree in which Tribe to place it, and therefore leave it indifferently to either.

To the Tribe of *Simeon* is ascribed the Cities and Towns of *Geray*; *Siceleg*, or *Ziglag*; *Haijn*, a City of *Levites*; *Cariath-Sepher*, Interpreted the City of Books, within the Borders of *Simeon*, but appertaining to *Judah*; and *Chorma*, with others of smaller note, rather Villages than Towns.

The Tribe of *Judah*, so called from *Judah* the Fourth Son of *Leah*, had for its Lot *Arda*, Scituate in the Entrance of *Judea*; *Hebron*, one of the Antientest Cities of the *Canaanites*, formerly Inhabited rod by the Giant-like Sons of *Anakim*, or *Anak*, the Word signifying a Chain, and here it was that *Abraham* bought a Buryal Place for his Dead, and Buried his Wife *Sarah*; *Tecoa*, the City of *Amos*; *Jether*, or *Jutter*; *Maresa*, where the Prophet *Micah* was born; *Emmaus*, since called *Nicopolis*; *Hasor*, or *Chatsor*, one of the Frontier Towns of *Idumea*; *Odalla*, or *Hadullun*; *Ceila*, or *Keila*, where David hid himself when he fled from *Saul*; *Eleutheropolis*, or the free City, not far from *Hebron*; *Azeca*; *Beth sur*, or *Bethsora*, signifying the House of Rocks, alluded from its standing on a Rocky Hill; *Adoram* bordering on the Dead Sea; *Zore*, in former times called *Bela*, but took its Name from the words of *Lot*, the word *Tsobor*, Importing Refuge, Safety, or Deliverance; *Massada* a strong Hold; *Libna* a strong Fortified City, seated in the Corner of *Juda* between the Tribes of *Dan* and *Benjamin*; *Ziph* in the Wilderness, where *Saul* came to pursue *David*.

BETHLEHEM call'd *Bethlehem-Judah*, to distinguish it from one of the same name in *Zebulon*, the Birth place of our Blessed Saviour, and the Grave of those Innocents that suffer'd on his account by the Cruelty of *Herod*. As for the Territories of these Cities and Towns, they are exceeding fruitful, and in many of the Valleys are Gardens of Balsam or Opobalsamum Trees.

The Tribe of *Benjamin* had for its Portion the Cities of *Mizpeh*, *Gebah*, *Gibeah*, *Ai*, *Gibeon*, *Jericho*, *Anathoth*, *Nob*, *Gilgal*, *Bethel*, *Ramath*, different from what has been mentioned; *Chadi*, or *Haidi*, *Lod* and *Ono*; but the chief Magnificence of this Tribe, was the Famous City of *Jerusalem*, scituate upon a Rocky Mountain, yet in most parts easie of ascent; Invironed with Neighbouring Hills, and consisted in its most flourishing time of four parts, separated by several Walls, resembling distinct

stinct Cities, divided into the upper, lower, and new Cities; together with the City of *Herod*, which made the Fourth division; all the Walls fortified with Towers and Castles, and the Cities stor'd with stately Buildings, Fountains, and pleasant Gardens; but all these exceeded by the magnificence of the Temple, held to be the chief wonder of the World; the Description of which is lively set down in the Old Testament; wherefore it will be superfluous here to delineate it, though at this day its Glory is laid in the dust.

The Tribe of *Levi*, though properly a Tribe of the *Israelites*, had no Possessions assigned it, but had the Priesthood for its Inheritance; and therefore scattered or planted in divers Cities, assigned for the Levitical Residence; being as *Jacob* their Father had before Prophesied: divided in *Jacob*, and scattered in *Israel*, their Portions being to live on the Altar, and the Tenths of the Offerings, &c. and as it is in *Joshua* 18. 17. *The Priesthood of the Lord was their Inheritance*. And of these there were four Kinds or Distinctions. 1. *Punies* or *Tirones*, which from their Childhood, till the 25 year of their Age, were obliged to Learn the duty of their Office. 2. *Graduats* which were obliged for 4 years to study the Law, or till they were well grounded in it. 3. *Licentiates* who actually exercised the Priestly Office: And 4. the Doctors or Rabbins, who where of the highest Order, and expounded the Law to the People.

IDUMEA is a part of *Palestine*, separate from the Tribes commonly called the Land of *Edom*; bounded on the East and South with *Arabia* the Stony; on the North with *Judea*; on the West with the *Mediterranean Sea*; Inhabited by the Children of *Esau* Brother to *Jacob*; and is a very fruitful Country towards the Sea coast; but that bordering on *Arabia* is somewhat Barren and Mountainous

though

though they heretofore afforded Balm, and now a great many Palm-trees grow there; as for the People, they are, and anciently were, rude, boisterous and untractable, given much to Violence, and were no small contributers, by raising a Sedition in *Jerusalem*, to the Destruction of that famous City by the *Romans*, under *Titus*; and had for their chief Cities and Towns, *Dinhabath*, the City of *Bela*, the first King of *Edom*; *Aniath* the City of *Hadad*, and *Pan* the City of *Hadar*; two other Kings of this Country, mentioned in *Genesis*, *Berzamna*, *Caparosa*, *Gamurarii*, *Elasa*, *Rossa*, *Rhinocurura*, *Raphia*, and others, with many scattered Castles and Villages; and of this Country the *Horites* are thought to be the first Inhabitants; amongst whom *Esau*, upon the discontent he received by his Brothers circumventing him of the Blessing, went to dwell, and took to him Wives of the Daughters of the People of the Land; and as though the two Brothers Difference had been inherent to Posterity, the *Edomites* alwaies proved mortal Enemies to the *Israelites*, not only siding with their Enemies, but making continual War and Inroads upon them their selves.

The other Parts of *Palestine*, which may properly be so called, are the Divisions of *Peræa* and *Ituræa*, and the first of these lies between the Mountains of *Arnon*, and the River *Jordan*, abounding with Olives, Vines, and Palm-Trees, the Soil every where being exceeding Rich, and was formerly the Habitation of the *Midianites*, *Moabites*, and *Ammonites*, as also of the two Tribes of *Gad* and *Reuben*.

The Quarter of the *Midianites* was at the South Side of the Dead Sea, at the very entrance of the Country, and were held to Descend from one or more of the 5 Sons of *Madian* the Son of *Abraham*, by *Keturah*, mentioned in *Gen.* 25. 4. and had

G for

for their chief Cities *Recome*, Built by one of the 5 *Midianitish* Kings, slain by *Joshua*; and *Midian* on the bank of the Dead Sea; and these were they, that by the advice of *Balaam*, sent out their Beautiful Women to Insnare the *Israelites*, upon their entrance into the Land of *Canaan*.

The *Moabites* Possessed all that part of the Country, from the boundards of the *Midianites* on the South, as far as *Esebon* on the North, on both sides the River *Arnon*, having the River *Jordan* on the West, and the Hills of *Abarim* on the East, first possessed by the *Emmims*, a Race of Giants, whose Principal City was *Sheneth Kirjathaim*, but they being Vanquished by *Chedorlaomer*, and driven thence, their forsaken Seats were possessed by the *Moabites*, Descended from *Moab* one of the Sons of *Lot*, and had for their Cities in chief *Rabbat*, the Regal Seat of *Balak* King of *Moab*; *Diblathum, Gallim, Muthana, Nathaliel, Bamath, Mispha, Hor, Kirhajareth*, and some few others of little note; and this Country God commanded *Moses* to spare, because he had given it for an Inheritance to the Sons of *Lot*.

The *Ammonites* had their Habitations on the North-East of the River *Arnon*, and possessed all that Tract from *Arnon* on the Head of the River, to the City *Rabbah*, and on both sides the River *Jaboc*, as well within as without the Mountains of *Galaad*, Antiently the Seat of the *Raphaim* and *Zamzummins*, a Race of Giant-like People; and had for their chief Cities *Rabbah*, before which *Uriah* was Slain on the account of his Wife; *Dothema, Mitspa*, and others of lesser note, and had continual War with *Israel*, God appointing them as a Thorn in their side, because they had not at first rooted them out of the Land.

The *Reubenites* or Tribe of *Reuben*, had their Dwellings appointed on the East side of *Jordan*, having

having the *Gadites* on the North, and the *Arabian* Desarts on the East, and on the South the Land of *Moab*, parted by the River *Arnon*; whose chief Cities were *Abel*, *Sittim*, *Bethabara*, or *Beth-bara*, *Macherus*, *Lasa* or *Lesha*, *Medeba*, *Bosor* or *Bozra*, a City of Refuge to the *Levites*; *Livias*, a Town Built by *Herod*, in Honour of *Livia* the Mother of *Tiberius Cæsar*; *Kedmoth*, *Adom*, *Heshbon*, *Bamoth-bal*; and within their Territories is the Mount *Nebo*, from whose Top *Moses* took a view of the Land of *Canaan*; and joyning to it is the Hill *Pisga*, or to say more truly, one of the Tops or Spires of the same Mountain.

The *Gadites*, so called from *Gad* the Seventh Son of *Jacob*, begot on *Zilpha* the Hand-maid of *Leah*, had their Lot of the Promised Land, between the *Reubenites* on the South, and half the Tribe of *Menasses* on the North, the River *Jordan* on the West, and the Mountains of *Arnon* on the East; and inhabited the Cities of *Aroer*, upon the Banks of the River *Arnon*, *Dibon*, towards *Jordan*; *Bethnimrah*, *Natoroth*, *Beth-haram*, *Beth-ezob*, *Mahanaim*, so called from the Apparition of Angels; *Succoth*, *Jahzor*, *Ramoth*, *Penuel*, &c. All the Plains of this Country being exceeding Fruitful, as on purpose prepared for the Favourites of Heaven; yet the People who had been brought out of Slavery with a mighty hand, growing fat in these fruitful Fields, soon forgot their Maker, and went a Whoring after the Gods of the Strangers, for which the *Canaanites* had been cast out of the Land.

There were moreover in this Tract, called the Land of *Palestine*, the *Trachonites* inhabiting the Hilly Country, bordering on the *Ammonites*, called the Mountains of *Gilead*, extending Northward as far as *Libanus*, living, as *Josephus* tells us, for the most part, in Woods and Caves, upon Prey and Spoil, &c.

The *Batanea* a People living in a part of the Kingdom of *Basan*, but their Kingdom, upon the Arrival of the Children of *Israel*, was given to the other half Tribe of *Manasses*, and contained many fenced large Cities: The chief was *Pella*, formerly called *Butis*, but the Name changed by *Seleucius*, the great *Assyrian* King, of the Greek Race; destroyed by *Alexander Janæus*, a King of the Jews, for refusing to admit the Law of *Moses*, but afterward by *Pompey* the Great restored to its former Luster: And more memorable in Church History, for the Voice heard from Heaven, admonishing the Christians then in *Jerusalem* to retire thither, that they might escape the Destruction that the *Roman* Army, under the leading of *Titus*, was about to bring upon that great and sinful City.

Gessur, since called *Aurantis*, the last Division of *Ituræa*, is North of *Basan*, and was once accounted a Kingdom; and had for its chief Cities *Hauran*, *Gessur*, *Mahacath*, *Chatsar*, *Hevanus*, and others of lesser note.

As for the Country of *Palestine* in general, or the promised Land, it is taken by some to be the place where the Terrestrial Paradise stood, and is indeed Fruitful, even to a miracle; for in most places there is an Eternal Spring, and in Summer the Flowers alwaies smiling, and the Vernant Trees seldom casting their ripe and mellowed Fruit before Blossoms and green Fruit take place, and are naturally of extraordinary growth; insomuch, that we read, when *Caleb*, *Josuah*, and others, went up to spie the Land, they brought a cluster of Grapes, as an earnest of the rest, so large, that they were obliged to carry it upon a Staff, between two of them. And thus much for the Land of *Palestine*, as it flourished in its most glorious daies, but now its antient Inhabitants are scattered over the face of the Earth, and *Turks* possess their pleasant places.

The

The three ARABIA'S Describ:d, in their Countreys and Provinces.

1. ARABIA DESERTA, called by the *Turks* Be-*riara*, is bounded on the East with the Babylonian Territories; on the West with some part of *Palestine* and *Arabia* the stony; on the North with *Mesopotamia* and *Palmyrene*; the first of these parting it from *Euphrates*; and on the South with *Arabia Petræa* part, and *Arabia Felix*; and takes the name of *Deserta* from the great Desarts that are found in it, all of loose Sands, taking eight daies in passing over them, which at certain times are carried so violently by the Wind, that Travellers are overwhelmed under heaps and mountains of Dust, and buryed Alive: as also are the Shepherds, who build little Cots on the borders of these Desarts, though very poor and despicable: as *Lucan* has it in his *Pharsalia*; and thus Englished.

> The greatest part of Land, the Winds do bear
> Unto the Skies, which hangs not fixed there.
> His House and Land, the *Nasamonian* Seas,
> Fly in the Wind their little Cottages,
> Blown o'r their Heads into the Air as high,
> As from a Fire the Smoak and Sparkles fly,
> Till mounted, Dust like Smoak obscure the Sky.
> Mountains of Dust, the South Winds furious hand,
> Rolls o'r them till their drown'd in heaps of Sand.

And indeed this whole Division of *Arabia* yields nothing pleasant, being mostly inhabited by Thieves and Rovers, who having committed Robberies and Outrages, in more populous and wealthy Countries make this their retreat, as knowing few will give themselves the trouble of looking for them in so waste and desolate a Country; yet there are some

some few Cities and Towns found in it, but those mostly on the Borders, *viz. Sabe* or *Saba*, the Habitation of the *Sabæans*, that was so called from the Grandson of *Abraham* by *Keturah*, mentioned *Gen.* 25. 3. And these were they that plundered *Job* of his Cattle; *Thema*, supposed to be the City of *Eliphaz* the *Themanite*, one of *Job*'s Visitants; *Shua*, *Tharsacas*, *Zagmais*, *Phunton*, *Oboth*, and *Reganna*; though they had no formal Government, as being a disjoynted People, the poverty of the Country obliging every one to shift as he could; although now counted part of the *Turkish* Empire, it is so only in name rather than in effect, as paying little or no Tribute to the Grand *Signior*.

2. *Arabia Petræa*, or the Stony, is bounded on the East with *Deserta*, and a part of *Sinus Persicus*, on the West with the *Isthmus*, that joyns *Africa* to *Asia*, and part of the Red Sea, or *Arabian* Gulph, on the North with *Palestine*, and on the South with a long ridge of Mountains, dividing it from *Arabia Felix*, and is called *Petræa*, from its rockyness, and the abundance of large Stones that are found every where in it; and is indeed barren in a manner, as the former, but more firm and solid, which gives it the preheminence in Fruitfulness; and is full of woody Mountains, wherein the wild *Arabs* lurk and fortifie themselves, being reduced under Captains of Tribes, as also untravell'd Desarts, unless by such as carry their Provision with them for fear of starving, and for that they are many times set upon and murthered by the Thieves and Rovers; so that the general passage to *Egypt* and *Babylon* is by Caravans, to defend which there seldom go less than 4 or 500 armed men, where they carry their Merchandize upon Camels, one of these Beasts carrying ordinarily 6 or 800 weight, and sometimes a 1000, and are the fittest of all Creatures
for

for this Journey, becaufe they will endure three or four daies together without drink, in a Country where Water is not to be found, but rather by chance than any certainty; and of thefe Defarts the moſt memorable are thofe of *Sinan, Pharan*; the Inhabitants faid to defcend from *Chus* and *Iſhmael*, intermixed with the *Medianites*, who are held to be of the poſterity of *Madian*, the Son of *Abraham* by *Keturah*, and have for their chief places, *Petra*, memorable for the many Sieges it has held out againſt the *Syrians, Jews*, and *Romans,* &c. And was much aimed at in the time of the Holy War, even coveted by the Turks and Chriſtians, as a Gate or Inlet to *Paleſtine*; *Boſra*, faid to be built, or rather repaired by *Auguſtus Cæfar*, to curb that wild and untractable Nation; *Phara, Bernice, Sur, Havilah, Madian, Rephaim, Kadeſh-Barnea*, and *Thara* ; and in this Country ſtands the famous Mount *Sinai*, on which the Law was given; and here for the moſt part it was that the Children of *Iſrael* ſuffered ſo much in the Wilderneſſes and Defarts, during their progreſs to the Land of *Canaan*. And the Character *Marcellinus* gives more particularly of thefe *Arabians*, is viz.

That they are a martial People, half naked, clad only as far as the Groin, with painted Cloaths, ranging up and down upon Camels, ſwift Horſes, and Dromedaries, as well in Peace as times of Trouble, not uſed to Plough, plant Trees, or get their Living by Tillage, but wander for the moſt part, from one place to another, without any ſetled Habitation; nor have they the uſe of Laws, neither can they long endure the Air or Soil in one place: Their Food is chiefly upon Veniſon, and ſtore of Milk, Herbs, Fruits, and Wild Foul; but as for Corn and Wine they have none: their Wives are hired only for a time, though

though for a shew of Marriage they present their Husbands with a Spear and a Tent, as their Dowry, though they part when they please; and both Sexes are extreamly given to Lust, the Women as rambling as the Men, leaving their Children to the help of Providence, where they fall without any further care of them.

As for the Rivers in this thirsty Land, there are but few, and the chief are *Trajanus Amnis*, *Trajans* River passing through the Country, and ending its course in the Red Sea, *Rinocorura*, called in Scripture the Torrent of *Egypt*, rising in this Countrey, and passing by the Borders of *Idumea*, falls into the Lake of *Sirbon*.

3. ARABIA FELIX, or the Happy *Arabia*, so call'd from its Fruitfulness, supplying in a manner the defect of the foregoing, is bounded on the East with the *Persian*; and on the W th the *Arabian* Gulphs; on the North with a continued ridg of Mountains; and on the South with the main Ocean, whose bounds is not known.

In this *Arabia*, the Fields, Valleys and Hills are exceeding Fruitful, abounding with Myrrh, Frankincense, Balsamum, Spices, Fruits of sundry kinds, very delicious; as also Gold, precious Stones, &c. and lying so commodiously on the Seas, is acquainted with whatever Blessing, either Element can afford, well furnished with quiet Harbours, and Roads for Shipping, the Towns of and Merchandise standing near together, and the retiring Houses of the Kings neat and very sumptuous, the Countrey being generally accommodated with wholsom Fountains, and Medicinal Waters, with sundry Brooks and Rivers cool and clear, and the temperature of the Air exceeding healthful.

And

And this Countrey by the *Arabians* themselves is called *Jeman* and *Al-jeman*; and although the people are more Civil here than in the other parts, yet they had and have many Barbarous Customs amongst them, as Carnally knowing their nearest Relations, holding Community of Wives; and of dead Bodies no care is taken, but they cast them into some Ditch or a Dung-hill, and are frequently a bragging of their descent from *Jupiter*, foolishly neglecting all Arts and Sciences, as disparagements to so great a Nobility; however there are some amongst them that apply themselves to Grazing, the Countrey abounding with Cattle and rich Pastures, and others to Merchandize, tho the chief Product of the Countrey is managed by Strangers.

The chief Cities or Towns that are at this Day found in this Tract are *Elgra*, on the Shoar of the Red Sea, called *Sinus Elgranaticus*; *Jathrib*, or *Jatrib*, in the way between *Algiar* and *Medina*, the Birth-place of *Mahomet* the Impostor; and in the City of *Medina* (to which is added the Name of *Talmabi*, signifying the City of the Prophet) is the Sepulchre of *Mahomet*, not drawn up with a Loadstone as the Vulgar rumour goes, but inclosed in the manner of our Sepulchres with an Iron Grate, and covered with a green Velvet Carpet, which the Grand Seigniour sends every Year as his Offering; so that when the New arrives, the Old is cut into innumerable Shreds, and Sold to Pilgrims by the Priests at large rates as Holy Reliques; and in this Temple, which is large and Magnificent, are 3000 Lamps continually burning: *Meccha* a Town Scituate in a barren Soil, not far from *Medina*, but of greater Resort and Traffick, the Commodities not only of *Arabia*, but of *Persia* and *India* flowing thither, from whence it is dispersed into all parts of the Turkish Empire; and here it is made Death for any Christian to come, so made to prevent the

G 5   Dis-

Discovery of the Fopperies in their Religion, and is utterly destitute of Waters, except such as is taken in Cisterns when it Rains, or brought on Camels Backs from distant Places, though three Carravans with Troops of Merchants and Pilgrims Visit it every Year: *Zidon* accounted the Haven Town of *Meccha*, though distant 40 Miles, Scituate on the Red Sea; *Zebit*, held now the Metropolis of the Country, much Traded to for Spices, Sugar, and Fruits; *Eltor* a Port Town, where the Christians are suffered to Inhabit. *Aden* on the entrance of the Red Sea, and is the most Famous Empory of this Country, well Fortified, and has a very capacious Haven for the reception of Shipping, once the L... of a distinct Kingdom, but now in Subjection to the *Turks*, being Treacherously surprized by them in the Year 1538, and soon after all the rest of the Country, *Hor*, *Zarnal*, and *Muskahat*, over-against *Surat* in the *East-India's*: As for the Woods that are found here, they naturally abound with Spices, and Odours, which in their Bloom send forth a grateful Smell, which accosts the Mariners before they can see the Land, and the Rivers are many, the chief *Harman*, *Lar*, *Prion*, *Messinatis*, *Betius*, &c. and in the *Arabian* Fields, or no where, the Phœnix is said to Inhabit.

A Description of Chaldæa, Assyria, and Mesopotamia, *in their Countries and Provinces*, &c. *As also the Mountains Kingdoms*, &c.

THESE three Countries or Provinces, are held to have been the Principal Body of the *Assyrian Empire*, wherefore it is thought fit to place them

them together, though in our Proceeding to Describe them, we shall do it severally; and First

1. *CHALDÆA*, is bounded on the East with a Persian Province, called *Susina*; on the West with the Desert of *Arabia*; on the South with the rest of *Deserta*, and the *Persian Gulf*; and on the North with *Mesopotamia*. As for the Original from which this Country has its Name, is uncertain; however it is exceeding Fruitful, yielding Corn in many places 2 and 300 Fold; and *Pliny* affirms the Babylonians Mow their Corn twice a Year, and Seed it a third time, or else it would Produce nothing but Blades; and here many hold the Terrestrial Paradice, a Select Garden, more Inriched by the Bounty of Heaven, than any other part of the World; and the Reason they give for it is, because the Rivers mentioned in Scripture to flow from it are found in this Tract, according to all circumstances the same, though length of Time has caused corruption or alteration, but rather in name than place, &c. and in this Country, on the large Plains of *Shinar* was founded *Babel*, signifying in the *Hebrew* Confusion, where happened the first Confusion of Languages, a work so Stupendious, being the Business of almost all the Inhabitants of the Earth, that before it was left off, it began to rear a Head of Majesty, 5146 Cubits from the Ground, having proportionable Basis and Circumference, the Passages going up winding, and so easie of Ascent, that Horses and Carts might not only pass up it, but meet and turn, having Lodgings and Stations in them for Men and Beast, and Earth spread upon the mighty Work for Corn Fields; and all this foolishly undertaken to secure themselves in case of a second Deluge; and would however (had it not been prevented by the Divine Power) according to the Model devised, have Transcended the Clouds. In this Tract was the City of *Babylon* in its Antient
Glory,

Glory, the Walls of which was 46 Miles in Circuit, 50 Cubits in heighth, and of such a thickness, that Carts and Carriages might meet on the top of it, Finished in one Year by the daily Labour of 20000 Work-men, Built on both sides the River *Euphrates*, having its Communication by stately Bridges, and is said when taken by *Cyrus* the Persian, that he had possessed one part of it three days, before the more remote Inhabitants knew the Enemy was entered; but it has been since that time destroyed and removed; so that at this day *Bagdat* is taken for *Babylon*, Scituate on the River *Tigris*, and now in the Possession of the Turk; the other Places of note are, *Ctesiphon*, *Sipparum*, *Apamia*, *Vologesia*, *Borsipha*, and *Balsora*, the Port of *Bagdat* or new *Babylon*, Scituate at the Fall of *Euphrates*, into *Sinus Persicus*, a Place of great Trade and Wealth, now in the hands of the Persians.

As for Mountains this Country affords not any; and for Rivers, the chief are *Euphrates* and *Tigris*: The People anciently were much addicted to Sooth-saying and Divination, and held to be first Idolaters, but now they are divided into several Sects, and become a mixture of Christians, Jews, and Mahometans, though once the Christian Faith Flourished here altogether, as Planted by St. *Peter*, who assures us that he was at *Babylon* in the latter end of his first Epistle.

2. *ASSYRIA* is bounded on the East with *Media*; on the West with *Mesopotamia*; on the South with *Susiana*; and on the North with some part of *Turcomania*, and part of *Chaldæa*, taking its name from *Assur* the Son of *Sem*, who first Inhabited it, though of late it has been called by other Names, but this being warrantable by Scripture, we shall the rather continue it.

As

As for the Countrey, it is free from Hills, unless such as render it very Commodious, so that being watered with pleasant Springs and Rivers, it is every where very Fruitful, and the People were anciently very Warlike, making themselves by their Arms Lords of the greatest part of the East, extending their Dominion from the *Mediterranean* Sea to the River *Indus*; the Men especially very formal in their Habit, wearing Robes trailing on the ground, their Hair exceeding long, and their Caps so steeple Crowned, that they seem like Pyramids, Perfuming themselves, and Adorning with Jewels, Rings, &c. and a Staff of Ivory, Rich Wood, or some precious Mettal in the form of a Scepter in their Hands; and as for the ancient Custom, it was to expose the fairest Women to Sale in open Market, not as Slaves, but to be purchased as Wives, and with the Money they put off those of the courser sort that were more deformed; happy for our *English Doudies*, were the Custom in use amongst us: And as for the Celebration of Marriage, it is a little strange; *viz.* The Bride-groom sees not his Bride before the Wedding-day, but takes her upon the good report of his Friends and others, when having made the Bargain with her Parents, they meet in the *Chancel* of the Church, and there the *Caſſiſſe* or Priest obliges the Bride-groom to put his hand through the hole of a Partition, and take the Bride by the Hand, which done, her Mother with a sharp Bodkin pricks his hand all over with much eagerness; and if so, for all that he holds her fast, and wrings her hand till she squeak, they term it a presage of lasting Love, but if he let go, the contrary; and if the first Year a Male child is born, the Father loses his Name, and is called *Abba* or Father, the Sons Name being added to it.

ASSYRIA is principally watered with the *Tygris*; so named from its swiftness and rapidity: Into which, as *Ptolomy* affirms, discharge themselves, the Rivers *Cuprus*, *Lycus* and *Gorges*, with some other Streams, or Rivulets, and the whole *Assyria* was divided into six parts, *viz*. *Araphachits*, *Adiabene*, *Calacine*, *Sitacene*, *Arbelites*, and *Apoloniates*, and has for its chief Cities *Calach*, one of the four Cities built in the Land of *Assur* by *Nimrod*; *Sittaca*, about Two Miles from the Banks of *Tygris*; *Athela*, *Apollonia*, *Geguamela*; Memorable for the first great overthrow given by *Alexander* to *Darius* the *Persian*, wherein 90000 *Persians* are accounted to be slain, with the loss of 300 *Macedonians* only; *Reboboth* another City, said to be built by *Nimrod*, but now supposed to be that called *Birrha*, On the *Tygris*; *Rhesen* another, said to be built by the same party; *Ninive*, first built by *Nimrod*, and so named from *Ninus* his Son or Nephew; the City to which *Jonah* was sent, and in those days accounted Sixty Miles in Circuit, which may properly enough in those hot Countreys be accounted three days Journey: *Mosul*, seated on the *Tygris*, *Arzeri* and *Scheheruzal*, the chief Residence of the Turkish Bassa, Governour of this Countrey. As for the Profession of the Natives, and some Strangers mingled amongst them, 'tis that of the *Nestorians*, but the standing Religion is Mahometism imposed by the *Turks*.

3. *MESOPOTAMIA* has on the East for its boundard the River *Tygris*, parted by it from *Assyria*; on the West the *Euphrates*; on the North Mount *Tauryus*; on the South *Chaldæa* and *Arabia Deserta*, and is frequently in Scripture called *Padan-Aram* which in the Latine signifies *Syria Culta*, and was, anciently Inhabited by the *Aramites*, and is full of Rich Pastures, the Soil very fruitful in Corn, abounds with Vine-yards and store of Cattel, and is in-

indeed so well furnished with all things necessary for Humane Support and Pleasure, that *Strabo* calls it *Mesopotamia Felix,* tho in the extream South, there are a few barren Desarts and some rough Mountains or Hills; and though it is a kind of a Compounded Countrey, yet the people are very Active and Industrious, improving Natures Bounty more than any in this Tract, though being but a small Countrey, it has always been in Subjection, and is watered with the Rivers *Tygris, Euphrates,* and *Caboras* or *Abaras.*

The chief Cities found in this Countrey, are *Edessa, Cologenbar, Nisibius,* and *Ur*; as for their Religion, as far as relates to Christianity, it is in a manner Orthodox, agreeing in most Points with the Reformed Churches of *Europe.*

I might now proceed to say something of the Two Kingdoms in the great Mountain *Taurus,* named from their two last Kings, the Kingdoms of *Aledeules* and *Bahaman*; the first subdued by *Selimus* the First Emperour of the *Turks,* and the last by *Abas* the *Persian Sophy*; but having nothing but Rocks and barren Mountains to deal with, and indeed the difficulties the Inhabitants struggle with, being more to be wondered at than any thing else, I shall thus briefly pass them over, and proceed to *Turcomania.*

Turcomania *described in its Provinces,* &c.

TURCOMANIA, or the Land of *Turky,* so called from the *Turks* Inhabiting it before they got by Stratagem the *Persian* Empire, is on the East bounded with *Media* and the *Caspian Sea*; on the West with *Cappadocia, Armenia Minor,* and the *Euxine Sea*; on the North with *Tartary,* and on the South

South with *Assyria* and *Mesopotamia*; and is properly divided into four parts, *viz. Armenia Major*, held to be the true *Turcomania*; *Colchis*, now called *Mengrelia*; *Iberia* now called *Georgia*; and *Albania* called by some *Zuirca*, and of these in their order.

ARMENIA MAJOR, now called *Turcomania*, is a very Hilly Countrey, as much overspread with the Spurs of Mount *Taurus* and *Anti-Taurus*, though between them are many fruitful Valleys, that produce store of Cattle: The greatest business of these people when exempted from War, being to feed Sheep upon the Mountains, and other Cattle on the lower ground, driving them from place to place where the Pastures are best, and where they find the most commodious Springs, carrying with them their Families, Tents, and Provision, and usually go Armed, not so much for fear of Rovers, as Wild Beasts that possess the Caves of those Mountains: The People being large of Body, comely of Personage, much used to the Bow and Spear; patient of all kind of Labour: The Women are very homely, but of a manly aspect, and when occasion requires, addict themselves in Disguises to the Wars, and mingled with the Men, perform equal Exploits; and in Towns, where they are setled, their Families are very great, by reason they co-habit under one Roof to the third or fourth Generation, the eldest commonly bearing Rule, and being in all things absolute as King of the Family, yet those live not idle, but employ themselves in making Tapestries, Gograms, Watered Chamlets, and other Manufactures, dispersed into all parts, and some, tho not many of them are considerable Merchants, dispersing themselves over the Eastern Countrey, and from a Mountain of this *Armenia* called *A'at*, has the great River *Araxis* its Fountain,

tain, and the people generally are Christians.

The chief Cities and Towns of this Country are, *Artaxata* the Royal seat of the Antient Kings of *Armenia*; *Sebastia*, now called *Suassia*; seated on the *Euphrates*, *Tigranes*, *Certa*, *Arsamosata*, *Clamassum*, *Cholna*, *Baraza*, *Chars*, *Colonia*, *Thespia*, and others of lesser note: as for Forrests or Woods, this Country has very few, and none considerable.

COLCHIS the second Division of *Turcomania* on the North of *Armenia* is Inhabited by a rude uncivillized people; however the soil is fertile producing naturally much plenty, and the Vines of their own accord, twist themselves about Trees, creeping up into the spreading Branches, and affording much Wine; but that which in Antient times rendred it most memorable, was the abundance of Gold found in the Sands of the Rivers issuing from the Mount *Caucasus*; for which *Jason* made his Expedition; and thereby gave the occasion of the Fable of the Golden Fleece: there were likewise found divers Veins of Silver in the Mountains, though at present for want of working, or being exhausted, the People deficient in Coin, are obliged to Barter Goods for such things as their necessities require; however they are much given to Riot and Excess, nor do they refuse to prostitute their Wives and Sisters, to the pleasure of their guests upon any slight Entertainment, as not thinking they can be otherways sufficiently welcom; nor do the Women refuse a complyance. And here the chief Cities are, or were *Dioscurias*, *Sibaris* once the Royal Seat of the *Colchine* Kings; *Siganeam*, *Æopolis*, *Neapolis*, *Phasis*; from whence the Phesants were first brought into *Europe* by the *Greeks*; *Alvati*, *Mechlessus*, *Zadris* and *Sirace*; though at present none of them considerable; however the Christian Religion continues here,

though

though the *Turks* have possessed themselves of the Country.

IBERIA takes its name from the River *Iberius*, running through it, though lately the name is changed to *Georgia*; as some will have it from St. *George* the *Capadocian* Martyr; who first planted, or at least greatly improved the Christian Religion amongst them.

The Country is Mountainous, Woody, and a great part of it covered with Snow three quarters of the year; so that the Soil not being very fruitful, the people addict themselves much to War; so that for a long time they lived in freedom under their own Princes, till the *Persian* War; at what time they partly by force, and partly by submission, became Tributary to the *Ottoman* Emperors; so that it contains not any Cities of note; however amongst them are reckoned *Artaxissa*, *Vasada*, *Lubium*, and *Armastica*, so named by *Ptolomy*; though at present *Cremen* at *achet* are in most esteem; and to keep the people in aw, the *Turks* have fortified many places; and amongst others the strong Castle of *Teflis*, the Key of *Media*, now called *Servan*, Garrisoned with 6000 men; and has in it besides other Ammunition 100 pieces of Ordnance.

ALBANIA in *Asia*, distinct from that in *Europe*, East of *Iberia* is accounted to be first peopled by *Gether* Son of *Aram*, and Nephew of *Japhit*, and rested out of the way of War till the *Romans* time; when siding with *Tigranes* King of *Armenia Major*, and *Mithridates* King of *Pontus*, they were brought under subjection by *Pompey*.

The Soil of this Country is very rich in many parts, as being watered with the Rivers *Saonia*, *Cyrus*, *Gerrus* and *Albania*; and on the latter is seated a City of that name, the chief of the Province; here are likewise found *Chabala*, *Thelbis*, *Getara*,

Na-

Namechia and *Teleba*: The chief commodities are Corn, Cattle, Wine, and some Manufactures, and has over it a *Turkish* Bassa; and from these Countries the *Turks* are held on all hands to descend, as in the History of that people, appears more at large.

Media *and* Persia *described, in their respective Provinces,* &c.

MEDIA (the first that occurs in order) is bounded on the West with *Armenia Major*, and some part of *Assyria*; on the East with *Parthia*, and some part of *Hyrcania*, and the Provinces of *Persia*; on the North with the *Caspian Sea*, and *Georgia*; and on the South with other parts of *Persia*; held to take its name from *Madai*, the Son of *Japhet*, who first planted it; though at this day it is called by the *Turks* (in whose possession the greatest part of it is) *Sheirvan*, or *Servan*; the word in their Language signifying a *Milky* plain; alluding thereby to the great plenty of the Country, and is of large extent; once famous for a warlike people, that over-run the greatest part of the East; yet this Country like all others, differs in degree of fertility, for although the South part is exceeding fruitful; yet the North part lying between Mount *Taurus* and the *Hyrcanian Sea*, is very barren; insomuch that the people make their Bread of dryed Almonds, and their drink of the Juice of certain Herbs; no Fruit trees flourishing there, nor any considerable quantity of Corn.

As for the Kingdom of *Media*, we may properly divide it into two Provinces; viz. *Atropatia* and *Media Major*; the first of these contains the northern parts of the country; and is held to be that, where *Salmanasser*, the *Assyrian* King placed the *Israelites*, whom

whom he carryed into Captivity, and is watered by the River *Gonza*; and had for its chief Cities or Towns *Hamadum*, *Gonzavia*, *Mandagarsis*, *Gelin*, *Bochu*, *Erea*, *Sumachia*, or *Shamaki*; the last built by *Cyrus* the *Persian*, and much Illustrated by others; and in it as a Monument, stands a Pillar Interwoven with the Heads of Noble men all of Flint, curiously wrought, &c. This Province is very Mountainous, as having the Spurs of the *Taurus* branching out, and the body of the Mountain it self, &c.

MEDIA-MAJOR, on the South of Mount *Taurus*, is a very pleasant Country; yielding Corn and Wine in abundance, with many pleasant Fruits, and good Pastures, watered every where with fresh streams; so that Cattle, especially Horses encrease in great numbers; the men being generally expert Riders, and much redoubted in War.

The chief Cities that were here found are the great *Ecbatana*, to which *Semiramis* took such liking, that she caused for its better Accommodation, water courses to be cut through the Mountain *Orontes*, reckoned to be in compass 24 *Italian* miles and fortified with a Wall of 70 Cubits high, 50 broad, with 100 Gates, and Towers built over them of smooth stone, and had formerly six lesser Walls, though now little of it remains. *Taurus* a City pleasantly scituate, under the shadow of *Orontes*; opening to a curious fertile Plain on the South; once a place of great Trading, but having been often ruined by the *Turks*, in their Wars with the *Persians*; it has lost much of its former splendor. *Arsacia* built by some of the *Parthian* Kings, in their Conquest of this Country: *Casbin* scituate in an open Plain, on the Banks of a small River, but of no considerable Trade, though the *Persian* Sophies have a Pallace in it: *Rages*, *Nassivan*, *Ardovile*, *Sultania*, *Turcoman*, and *Marant*. The Christian

ſtian Religion is held to be firſt planted here by St. *Thomas*; and though it was not Univerſally Embraced, yet it flouriſhed till *Mahometiſm* was introduced, more by the power of the Sword than the Peoples Inclination.

Perſia *Deſcribed.*

PERSIA has for its Eaſtern boundard *India*; for the Weſtern *Media, Aſſyria,* and *Chaldea*; the Northern *Tartary*; and the Southern the main Ocean; ſo named, (if you will credit the Story) from *Perſeus,* Son to *Jupiter* and *Danae*; though rather from *Perſis* a ſmall Province; or part of the Country which took its name from one of their Kings: and the whole Region of *Perſia,* is found to extend from 82 degrees of Longitude, to 120. 36 degrees in all, and in bredth from 32 degrees North Latitude to 42, ſcituate under the fourth, fifth, and ſixth Climates; ſo that the longeſt day in the Southern parts, is 13 hours and almoſt three quarters but in the moſt Northern 15 and a quarter; the Air for the moſt part pure and wholſom, though the Earth by reaſon of the great heat of the Sun, is dry, and ſandy in many parts, and deſtitute of water; having few Rivers, and not many Lakes; however taking the Country in general, it abounds with all things neceſſary, and may properly be divided into 12 Provinces, viz. *Suſiana, Perſis, Carmania, Ormus, Gedroſia, Drangiana, Aria, Parthia, Arachoſia, Paropamiſu', Hyrcania,* and *Margiana*; and held to be one of the Antienteſt Kingdoms of the Eaſt; the people as the *Chaldæans,* giving themſelves up to the Study of Aſtrology; and as to their Religion, its the Sect of *Haly,* differing in many things, from the Tenets of the Impoſtor *Mahomet*; tho amongſt them are many Chriſtians and more

Jews

Jews; and the chief Rivers that visit *Persia*, are *Araxis*, some windings of *Euphrates* and *Tigris*; and here are found Mount *Taurus*, the *Seriphian* Hills, and some others of less note: And has for the most material Cities, *Persopolis*, *Aracca*, *Tarsiana*, and others; the Country affording Dates, Myrrh, Drugs, Spices, Mines of Silver, Brass, Quarries of of Marble, Cedar-wood, and rich Manufactures of Silks, and Embroideries of Silver and Gold, and has been much traded to, by the *European* Merchants, especially the Island of *Ormus*; accounted the most fruitful in the World; so that those who have compared the World to a Ring, have allowed this to be the Jewel, that ought to be set in it; for the *Portugals* upon their first coming hither, so much inriched themselves, that they easily commanded the whole Trade of *Europe*.

As for the Persians, they are generally good natured, courteous to Strangers, exceeding obedient to their Prince, whom they in a manner Idolize; they are tall of Stature, well Limbed, and for the most part handsome (especially the Women) Patient of Labour, yet through the Plenty of the Country much given to Luxury, Valiant in Fighting, as well the Women as the Men, who accompany their Husbands to the War in disguise, and frequently die Fighting by their sides, as appeared by the great number of them found upon the stripping of the Slain in many Battles fought between them and the Turks. And within this Jurisdiction we may include *Bactria*, lying West of *Margiana*, watered by the River *Oxus*, so that it is partly Fruitful, and partly Barren and Desert, possessed by a rough and untractable People, and has many Woods and Forrests full of wild Beasts, which renders the Passage dangerous to Travellers, and has its Name from *Bactria* the Metropolitan City, Seated at the Foot

of

of the Mountain *Sogdij*, and is now in Subjection to the Persians.

Tartaria *Described, in its Kingdoms and Provinces*, &c.

TARTARIA, or *Tartary*, is a large Tract on the Northern part of *Asia*, and shooting out considerably to *Europe*, bounded on the East with *China*, and the Eastern Ocean; on the West with *Russia* and *Podolia*, a Province of the Kingdom of *Poland*; on the North with the Frozen-Scythian Ocean; and on the South with another part of *China*, from which it is separated by a mighty Wall, the River *Oxus* parting it from *Bactria* and *Margiana*, the *Caspian* Sea from *Media* and *Hyrcania*; the *Caucasian* Mountains from *Turcomania*, and the *Euxine* Sea from *Anatolia* and *Thrace*, and is possessed under the general Name of *Tartars*, by many powerful Nations, accounted to be 5400 Miles from East to West, and 3600 from North to South.

The People are generally Rude, giving themselves more to War and Rapine, than to Arts or Husbandry, big Bodied, broad Faced, ▪▪le and hollow Eyed, thick Lipped, and flat Nosed, Swarthy of Complexion, tho distant enough from the Sun, hardy and capable of induring extream Hardships, loving to ride, tho on Cows, Oxen, and other Beasts, not used in other parts in such Services; their Speech carries a kind of a whining Tone with it, and when a Company are got together a Singing, one would imagine them a consort of Wolves a Howling, and have indeed in their many Excursions and Wars proved the Terror of the World, yet are seldom Covetous, of more than is sufficient to support them, as being altogether regardless of Silver, Gold, or costly Apparel, going for the most part clad with the Skins and Furrs of Beasts they take by Hunting, and are by some held to be the Off-spring of the Ten Tribes removed out of *Palestine* by *Salmanasser*; for many of the great Lords of the Tartars stile themselves *Naphthalites*, *Danites*, &c. and Canton themselves into Families and Tribes.

This Countrey is usually divided into these following Provinces, viz, *Precopensis*, *Asciatica*, *Antigua*, *Zagatha* and *Cathaia*: The first contains *Taurica Chersonesus*, and the *Asciatican* Banks of *Tanais*, taking its name from *Precops* the chief City, and has in it, beside the Towns of *Ozaclow*, *Capha*, *Crim*, and others of lesser note. The second contains *Asciatica Deserta*, or *Deserta Muscovita*, held to be the ancient *Sarmatia Asciatica*, remaining unciviliz'd at this day; as feeding upon Raw Horse-flesh, sucking Blood from living Creatures, and oftentimes preying upon each other, and neglecting all manner of Tillage. The Third contains the Cities of *Noyhan*, *Cashan*, *Charackzicke*, *Astracan*, and some others of lesser note, as *Coras*, *Caracora*, and the whole Kingdom of *Tendock*, and affords the Drug called *Rhubarb*, not any other where to be found. The fourth Division contains *Scythia*, *Inter Imaum*, inhabited by a more civiliz'd People of the *Tartars*, and have for their chief Cities *Istigias*, scituate in a very fruitful Plain, to which flow the principal Commodities of the whole Kingdom, and *Samarchand*, usually the Residence of the *Tartarian Chams*, where *Tamerlain* the Great was born and died; but the most pleasant of all, and indeed the Glory of the whole Countrey, is the Kingdom of *Cathia*.

The Soil of this part of *Tartary* yields a superabundance of Fruits, Corn, Hemp, Flax, &c. and the other Merchandise are Woolls, Rhubarb, Musk, Silks, and Manufactures of its own, and also those of *China*, that are brought hither, and has for its
Chief

Chief Cities *Cambalu, Tebeth, Carraran,* and *Xeandu,* all of them very stately; containing in their large Circumferences, Pallaces, fixed and moving, Parks, Pastures, with many other Rarities; but in all these Countreys, the Government is Arbitrary, the Lives and Estates of the People depending upon the pleasure of the Prince.

There are yet another sort of this people called *Crimesian Tartars,* inhabiting the *Crim,* on the Fenns of *Mæotis* and borders of *Moscovy* and *Poland,* but much of the nature of those already mentioned. As for Religion, they are in many places divided in Opinion, as being a mixture of *Armenians, Christians, Jews, Mahometans,* and some *Idolaters.*

The chief Rivers that Water this Countrey, are the *Tanais* and *Volga,* and the principal Mount *Imaus,* which runs in a long Chain or Ridge, branching however into divers Spurs, *&c.*

A description of the Kingdom of China in its Provinces, &c.

CHINA is a large Kingdom, though not well known, till the latter times to the *Europeans,* bounded on the North with the *Eastern Tartars,* and *Altay;* separated from them by a continued Chain of Hills, and a Wall of 400 Leagues in length, furnished with Towers, and so broad, that a Cart may be driven on the top of it, built (as they give it out) by *Tzaintzon* the 117th King of *China.* The Southern boundards are partly *Cochin-China,* a Province of the *East India,* and partly the Ocean; on the East with the *Oriental Ocean,* and on the West with part of *India* and *Cathaia*; and is indeed on all parts so hemm'd in with Mountains, Seas, and Artificial Fortifications, that it is no wonder Travellers missed it in their way to other Countreys. This

H

This Kingdom, according to the account of the Natives, contains 15 Provinces, viz. *Canton, Foqueit, Olam, Sifuam, Tolenchia, Canfay, Miuchian, Ochian, Hionam, Paguia, Taitan, Quinchen, Chagnian, Sufnam,* and *Quinfay,* in which are computed 591 Cities, 1593 Walled Towns, 4200 Unwalled Towns, and 1154 Castles; the whole Countrey being accounted 3000 Leagues in Circumference, reaching from 130 to 160 Degrees of Longitude, and from the Tropick of *Cancer* to the 53 Degree of Latitude, lying under all the Climes from the Third to the Ninth, so that the Air is very Temperate and Healthful, by which the Natives are for the most part exempted from Sickness, and live to an extream Age: As for the Riches and Fertility, it is very much, even to admiration, the people being very Industrious, and the Soil as suitable; so that in many places they have two, and in most parts three Harvests in a Year, nor do they spare to Plant and Sow, the best of all kinds they can compass.

The chief Commodities coming from hence are Pearls, Bezora Stones, Wooll, Cotton, Olives, Wine, Flax, Metals, Fruit, *China* Ware of sundry kinds, Stuffs, Carpets, Embroideries, Musk, Amber, &c. The People are of a Swarthy Complexion, especially those living towards the Southern parts, short Nosed, black Eyed, with thin Beards, wearing long Garments, with loose Sleeves, and Hair at its full growth; they are much given to often eating, but then they do it very sparingly, not touching their Victuals with their hands, but take it with a Fork made of Ebbony or Ivory, from whom the *Europeans* learned the Fashion. The Men are very Jealous of their Wives, insomuch that they will not suffer them to go abroad, nor sit at the Table with them if any Stranger be there, unless some very near Kinsman; however they permit them

them to go as Gay as they please about the House, and one Trick has been brought into a Custom, to prevent their desiring to ramble, the which is by the hard binding up their Feet when Children, to render them small, that being accounted the greatest Ornament or Beauty, so that being Cripled by that means, they cannot go without pain. As for their dead, they bury them in Fields fifteen days after their decease: They that are buried within the Walls of Cities, &c. being by them accounted most miserable. Knowledge they have of the Deity, and some marks and foot-steps of Christianity is remaining amongst them, but so obscured, that they live for the most part after the manner of the ancient Gentiles, offering Sacrifices to the Devil, thereby to appease him, that he should do 'em no Mischief; and will needs have the date of their Actions, or the beginning of their Kingdom, long before the World was made, telling many strange and incredible Stories about the Creation, &c. In their Building, and indeed in all their Actions, they are very neat, and the Countrey so populous, though the Wars with the *Tartars* have somwhat lessened the number; that some of their Kings have brought a Million of People into the Field, and has seldom less, than 1000 Ships of War, though of no great Service, in a readiness, and 10000 lesser Vessels on several Rivers, for carrying of Goods and Merchandise from place to place; yet so jealous are they of Strangers prying into their Affairs, that in some Cities 'tis Death for any but a Native to lodge a Night within the Walls, nor is he permitted in the day time to enter, without giving his name to a *Publique Notary*, which when he returns, he must see crossed out, or where ever he is found, he suffers for it.

The Towns and Cities are too Numerous to be particularly recited, but the principal are *Quinsay*, 100 Miles in Circuit, with a Lake of 30 Miles compass within the Walls, in the middle of which is an Island, where the Emperor (as he stiles himself) has a Magnificent Pallace, and is thought to contain Two millions of People. *Pequin* or *Pekin*, not much inferiour to the former in bigness, but nothing in Trade, and all the Countrey is so free from Hills or Mountains, that the *Chinese* ride in Charriots made of Reeds, or Canes, which by the help of Sails is driven by the Wind, as if drawn by Horses, or floating upon the Water. As for the Rivers, they are but few, and those proceed from great Lakes, as wanting hills to give them Springs; the principal are *Aspthara*, *Senus*, *Ambaƈlu*, and *Cotiaris*, all Navigable; and have over them a great Number of Bridges, the Arches of some of them rising so high, that a Ship under Sail may pass with as much ease as a Boat: And as for the Customs arising by Trade, they are so great, that no Prince whatsoever receives so much upon the like occasion.

East India *described, in its Kingdoms and Provinces*, &c.

*I*NDIA the largest Tract in the World, going under one entire name or denomination, except *Tartary* and *China*, is bounded on the East with the Oriental Sea, and a part of *China*; on the West with the Dominions of the *Persian Sophy*; and on the North with Branches of Mount *Taurus*, that divide it from *Tartary*; and on the South with the *Indian Ocean*: The whole Countrey (as most considerate persons affirm) taking its name from the River *Indus*, the most famous and noted in that part of

Asia; tho some will have it to be so called from the end or furthest extent of *Asia*, and is extended from 106 to 159 degrees of Longitude, and from the Equinoctial or Equator, to 44 degrees of North Latitude, as to the main Continent, tho some Islands reckoned within the compass of *India*, extend to 9 degrees South Latitude.

This Countrey, to give it its due, is in most parts exceeding pleasant and flourishing, enjoying healthful and Temperate Air, unless at some Seasons, when the heat is excessive in the Southern parts, the Summer continuing there much longer than with us, so that they have in a manner Two Summers giving a double increase; so that they want nothing fit for the sustaining the Life of Man, or whatever may tend to Recreation or Delight: The Kingdoms and Provinces generally abounding with Precious Stones, Spices, Perfumes, Medicinals, Mines of Gold and Silver, and Minerals of all other kinds, Copper and Lead excepted; and that they may not so abound as to reject the Traffick of other Countries, they are deficient in Wheat and Vines, and have but few Horses; the Creatures they use for Service, being Camels, Elephants, and Dromedaries, with other Creatures of lesser note: Though the Woods, Plains, and Rivers abound with Tygers; some Lyons, Rhinocerots, Apes, Serpents, and Crocodiles; and in the Seas are found Whales of a monstrous size, as 66 Cubits in length, and 20 in thickness, with lesser Fish of sundry forms, not found in the *European* Seas, nor perhaps in any other. The Natives of *India* are different, according to the Climates they inhabit; but in general of a Swarthy Complexion, Tall of Stature, Strong of Body, and in most places very much Civiliz'd, and Exact Dealers; and altho the common sort are but meanly clad, and many only with Garments capable of hiding their Privities, and others meerly for

H 3 Decency,

Decency, yet those of the better rank observe a Majesty in both *Sex*, as to their Raiment and Attendants, Perfuming themselves, and wearing besides Rich Attire, Jewels, and other Ornaments of great value; and tho the Women are barred of that Perfection of Beauty the *Europeans* possess, yet have they many lovely and attractive Features, wearing their Hair long and loose, yet covered with a Veil of *Calicut* Lawn; their Ears hung with Rings and Jewels, so heavy, that the weight distorts and disproportions them; they have also Jewels in their Noses, according to their degree, and are very submissive and loving to their Husbands, insomuch that they frequently leap into the Funeral Fires, and perish with the dead Body, in hopes to enjoy him in another World; those that refuse it, being looked upon worse than common Prostitutes, and not only hated, but severely persecuted, to the hazard of a worse Death by their own Relations.

The Religion of the *India's* is mostly that of Gentilism, tho Mahometism has made a considerable progress; and since the *Europeans* have Traded here, Christianity has considerably prevailed or rather revived; it being held on all hands that St. *Thomas* the Apostle planted the Christian Religion in these parts, of which upon the first Arrival of the *Portugals*, many marks remained; and in this Countrey it is held he suffered Martyrdom, being run through the Body with a Spear as he was at his Devotion, by the Command of an *Indian* King; and if we take *India* in general, it consists of a mixture of five sorts of people more especially, *viz.* Indians, Moors or *Arabians*, *Jews*, *Tartars*, and *European Christians*, who have planted divers Colonies on the Sea Coast, and in the Islands, strongly fortifying themselves against the Power of the Natives and other Strangers.

This

This large Countrey, especially on the Continent, is principally divided into *India intra Gangem*, and *India extra Gangem*, and then subdivided into Kingdoms and Provinces, and the chief contained in the former, are *Narsinga, Mallabar, Balassia, Cambaia, Mandoa, Bengala, Ostrian, Conora,* and *Dellie*; and of these in their order.

NARSINGA lies on the East of the Golf of *Bengal*, properly accounted a Kingdom, and is 3060 miles in Compass, the King whereof is not subject to the Great *Mogul*, but for his support, and the defence of his Countrey, keeps 40060 Men in pay, and can raise upon occasion a far greater Number; the Countrey is very fruitful, as being watered with many pleasant Streams, besides what the *Ganges* contributes towards it, and has for its Chief City *Melleaper*, otherwise called St. *Thomas*, in Memory of the Apostle said to be Martyred in it; *Bisnagar* a Town of considerable Beauty and Trade; as also *Narsinga*, from whence the Kingdom seems to take its Name; and here the Women burn themselves with their Husbands.

MALLABAR, formerly called *Aurea Chersonesus*, is a Countrey extreamly well peopled, yielding Corn, Spices, Cocoes, Jaceroes, and although it has not above 25 Leagues of Sea Coast, yet it has in its Tract the Provinces of *Kanonor, Calecut, Cranganor, Cochin* and *Cariolam*, and is of large Inland extent; the people upon many parts of the Coast addicting themselves to Piracy, and prove very inhospitable to Strangers, eating Humane Flesh, and giving their Virgins to the Priests or Strangers to be deflowred, before they suffer them to be Bedded by themselves when Married; with many other Barbarous Customs, as their changing their Wives, and their having sometimes but one between seven or eight of them.

BALASSIA, called the Kingdom of *Bocan*, tho but very small, is nevertheless famed for the Mines of Gold and Silver found therein, by which the Neighbouring Countreys are enriched, having for its Chief Towns *Senergian*, *Balaſſiá*, and *Bocan*, very Fruitful in many parts, and much Traded to.

CAMBAIA, called by some *Guzant*, is accommodated with 500 Miles of Sea Coast, very Fertile, and is full of Cities and Towns, many of them considerably Traded to, and altho Cattle of sundry kinds abound here, the people are so Superstitious, that they will eat no Flesh, but live upon what else the Countrey affords, fancying, like the *Pythagoreans*, that the Souls of Men pass into Beasts, *&c.* though they spare not to kill the Elephants for their Ivory, and have for their Chief Sea Towns, *Daman*, *Curate*, *Bandora*, *Ravelbon*, and for those more inland, *Campanel*, *Tanaa*, *Mollar*, and *Cambaia*; the last giving Name to the whole Kingdom.

MANDOA, a Province very Fruitful, and stored with considerable Towns, and above the rest *Mandoa*, from which it takes its name, being 30 Miles in compass, and said to be so well Furnished for Defence, that it held out a Twelve years Siege against the Armies of very Powerful Kings; *Molta*, where the Women imitating the Men, ride a stride with Boots and Spurs on, *&c.*

BENGALA, is a very large, and no less Fruitful Kingdom, lying upon the great Golf of the Sea, to which it gives Name, making 120 Leagues of Sea Coast, watered by the River *Chaberis*, on which are seated many considerable Inland Towns, full of people, but such as are exceeding Crafty and Deceitful, thinking it no crime to cozen or over-reach Strangers, nor the Women to prostitute their Bodies to any that will give them Money; the Fathers letting the Daughters to hire for so long as is desired to do the Work at Bed and Board, it being the

Custom

Custom of the Countrey, being a place much resorted, by reason of the rich Commodities found there, as Ginger, Long Pepper, Silks, Cottons, and others, &c. As for the Chief Cities, they are *Bengala*, scituate on the Bay or Golf *Chatigan*, or *Satigar*, and *Gouro*, and in this Tract the beast called the *Rhinoceros*, is chiefly found.

ORISTAN or *Orixa* is a Province not very large, yet furnished with Rice, Cloath of Cotton, a fine Stuff like Silk made of Grass, and there called *Teva*; Long Pepper, Ginger, Mirabolans, and other Commodities; So that from the Haven of *Orissa* 25 or 30 Ships have been laden with the Commodities of this Province in a Season; and here the people differ from the foregoing, as being very honest and just in their Dealings, and has for its Chief City *Raman*, where the Governour for the *Mogul* resides.

CANORA is a Kingdom of considerable strength and largeness, but famed for nothing more than the Quarries of Adamant, where likewise Diamonds of Considerable Value are found, and that none may purloyn them, a Wall is drawn about the Hill, and a Guard set upon the Gates: As for the chief Cities or Towns, they are *Lispeo*, *Dangar*, and *Ultabat*, with some other of lesser note.

DELLIE is accounted as the former, a Kingdom, the Prince, or rather Governour of it living in great State, and is so highly Reverenced by his *Subjects*, that they not only kneel when he passes in a Rich Chair of State carried on Mens Shoulders, but upon Notice given that he shaves his Beard, or has his Hair Cut, a Jubile is kept throughout his Countrey: As for the Soil, it is not very Fruitful, as lying considerably Northward, and more subject to Frosts than the rest: Its Chief City is *Dellie*, from whence the Kingdom takes its Name; besides which, there are of note, *Fremel*, *Fultaber* and *Besmer*; and these People above other *Indians* addict

dict themselves much to the study of Magick.

In this Tract of *Intra Gangem*, are found the Provinces of *Cochin*, where the *Portugals* hold a considerable Trade, and have some Collonies; *Crangan* a small Kingdom, mostly inhabited by such as stile themselves the Christians of St. *Thomas*, and is very plentiful as well in Product as Manufacture: *Conlam* is a small Dominion of about 80 Miles extent, Governed by a Petty King; but for want of good Havens or Sea-coast, not much Traded to, though it comprehends Three and twenty Walled Towns.

India *Extra Gangem*.

IN this part of *India* are found divers Rich Countreys, *viz.*

ARACHAN, an Inland Region invironed with *Mountains* and *Woods*, yet exceeding Fruitful, and in it are gathered from the Rough Rocks, &c. great quantities of *Precious Stones*; as for the Chief City it is *Arachan*.

MACHIN a little Kingdom, wherein grows the Wood *Aloes*, much esteemed and valued, and has *Machin* for its Chief City.

CAMBOIA a large Countrey full of People, abounding with *Elephants* and *Rhinocerots*; also with Gold Silver and *Aloes*, and other *Commodities* of considerable value, put to Sale in *Camboia* its Chief City.

COCHIN, *China* a Countrey (once belonging to the *Chinese*, but now under the *Mogul*, Governed by his Deputed Kings) abounding with *Porcelain*, *Aloes*, *Silks*, *Gold*, *Silver*, &c. having its Chief City of the same Name.

BRAMA once a Kingdom of no account, but now by the Conquests the Kings have made, it has under its power *Calam, Prema, Melinta, Meranda, Decan,*

Decan, Tangu, Ava, Machin, Aracan, Odia, Pegu, Siam, and others; so that it is the most powerful in this Tract; and the City of Pegu is the Royal Residence of that King.

SIAM, once a powerful Kingdom, the King thereof styling himself Mighty, but now, as before intimated, it is Tributary to the King of Brama, and is however a very Fertil Countrey, having Malacca for its Chief City, possessed by the Portugals, and much Traded to by other Nations for Spices.

PEGU was formerly so powerful, that the Kings thereof have brought Armies of 11 and 900000 men into the Field, extending their Conquests very wide, but now the good Fortune of the Brananian holds it in subjection. These are the places of Chief Note upon the Continent; however there are found in this large Tract the Provinces or Kingdoms of Dulsinda, Pengab, Agra, Sanga, Camboia, Decan, Bacaster, Patanaw, and Jangoma; many of them very spacious, abounding with Fruits, Cattle, Minerals, Precious Stones, and the like. This Countrey rarely failing any where to produce something worthy of Note.

The Principal Rivers are Ganges, Indus, and Hydaspes; the last is in esteem with the Natives, that they come many miles on Pilgrimage to it, Superstitiously imagining, that if they sink the Waters of this River before they die, they shall undoubtedly possess their Imagined Felicity in another World; and in the last are found a great number of Perfect Ossier, washed from the Rocks and Mountains, by the English Side adjoyned to these Streams thereof; besides all, Nilus contributes farning and enriching the Soil in every part where they flow. As for Mountains of note, except some Branches of Taurus, there are but few.

A Geographical and Historical Description OF 𝕬𝖋𝖗𝖎𝖈𝖆,

In its Kingdoms and Provinces, &c.

AFRICA larger than *Europe*, but less than *Asia*, is bounded on the East with the *Red Sea* and *Arabian Bay*, parted by them from *Asia*; on the West with the Main *Atlantick Ocean*, separating it from *America*; on the North with the *Mediterranean Sea*, dividing it from *Europe* and *Anatolia*; and on the South with the *Æthiopick Ocean*, separating it from the *Southern Continent*; and joyns only to *Asia* by an *Isthmus* of 60 Miles, over which *Cleopatra* the Queen of *Ægypt* when she fled with *Antony* from the Naval Fight at *Actium*, purposed to draw by main force her *Ships and Galleys* into the

Red

Red Sea, but was diffwaded from it, by being put in hopes of a better Fortune.

AFRICA is held to have taken its name from *Affre* or *Apher*, descended from *Abraham*, and is properly held to contain Six principal Regions, besides other of lesser note, *viz. Barbary, Egypt, Numidia, Sarra*, the Countrey of the *Negro's*, and the Dominions of *Prestor John*, and is in form like a Pyramid reversed, the Basis of which, from *Tangier* to the Straights of *Gibralter*, to the Point where it joyneth to *Asia*, is counted 1920 *Italian* Miles, the Cone of it very narrow, but to reckon from the Cone or Pyris, to the Northern parts of the Basis, it extendeth it self 4155 Miles, and is scituate for the most part under the *Torrid Zone*, being crossed by the *Equator* almost in the midst, which made some of the Ancient Writers conceive it not habitable, by reason of the excessive Heat in the middle and more southern parts, in which they deceived themselves; for al-tho in some places it is full of Sandy Desarts, yet the greatest part of those Regions that lie near or under the Line, are furnished with so many Fountains, Rivers, and little Brooks, *Cedars* and other lofty *Trees*, casting a large Shade as well as bearing delicate Fruits, and at all times stored with Blossoms, that the place is not despicable, but much to be desired, and especially places more Northward, but leaving it in general, we proceed (for the better satisfaction of the Reader) to particulars.

A Description of Egypt, *&c.*

EGYPT, once a Famous and Flourishing Kingdom, now in the hand of the *Turks*; is bounded on the East with *Idumea*, and the *Arabian Bay*; on the West with *Numidia, Barbary*, and part of *Libya*;

Lybia; on the North with the *Mediterranean Sea*; and on the South with *Æthiopia Superiour*, containing in length from the *Mediterranean* to the City of *Asua* or *Syene* bordering on *Æthiopia*, 562 *Italian* Miles, and in breadth from *Roseta* to *Damiatia*, or from the most Western Branch of *Nile* to the farthest East 160 of the like Miles; said to be first Inhabited by *Misraim* the Son of *Chus*, and Grandchild to *Cham*, scituate under the Second and Fifth Climates, making the longest Summers day but 13 hours and a half, and altho by reason of its Southerly scituation, it must consequently be in a hot and sultry Air; it has nevertheless fresh Gales of Wind to temperate it, and once a Year the over-flowing of the River *Nilus*, which renders it so Fruitful, that it abounds with rich Pastures, store of Camels, Horses, Oxen, Asses, Sheep and Goats of extraordinary growth; also with infinite store of Wild and Tame Fowl, with plenty of Minerals, Precious Stones, Wine, Choice Fruits, as Oranges, Lemons, Citrons, Pomegranats, Cherries, &c. and has Palm Trees in great numbers growing Male and Female, and the Female bears not unless she grows by the Male; a Tree universally useful, as serving to above twenty ends.

As for the People, they are of a Swarthy or Tawny Complexion, very much inured to Labour, tho the Countrey yields great Encrease of its own accord, very servile and obedient to their Conquerers, who Lord it over them; the Richer sort generally addicting themselves to *Necromancy* and *Sorcery*, and are said first to Teach the use of Letters to the *Phænicians*, though the *Magi*, and those that were stiled their Priests, strugled all that in them lay to obscure Learning, by representing the meaning of what they intended to express in *Hieroglyphicks*, shadowing it under divers forms of Birds and Beasts, &c. and here are to be found the Ruins of mighty

Stru-

Structures, as the Pyramids and Tower of *Pharo's*, built of Marble, exceeding high, nightly hung with Lights, as a Sea-mark to *Sailors*, and many other rare Matters to demonstrate the Magnificence of a Plenteous Kingdom.

As for the Cities of *Egypt*, they are generally built upon Hills or high rising Ground, to stand dry during the over-flowing of *Nilus*, from whose Waters the Countrey receives its Fertility; so that whilst it carries its Stream over the Land, they Commerce with each other by little Boats, which beginning on the 15th of *June*, lasts 40 days, standing 15 Cubits in many places, and in 40 more gathers its Waters within the Banks, by which means the Earth is so well tempered (for in this Kingdom there falls no Rain) that the Encrease is sixty and eighty fold, their Harvest being commonly in our *March* and *April*; and if the River flows too scanty or too immoderate, then it betokens scarcity, or some misfortune to the Prince, Governour, or State, and whilst its Waters are abroad, which at the first issuing create a *Plague* for the space of a day: The Cattle feed on the Hills; and when the Famine was here in the Reign of *Pharaoh*, this River refused to pass its bounds, or give any Assistance to the Thirsty Land.

This Countrey was formerly divided into two parts, *viz. Delta* and *Thebais*; the first lying between the two extream Branches of the River *Nilus*, in form of the greek Letter, from whence it takes it's name, and the last taking name from the City of *Thebes*, containing all the rest of the Rivers Course; and these again with some odd Angles, are divided by some into many *Parts*, *Shires*, or *Counties*, and is said in the time of King *Amasis* the Second to contain 20000 *Cities*, *Towns*, and considerable *Castles*, but now a far less number; as being ruined in their several *Wars*, &c. they being

Caire

Cairo or *Grand Cair*, *Alexandria*, *Pelusium*, since called *Damiatia*, taken and possessed by the *Christians* in the Holy War, yet held out so obstinately upon the Siege, that 70000 persons died of the Famine and Pestilence: *Heros* or *Heroum*, scituate on the *Arabian Isthmus*, at the very bottom of the Golf, where *Jacob* and *Joseph* had their first interview: *Heliopolis*, the City of the Sun, now called *Betsames* in the Land of *Goshen*: *Arsinoe*, on the Shoar of the *Red Sea*, *Cleopatris* built by Queen *Cleopatra*: *Gleba Rubra*, by the *Greeks* called *Hierabolus*, and sometimes *ErithiaBolus*, of which there goes a Story, That King *Amenophis* the Fifth being Blind, was informed by one of his *Magi*, that if he could procure the Water or Urine of a Woman that had been Married a Twelve-month and upward, who had known no Man but her Husband, it would restore him to Sight, when having tried in vain a great number, at last one was found, whose Urine effected it, upon which he took her as a mark of Honour, to be his Queen, and caused the rest to be brought into this Town, and to be burnt together with it.

As for the *Egyptians*, they are a great many of them *Mahometans*, and some maintain their first Idolatrous Custom, in Worshipping an Ox, Onions, Leeks, and other Foolish Matters, and when they have a great Increase, they Offer to the God *Nilus*, as they term the River, in which Feast the poorer sort spend almost all they have Laboured for through the course of the Year; and indeed, this Country in Fruitfulness, occasioned by that River, affords them no small Store, alluding to which, thus the Poet *Lucan*;

Terrâ suis contenta bonis, non indiga Mercis,
Aut Jovis; in solo tanta est Fiducia Nilo.

The Earth content with it's own Wealth doth crave
No Forreign Wares, nor *Jove* himself they have,
Their Hope's alone in *Nilus* Fruitful wave.

And one thing extraordinary in this Kingdom, we think not fit to pass by, which if true (as indeed it is confirmed by People of known Credit) may justly create a wonder in all, coming to pass by a supernatural means, and not the work of Art and Nature, *viz.* about five Miles from *Cair,* there is said to be a place which every *Good Friday* shews the appearance of the Heads, Legs, Arms, &c. of Men and Children, as if rising out of the Ground, to a very great Number; however if any Person approach them, they shrink in again: A strange forerunner, or earnest, if true, of the Resurrection of the whole Body, presented Yearly by the rising of the Members; and to confirm the Truth hereof, *Stephen Dupleis* (held to be a sober discerning Man) affirms to be an Eye Witness of the Wonder, and that he had touched diverse of the rising Members, and as he was once about to do it to the Head of a Child, a *Carian* forbad it, telling him he knew not what he did. Another Wonder is the *Crocodile,* which coming from a small Egg, not exceeding the bigness of a *Turkies,* grows to be 30 Feet in length and proportionable in thickness, living at Pleasure in the Water, or on the Land, destroying not only Fish, but Men and Beasts; and with these the *Nilus* abounds, as also with a Fish called the River Horse; and thus much for *Egypt.*

A Description of Barbary.

BARBARY, (a considerable part of *Africk*, so called) is bounded on the East with *Cyrenaica*; on the West with the *Atlantick Ocean*; on the North with the Streights of *Gibraltar*, and some part of the *Atlantick Ocean*; on the South with Mount *Atlas*, separated by that Mount from the *Desarts* of *Lybia*, scituate under the third and fourth Climates, so that the longest Summers Day in the most Southern parts, amounts to 13 Hours 3 Quarters, but in the North 4 and a Quarter, accounted in Length 1500 Miles, and in Breadth in some places 100, and in others near 300 Miles, taking its Name from the Word *Bar* made double, signifying in the *Saracens* Language a Desart.

The Part of *Barbary* lying towards the *Mediterranean*, is full of craggy Hills and Mountains, shaded on the Top with Woods, where Lyons and other Beasts of Prey shelter themselves, though the Valleys are very Fruitful, but deficient in Wheat, insomuch that the Inhabitants Eat Barley Bread, yet between these and Mount *Atlas*, the Country is Champian, watered with many Pleasant Rivers, issuing from that Mountain, rendering the Soil rich and fertile, so that it affords great store of Plums, Pears, Figs, Cherries, Apples of sundry Kinds, Oyl, Honey, Sugar, and some Mines of Gold, called *Barbary Gold*, being the finest of all other; And *Pliny* reports that near *Leptis* we may behold a Date Tree over-shadowing an Olive, and under the Olive a Fig-Tree, and under the Fig, a Pomegranate-Tree, and under that a Vine, and under the the Vine, Pease or Corn, &c. all Flourishing at the same time, and this they do the rather, that they may shelter each other from the heat of the Sun.

The

The People are of a Dusky Colour, inclining to Bla' :fs, held to Descend from the *Arabians*, so that the Language they Speak in most parts is the *Arabick*, or so bordering upon it that it may be easily understood, and are Impatient of Labour, Covetous of Honour, Crafty and Deceitful, yet studious in matters of their Law, and some Sciences, more especially *Philosophy* and the *Mathematicks*, and are in Religion generally *Mahometans*; they are also stately of Gate, exceeding Mistrustful, Implacable in their Hatred, and Jealous beyond compare; for the Women indeed are comely of Body, well Featured, delicate, soft Skinn'd, and want nothing but Colour to make them Accomplish'd Beauties; nor has this Country failed to produce Persons, not only Famous for Arts and Arms, but for Piety and Learning, as, *Amilcar*, *Hannibal*, *Septimus Severus*, *Massinissa*, *Tertullian*, *Cyprian*, *Arnobius*, *Lactantius*, *Augustine*, and others of no less Note; and here once Ruled Queen *Dido* in the Famous City of *Carthage*, which City so long and strongly contended with *Rome* for the Empire of the World, but at last was destroyed through the Importunity of *Cato*, at which time there was found in it (notwithstanding the charge of a tedious War) 470000 pound weight of Silver.

As for the whole Country, called *Barbary*, it was Divided into 7 Parts, viz. *Africa Propria*, called also *Zugitania*, *Byzantena*, *Tripolitana*, *Numidia*, *Maurtania*, *Cæsariensis*, *Sitifensis*, and *Tingitania*, under diverse Kings and Governours, who then held it as Tributaries to the *Roman* Emperors, but since reduced to four Divisions, viz. *Tunis*, *Tremesen* or *Algiers*, *Fesso*, and *Morocco*; and of these in their order.

TUNIS is accounted a Kingdom, containing whatever the *Antients* called *Africa Propria*, or *Minor*, and *Numidia Antiqua*, the Air very Temperate,

rate, considering the degree it lyes in; the Soil very Fruitful, divided again into 5 parts, *viz. Bugia, Constantia, Tunis, Tripoley* and *Ezub*, accommodated with many curious Havens, the chief being *Tripoley*, where the *Turkish* Bassa resides; and *Tunis* a considerable City giving Name to the Kingdom, supposed to be founded on the ruins of the Antient *Carthage*; and hath in it a Temple of singular Beauty and Greatness.

TREMESEN, or the Kingdom of *Algiers*, commonly called *Argie*, now in the hands of the Piratical *Turks*; has for its chief City *Algiers*, from which the Country takes its name, Scituate near the Sea in the form of a Triangle with a Haven, but neither great nor secure from the fury of the North Winds; though the City is strong and beautiful, having not only in it spacious Inns, but Baths, and Mosques, very commodious and sumptuous; and here every Trade takes a Street to themselves; the Streets standing even one above another, upon the rising of the Hill; which renders it a very pleasant prospect, to such as sail by it, and the Harbour or Mole defended with strong Castles, and other works, which render the Approach inaccessible and was formerly a place to which Merchants traded; but now only a nest of Pirates, studying and striving all they can, to endamage and molest, such as sail those Straits or Seas; and though they have been often curbed by the *English*, *French*, and *Dutch*, &c. and brought to terms of Peace; yet like thorow paced Thieves, they never kept it longer than they found an opportunity, to break it to their advantage; and were in the year 1688, so resolute when the *French* Fleet lay before it, and had with their Bombs fired the Town about their Ears, not only to reject the offer made, but in contempt to that puissant Monarch, to shoot his Consul out of a Mortar, or piece of Cannon, towards

wards the *French* Ships in the Road, &c. As for the Upland Country, it has many pleasant Towns and Villages in it, abounding with Gardens, Vineyards, Pastures, Cattle, Corn-Fields, and Fruits of sundry kinds.

FEZ and *MOROCCO*, are now joyned under one King, who fondly stiles himself Emperor; and contain the whole Country of *Mauritania*, properly so called, which took its name from the *Mauri*, a people that Anciently Inhabited it; and the first of these has *Fez* for its chief City, giving name to the Kingdom; and here was scituate the City of *Tangier*, lately demolished by the *English*, as not worth the keeping; nor is the Country wanting in large Forrests, Green Fields, Vineyards, flourishing Gardens, abounding with Fruits, and producing an infinite number of Cattle, a breed of excellent Horses, and the Mountains many wild Beasts, watered with the Rivers *Buringrug* and *Inavis* for the space of 100 Miles.

MOROCCO is Scituate in a warm breathing Air, which renders the Country very fertile; so that it abounds with Figs, Dates, Grapes, Apples, Olives, Honey, Sugar, and Cattle; the whole Country being divided into 7 parts, viz. *Guzzula, Morocco, Hea, Duccala, Hascorasus* and *Tedles*, all holding under the King of *Morocco*, and paying him Tribute, his Power being Absolute and Tyrannical; insomuch that he causes whom he pleases to be put to Death, that is, cast to the Lyons, or other wild Beasts, to make him sport; nor can any of his Subjects, account what he has his own; as for the Profession of Religion these people make, it is *Mahometism*, though there are a great many *Jews*, and some *Christians*, living amongst them; as for Rivers there are not many in this Country, the Land being watered mostly by Brooks, and little

Springs;

Springs; nor do they know in most parts what Winter means as never having seen Ice or Snow, but what hangs on the Top of the *Atlas* a huge Mountain, held to Transcend the Clouds; the top of it Crowned with Pines, and so steep and rugged, that it cannot but with great difficulty be ascended; lying in the upper part, so near the Cold Region; that not withstanding the people beneath fry with the scorching Heat of the Sun; it is covered with Snow and Ice: of which *Virgil* thus writes.

Atlantis Cinctum, &c.

Atlas whose Piny Head, with Clowds inclosed,
Is to the Storms of Wind, and Rain exposed;
Now hides the Snow his Arms, now tumbleth down,
Upon his Chinn, his Beard with Ice o're-grown.

Lybia Interior *Described,* &c.

LYBIA INTERIOR, has for its Northern bound *Mount Atlas,* parted by it from *Barbary* and *Cyrenaica* on the East; *Lybia Marmarica* on the South; *Æthiopia Inferior,* and the Land of *Negro's* and bounded with the *Atlantick Ocean* on the West distinguished from the other *Lybia* by *interior,* as lying more in the main Land of *Africk.*

This

This Countrey, however it anciently was distinguished into parts, stands now divided into *Biledulgerid* or *Numidia*; *Lybia Deserta*, or *Sarra*, and a confiderable Portion of the Countrey called *Terra Negritarum*, or the *Negro's Countrey*; and as for *Numidia*, it abounds in many places with Cattle, Palm Trees, and Forrests of Wild Beasts, not more Salvage than the People, who live for the most part by Rapine and Murther, inhospitable to Strangers, neglecting Tillage, and giving themselves up chiefly to the feeding of Cattle upon the Mountains, Carrying like the *Tartars* their Families and Tents, with other Provisions from place to place, by reason of the scarceness of Water; for where this day a Spring is found, the next it may perhaps be sunk again; yet near the River *Dara*, and in some other parts, the Countrey people have scattered Villages, and those of better Rank Castles. As for the Towns we find of Note, they are or were *Tunugedit*, *Tafilete*; *Tulfet*, a Town of 400 Houses, but no place confiderable near it in 300 Miles: *Techort*, where inhabit the most Courteous People of all the Countrey, and chose rather to Marry their Daughters to Strangers than to Natives, with some other of lesser note, not worth mention, as being exceeded by most of our Countrey Villages.

LYBIA DESERTA, is a place so destitute and poor, by reason it mostly consists of wide Desarts, and barren Sands, breeding numbers of Poisonous Serpents, that few People Inhabit it, unless Thieves and Robbers, who live upon the Spoil of those that attempt to pass them; yet near the Borders, where there is any Green, they have some petty Towns, such as go for Cities in those Parts, as *Tagaza*, 20 Days Journey from any other Peopled Place, yet affords Veins of Salt, which they Exchange for Victuals with the *Tombutan* Merchants, or else must Perish for want, and are many times

over-

over-whelm'd with the Sands, driven like Clouds upon them by the South Wind; *Guargata*, Scituate on the Brink of a Lake; *Huaden*, and *Tomburaum*; nor was this Country ever sought after by the great Conquerors, as not being worth their Travel, &c.

TERR-ANIGRITARUM, or the *Land* of *Negroes*, Is partly in *Libya Interior*, and partly without it, and is exceeding Hot, by Reason of its Scituation under the *Torrid Zone*, yet full of Black People; and though a great part of it be Desart, yet some places by the favour of Springs are so well knit and fastened, that they appear Green and Flourishing, and especially those that lye within the compass of the over-flowing of the River *Niger*, insomuch that they have Pleasant Gardens, Pastures, Corn Fields, and store of Cattle, Woods full of Elephants, and other wild Beasts, whose Flesh they Eat, when taken by Hunting, and Clothe themselves with their Skins, but have very few Fruit-Trees, unless such as bear a kind of a Fruit like a Chesnut, very bitter, nor have they, unless very rarely, any Rain in this Country, but are supply'd, like *Egypt*, by Dews, and the over-flowing of *Niger*.

The People of this Tract were so simple, that at the first coming of the *Portugals* hither to trade, they took their Ships to be great Birds, with white Wings, and the Roaring of their Guns to be the Voice of the Devil; nor could they conceit their Bag-pipes to be any thing but Living Creatures, and when they were permitted to convince themselves of the contrary, they would not yet be beaten out of it, but that they were Immediately the Work of God's own Hands; yet are they very Reverent or Respectful to their King, who exceeds not in Manners, or Breeding one of our Coblers, never daring when they come before him

to

to look in his Face, but cast their Eyes downward, and when they sit, though the chiefest of his Favourites, it is at his Feet, Flat on their Buttocks.

As for the Religion (if it may be so termed) of these *Negroes*, it is a mixture of *Idolatry* and *Mahometism*, though formerly, as appears by some footsteps yet left, Christianity was predominant in divers parts of the Land; and through this Countrey the River *Nilus* passes, and 'tis Watered likewise with *Senaga*, a River arising out of the Lake *Guaga*, little inferior to the former, and has divers Mountains, as *Arualtes*, *Arangus*, and *Deorum Currus*, thrusting into the Sea, and reaching in a manner the Clouds.

The chief Cities of this Countrey in the time of *Ptolomy*, were *Nigra*, *Thumondacana*, *Malachath*, *Seleuce*, *Anigath*, *Panagra*, with some few of lesser note, but most of them are ruined, and scarce any thing but their names remaining; however there are some crept up in their steads, but those not many, as *Argina*, *Porto Dio*, *Porto del Riscato*, either built or so named by the *Portugals*.

In this Tract (for it is a very large one, taking up above a third part of *Africk*) are *Guinea*, extended from *Sierra Leona* in the 10th Degree of Longitude, to *Benin* in the 30th. where they have the Juice of a Tree as strong as Wine, as also Mines of Gold: A place very Fruitful, and much abounding in Rice, Barley, Ivory, and *Guinea* Pepper.

TOMBUTUM, a Kingdom of it self, very Rich in Mines of Gold, yet a greater store is gained by his Warring on his Neighbours; as also *Mell*, *Cano*, *Gialofia*, *Guber*, *Guangara*, *Gaoga*, *Gambra* or *Gambea*, *Gialofi*, *Bito*, *Temiano*, *Zegzeg*, *Zaffara*, *Gethan*, *Medna*, *Daum*, *Gualta*, *Agadez*, *Cano*, *Casena*, *Savaga*, most of them Petty Princes, not of any considerable Note.

BORNUM, a large and populous Countrey, accounted 500 Miles in Length, yet moftly Inhabited by keepers of Cattle that abound here, by reafon of the abundance of Paftures; and here they ufe no Marriage, but mix together as they think convenient, giving their Children Names by fome mark or token of their Body; however the Kings Revenues are great, his very Dogs being coupled in Chains of Gold.

BENIN, Eaftward of *Guinea*; the King whereof hath 600 Wives, with whom he Marches in State Twice a Year to fhow them to Strangers, and the Subjects following the Example of their Prince, get as many as they can, few having lefs than Ten, and here the Men and Women go naked till they are Married, and then have only a Covering from the Wafte downward, Superftitioufly raifing the Skin with three flafhes of a Knife, from the Navel to the Privy Parts, as a mark of their hopes of Salvation.

NUBIA, a confiderable Countrey, ftretching from *Gaoga* to *Nilus*, has *Dangula* for its chief Town, and fome other of leffer note, and affords, amongft other Drugs the mortaleft of Poyfons; infomuch that the tenth part of a Grain will difpatch a Man in a quarter of an hour; and affords moreover Civit, Sugar, Sanders, Ivory, &c. The Kingdom taking its Name from the *Nubiza*, a certain people that inhabit it, and is well refrefhed with Rivers and Lakes, and the people were generally *Chriftians*, a ftrong and potent Nation, well Skill'd in War, in fo much that *Cyriacus* one of their Kings, hearing the Chriftians were oppreffed in *Egypt*, raifed an Army of 100000 Horfe to fuccour them, but being about to enter that Kingdom, to the great Terrour of the *Turks* and *Sarazens*, he was met by the Patriarch of *Alexandria*, at whofe Supplication and Treaty he returned, without enterprizing any
thing

thing Memorable, nor has it been long since they, for want of Spiritual Guides to strengthen and confirm them, have faln off from the Christian Faith, and embraced the Superstitions of *Mahomet*.

Æthiopia Superior *described in its Kingdoms and Provinces.*

ÆTHIOPIA SUPERIOR has on the East *Sinus Barbaricus*, and the *Red Sea*; on the West, *Lybia Interior* and the Kingdom of *Nubia*; and part of *Congo* in the other *Æthiopia* on the North; *Egypt* and *Lybia Marmarica* on the South; the Mountains of the *Moon* parting it from *Æthiopia Inferiour*, and had its present name from the *Grecians*, and is scituate on both sides the Equinoctial, extending from the South Parrallel of 7 Degrees to the North end of the Isle *Meroe*, scituate under the Fifth Parallel on the North of that Circle, being accounted in length about 1500 Miles, and in breadth about half as much, in Circumference 4300 Miles; containing the whole Countrey of *Æthiopia*, as before limited; the greatest part of it being the *Abyssine Empire* or Dominion of *Prestor John*; the rest comprehending the Kingdoms of *Adel* and *Adea*, the Provinces *Quiola* and *Melindi*, though the last are reckoned parts of *Æthiopia Inferior*; the Island of *Meroe* in the North possessed by *Mahometans* Enemies to *Prestor John*, all on the South of *Nubia* and the West of *Nilus*, is Inhabited by the *Anzichi*, a *Cannibal* and *Idolatrous* People, who have a King of their own; and all the Coast of the *Red Sea*, as well within the Coast of *Babel-mandel*, the Port of *Erocco* only excepted, is in the Possession of *Moors* and *Arabians*, who pay Homage to the Kings of *Adel* and *Adea*.

As for the People of *Æthiopia*, properly so called, they were formerly held to be great Astrologers, the first Ordainers of Sacred Ceremonies, from whom the *Egyptians* had their Instructions, always counted good Archers, yet Treacherously shooting with Poisoned Arrows; they go ill Cloathed, and as bad Housed, for the most part extreamly inclined to *Barbarism*, and unless they Swear by the Life of their Emperor, not to be credited in matters of Weight; their Colour is an Olive Tawny, inclining more to Swarthiness, except their Emperor, who as a mark of the true Prince, and are held to be Converted to the Christian Faith, by the Eunuch of Queen *Candace*, Converted by St. *Philip* the Evangelist, which Flourishes amongst them to this day, and comes very near in all the Material Points, to the Orthodox Religion of the Reformed European Church, &c. and are under a Patriarch.

The Country of the *Æthiops*, is like all other Countries in this Tract, Fruitful in some Places, and Barren in others, yet it generally abounds in Rice, Barley, Beans, Pease, Sugars, Minerals of all kinds, Cattle, *viz.* Goats, Oxen, Sheep, Horses; and have great store of Flax and Vines, yet make neither Cloth nor Wine, unless peculiarly for the Emperor, Patriarch, or great Men, being much given to Sloth; nor do they indeed know how to bring their Minerals to Perfection, nor will they trouble themselves to Fish or Hunt, tho' the Woods and Rivers are infinitely stored with Fish and Venison.

As for the Provinces comprehended at this time within the bounds or limits of *Æthiopia*, they are, *Guagere*, *Tigremaon*, *Angote*, *Damut*, *Amma*, *Agdmedrum*, *Goijami*, *Adel*, *Adea*, *Barnagassum*, *Danculi*, *Debas*, *Fatigar*, *Xoa*, and *Barus*; though not all, as I intimated within the Circuit of the *Abassine*

bassine Empire; and of Note amongst these are; viz.

BARNAGOSUM Scituate upon the Red Sea, extending from *Suachen*, almost to the Mouth of the *Streights*, and hath for its Sea Port *Frosco*, the only Port of the Empire, held Tributary from the *Turks*, who sometimes since took it from the *Æthiopians*, with the Town of *Suachen*, for which they pay yearly 1000 ounces of Gold.

TIGRAMAON, lying between *Nilus*, *Marabo* and *Angote*, is a pleasant Kingdom, though of no great extent, and has for its chief City *Cazunia*, supposed to be the Regal Seat of Queen *Candace*, whose Enuch St *Philip* Baptized.

ANGOTE is a Province considerably Barren, lying between *Tigramaon* and *Amare*, insomuch that being deficient of Gold or Silver, or any other valuable Commodities, Iron, Plate, or Rings, and hard Loaves of Salt, made to sundry degrees of bigness, pass as Current.

XOA is more Fertile than the former, as having many green Pastures, where a great Number of Cattle Feed, as likewise abounding with Fruits, and is almost in all parts Grateful to the Husbandman.

FATIGAR is noted for having in it a Lake of that Name 12 Miles in compass, being on the Top of a high Mountain, from whence divers Rivers, well stored with Fish, descend to water the Country.

GOIJAMI is famed for the Mines of Gold found, as also for the Unicorn, who makes his abode in the Hills of the Moon, large Mountains so called, because the Moon upon her rising, appears first from behind them to that Country; and although the Beasts are rarely taken by reason of their *Swiftness*, yet their Horns, so famous for expelling Poison are found

found, which at a certain Period of Time they fled.

GUGERA, otherways *Meroe*, is an Island of which we intend to speak hereafter; and in this Country is found the Hill *Amara*, which is a Days Journey to ascend, and 30 Miles in compass, in Form round, and on the top of it are sundry pleasant Plains and Pallaces, the Air being much cooler than that beneath, and here the Princes of the Blood dwell. As for the Emperors Stile, by reason of the strangeness of it, we think fit to insert it, *viz.*

P. I. *Supream of his Kingdoms, and the Beloved of God, the Pillar of Faith, sprung from the Stock of* Judah, *the Son of* David, *the Son of* Solomon, *the Son of the Column of* Sion, *the Son of the Seed of* Jacob, *and the Son of the Hand-maid of* Mary, *the Son of Nahu, after the Flesh, the Son of St.* Peter, *and St.* Paul, *after the Spirit, Emperor of the higher and lesser* Æthiopia, *and of the most mighty Kingdoms, Dominions, and Countries of* Xoa, Goa, Caffares, Fatigar, Angote, Balignazo, Adea, Vangue, Goijami, (*where are the Fountains of* Nile) Amara, Banguamedron, Ambea, Vangucum, Tigremean, Sabaim, (*the Birth-place of the Queen of* Saba) Barnagosum; *and Lord of all the Region unto the Confines of* Egypt.

And is said to have for his Arms, a Lyon Rampant, in a Field Or, with this Motto, *viz. The Lyon of the Tribe of* Judah *shall overcome*. Which gives many occasion to think, he either descended of the Jewish Race, from the Stock of *David*, or from the Off-spring of the Queen of *Sheba*, or *Saba*, called the Queen of the South, supposed to be Begotten by *Solomon*; but leaving these Conjectures to those

that

that are disposed to make a more strict Inquiry into them, we proceed to the Inferior *Æthiopia*.

Æthiopia Inferior *Described, in its Kingdoms and Provinces*, &c.

ÆTHIOPIA Inferior has on the East the Red Sea; on the West the *Æthiopick Ocean*; on the North the Higher *Æthiopia*, and *Terra Nigritarum*; and on the South the Main *Ocean*, parting it from *Terra Australis Incognita*; being lower in Scituation than the former; a Country but little known to the Ancients, but since more fully Discovered, and is divided properly into 4 Parts, *viz. Zangebar, Monomotapa, Cafraria,* and *Manicongo*; and as for the People, they differ little from the other *Æthiopia*, either in Customs or Manners, going Clad with striped Plads, or Skins of Beasts, part *Mahometans* and part *Idolaters.*

ZANGEBAR is a Country Low and Fenny, by reason of the over-flowing of the Rivers, and so pestered with Woods and Forrests, that for want of the free motion of the Air it is very unwholsome; and so little are the people skilled in Shipping, that the *Moors* who dwell on the Sea Coasts use to adventure in little Vessels sowed together with Leather Thongs, and Caulk'd with Gum, having no other Sails than the Leaves of *Palm Trees*; and this Province contains 15 lesser Provinces, as *Melindi, Momboza, Quiola, Mosambique,* a very Fruitful, Populous Countrey; *Sofala,* supposed the *Ophir* of *Solomon* for its store of Gold, Ivory, and other Rich Commodities; *Moenhemago* or *Monemug,* an Inland Province, affording Mines of Gold, which the People barter with the *Portugals* for *Silks, Taffata's,* and the like, *Meneremge, Corova, Calen,*

Anzuga, Mombira, Mombiza, Bandi, Monzala, Macaos, Benda and *Embreo,* and has for its Chief Cities or Places of resort, *Mombaza, Ampaza,* both taken by the *Portugals; Quiola, Mosambique, Sofola,* and others of lesser note; and in this Region are divers *Cannibals* of a black and horrid Aspect, who War upon their Neighbours for no other end than that they may eat them when they take them Captive; and amongst others, having taken *Mombaza,* they made a great Feast of the King and such Citizens as escaped not their hands, and would have no Commerce held with them, were not *their Countrey* exceeding Rich.

MONUMOPATA lies mostly upon the Sea, and is in Circuit 3250 *Italian Miles*; the Air very Temperate, and wholsome and pleasant, and is Watered with the *Rivers, Panami, Aurug, Luanga, Mangeano,* in whose Sands is found much Gold, and as for the people of this Tract, they are black of Complexion, mean of Stature, swift of Foot, and very strong, covering themselves only with Cotton Cloath, and diet upon Flesh, Fish, Milk, Rice and Oyl of *Susman,* being Pagans in *Religion,* Worshipping a God called *Mozimo,* yet invisible, for they hate Idols; and here above all *Countreys* in *Africk,* the Women have the greatest priviledges. They punish Theft, Adultery, and Witch-craft with Death, yet have no Prisons, but execute the Offenders as soon as taken; and the lesser Provinces into which this greater is divided, are *Motuca,* Rich in *Mines* of *Gold, Torra* or *Butna, Boro, Quiticut, Inhambran,* and some others of lesser note, they being all very Fruitful, but most famed for their *Mines* of *Gold*; but their Towns are very inconsiderable, the people mostly living in stragling Cotts, the meaner sort not suffered to have any Doors.

CAFRA,

CAFRARIA, A third Division of this *Æthiopia*, is a Country greatly abounding with Herds of Cattle, Deer, Antelopes, Baboons, Foxes, Hares, Pelicans, Ostriches, Herons, Ducks, Geese, Pheasants, Partridges; exceeding well watered, but deficient in Corn, by the neglect of the Natives, who choose rather to live idly upon the bounty of Nature, than to improve it by Art; making their Aboads in Woods and Forrests, and building, for the most part, their Houses of Branches of Trees, interwoven Hurdle-waies, and are black of Colour, thick Lipped, flat Nosed, long Headed, but longer Eared, which reach beneath their Shoulders, occasioned by their hanging extraordinary Weights in them for Ornaments, as Rings, Chains, &c. And to render themselves more beautiful, slash their Skins in divers parts, carving it out into sundry Forms, in imitation of the Antient *Britains*; and the better to show it in all parts, they go mostly naked, unless a piece of a Beast's Skin over their Privities; and those that go best attired, it is only in Skins of Beasts, rough as they take them off, their Dyet being raw Flesh, and with the Guts of Beasts they adorn themselves, by hanging them about their Necks, and indeed are altogether Brutal and Bestial. And in this Tract live the *Imbians*, not far from the *Cape of Good-hope*, Tall, and of considerable Strength, living by War and Rapine, feeding on the Flesh of their conquered Enemies and dying Friends, whose Deaths they hasten, that they may the sooner Eat them, and make Drinking Cups of their Sculls; and in their Wars they fight with Poisoned Arrows, and a long Pole, hardened at the end with Fire, carrying likewise Fire before them, signifying thereby that they intend to Roast and Boil all they shall overcome; and these were they that Eat up the King of *Mambaza* and his People; their King if such a Monster deserve

deserve that sacred Epithete, accounting himself Lord of all the Earth; and when at any time the Heat or Rain offends him, he darts his Poisoned Arrows at Heaven, by way of defiance: As for Towns, they have none of any note, living in Hutts, stragling Villages, and Woods; and in these parts is the *Cape of Good-hope*, frequently touch'd by such as Sail to the *East-Indies*; and the better to discover the customs of these People, in the beastly and inhumane condition they live in, take the following account, *viz.* It happened that some English Ships, in their way home from the *Indies*, fortuned to take two of the Natives, near the Bay of *Soldania*, in order to learn from them, when they could be brought to speak English, a farther account of the Country, and one of them, named *Coore*, they brought to *London*, the other dying by the way, when the better to please him, they not only arayed him in fine Cloaths, but gave him Beads, Bells, and other things, wherein the Natives of his Countrey most delighted. yet nor these, nor the sumptuous Fare he met with, could alter his inclination, for he altogether appeared Dogged and Melancholy; and when he had a smattering of English, he would often throw himself upon the Ground, in a melancholy posture, and passionately cry'd out, *Home go* Saldania, *go* Coore *home, go.* So that all hopes being lost of bringing him to any better manners, than what he had naturally imbibed, they sent him back again by the next Ships, and set him, to his no small joy, on Shore where they found him: So that at any time when he saw Ships with English Colours, he would come running to the Bay with Gut and Garbidg about his Neck, to them, doing them all the good Offices he could, being more pleased with that Beastly manner of Living than any other.

MANI-

MANICONGO, is a very temperate Region, free from extream Colds, as being scituate under the Equator, rendring by that means the Soil exceeding fruitful, affording Fruits, Plants, Herbs, store of Pasturage; abundance of Bulls, Cows, Goats, Hares, Deer, Elephants, and Serpents so large that they will swallow a Man; Fowl of sundry kinds, they have in great plenty, both wild and tame, as being watered with the Rivers *Coanza, Bengo, Barbela, Ambrizi, Dande, Loza,* and *Zare,* and has in it the Mountains of *Siera,Complida*, the Chrystalline Mountain, where great store of Chrystal is found, the Mountains of the Sun, the Mountains of *Sal Nitri* affording great quantities of that kind of Minerals, and the Mountains of *Cabambe,* rich in Mines of Silver. And this Province of *Manicongo,* contains sundry lesser; the King stiles himself, King of *Bomba, Congo, Sango, Sundi, Bangu, Batti, Pemba, Abundi, Matana, Quisoma, Angola,* and *Cacanga,* Lord of *Congemes, Amolaze, Langelum, Anzuichi, Chucchi,* and *Zoangbi,* though several of them are undiscovered to the *Europeans,* the whole Coast being first discovered by the *Portugals,* who opened a way on this side of *Afric,* to the Wealth of *India* in *Asia*; and although the King of *Congo,* has no other Current Money but Cockle Shells, yet his Revenues are great by Presents, for none may come to him empty handed, as also by his share of Gold and Silver, digged out of the Mines; and in this Tract are sundry Nations of Cannibals, who greedily devour Mans Flesh, rather than that of Beasts, and of these there are the *Igges,* or *Giachi,* inhabiting the Mountains of the Sun, the which though they have Wives 10 or 20 a piece, yet have they no Children to be their Heirs, for they unnaturally strangle them as soon as Born, and Eat them as Dainties, supplying the Decrease

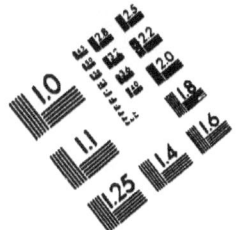
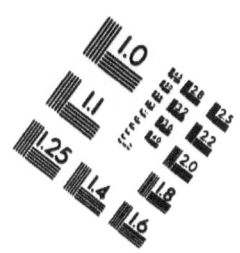

**IMAGE EVALUATION
TEST TARGET (MT-3)**

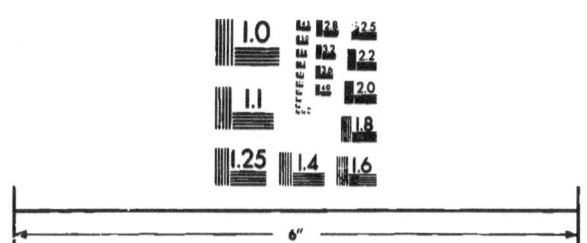

Photographic
Sciences
Corporation

23 WEST MAIN STREET
WEBSTER, N.Y. 14580
(716) 872-4503

in number by such as they take Prisoners of either Sex, stealing none under 16 or 20 years of Age, which by force and custom they bring to be as bad as themselves, against whom the *Batti*, a neighbouring Province, keeps 70000 Men in Arms, to prevent the Stealing or Eating the rest. Another sort there are of these Monsters in *Zazichana*, who Eat not only their Enemies but their Friends and Kinsfolks; and if at any time they can make to the value of a penny more of a Slave Dead than Alive, they kill him, and cut out his Body in Joynts, selling it publickly in their Shambles, as Beef and Mutton with us; and when they have any that are Lean, they fat them for the Slaughter. And great pitty it is, that so good and fruitful a Country, as these Regions of *Africk*, should be possessed with such impious Wretches; wherefore lest a further Relation of such a barbarous People, should prove ingrateful to the Reader, we will put a period to the Discourse of this Country, and of *Africa*, till we come to the Islands, and so proceed to the Description of *America*, the fourth and last part of the World, yet discovered Continent, &c.

A

A GEOGRAPHICAL AND Historical Description OF AMERICA,

In its Kingdoms and Provinces, &c.

AMERICA, the fourth Division of the World, so named by *Americus Vespucius*, an adventurous *Florentine*, who discovered a part of the Continent, is bounded on the East with the *Atlantick* Ocean, and the *Virginian* Seas, called *Mare del Noort*; on the West with the Pacifick Ocean, called *Mare Del Zur*; dividing it from *Asia* on the South, with part of *Terra Australis Incognita*, from which separated by a long

narrow

narrow Streight, called the Streight of *Magellan*, but on the North reaches, as some suppose, to the Artick Pole; the bounds are not known, and although this Country has been but lately discovered by us, yet it is conjectured to be as anciently Peopled as *Europe* it self, and though some have guessed it was known to the Antient *Greeks Romans* and *Carthaginians*, yet they are but Conjectures, only the Arguments or Probabilities, they bring to confirm or strengthen them, being much too weak to hold with a considering or Judicious Reader, and therefore coming to more certainty, we must be impartial, and ascribe the Honour of the Discovery of this great Country, called by many *A New World*, to the Honour and Memory of *Christopher Colon* or *Columbus*, a *Genoese*, born at *Neray* in the Signiory of *Genoa*, who being a man of considerable Abilities of mind, could not upon considering the motion of the Sun, perswade himself but that there must in reason be large Countries not found out, to which it communicated its influence, and being strongly possessed with these thoughts, he imparted them to the State of *Genoa*, in the year 1486, whereupon he sent his Brother *Bartholomew* to propose the Discovery to *Henry* the Seventh of *England*, who unluckily, by the way, was taken Prisoner, though some time after, being set at liberty, he performed his Trust, and was received with much chearfulness, insomuch that *Columbus* was sent for by the King: happy for the Natives had they fell into such merciful hands; but Providence otherways ordered it, for *Columbus* ignorant of his Brothers being taken by the *Pyrats*, not hearing any return or answer, concluded his Proposals rejected, and thereupon he made his Overtures to the Court of *Castile*, where after many delays and six Years Attendance, he was furnished with three Ships,

not

not for Conquest, but Discovery, when having Sailed sixty days on the Main Ocean, he could descry no Land, so that the disheartned *Spaniards* growing out of love with so tedious, and as they concluded, fruitless a Voyage, began to Mutiny, refusing to pass any further, at what time, as fortune would have it, *Columbus* espied a bright Cloud arise, growing still more light, from which he gathered, that they must ascend from the Fumes of the Earth, and not the Ocean, whereat taking Courage, he prevailed with them to stand three days course, and if in that time no Land was discovered, he would engage to return; when towards the end of the third day they espied Fire, which they afterward found to be on the Coast of *Florida*, where Landing his Men, he caused a Tree to be cut down, and making a Cross, he erected it on the firm Land on the Eleventh of *October* 1492, taking thereby possession of this *New World* in the name of the *Spanish King*, finding it exceeding pleasant and promising, and so by degrees proceeded further, and after him divers others, till they brought to light the Kingdoms and Countreys Intended here to be described.

The Countrey of *America* on the Continent, is properly divided into two great *Peninsula's*, whereof that toward the North is called *Mexicana* from *Mexico* the Chief City, computed to be 13000 *Miles* in *Circumference*; the South is called *Peruana*, the Sailing about which is reckoned 17000 *Italian Miles*, and the *Isthmus* that joyns them together, is very long, but narrow in some places, not above 12 *Miles* from Sea to Sea, and in many not above 17; called by the *Spaniards* the Streights of *Darien*, from a River of that name near the *Isthmus*, which *Isthmus* has been often proposed to be cut, that by the joyning the two Seas, the passage might be very much shortened to *China*, and the *Molucca's*, but never yet enterprized. The

The *Mexican* Province is properly divided into the Continent and Iſlands. The Continent containeth the *Provinces* of *Eſtotiland, Nova Francia, Virginia, Florida, California, Nova Gallicia, Nova Hiſpania,* and *Guatimalia,* and theſe ſub-divided into leſſer Countries. The *Peruan* Province, or the Southern Peninſula, taking in ſome part of the *Iſthmus,* hath on the Continent the Province of *Caſtela Aurea, Nova Granada, Peru, Chiele, Parognay, Braſil, Guiana,* and *Paria,* with their ſeveral Members, and particular Regions, of which in their order, and then of the *Iſlands* of the Univerſe.

Eſtotiland, *and its Regions deſcribed.*

UNder the name of *Eſtotiland* we comprehend the *Northern Regions* of the *Mexican Province,* as alſo thoſe on the Eaſt; and 'tis bounded Eaſtward with the Main Ocean; on the South with *Canida,* or *Nova Francia;* on the Weſt with undiſcovered Tracts of Land; and on the North with an Inlet or Bay of the Sea, called *Hudſons Bay,* taking its name from *Henry Hudſon* an Engliſhman, who firſt diſcovered it.

ESTOTILAND, properly ſo called, is the moſt Northern Region on the Eaſt ſide of *America,* the Soil ſufficiently inriched by Nature; the Natives Rude and void of Civility, Arts, or Tractableneſs, going many of them Naked, notwithſtanding the extream Cold, living by the Fleſh of Wild Beaſts they kill in the Woods, and is but little Inhabited but by the Natives, by reaſon of the laſting Winters; the greateſt Advantage drawn from this extream Region, being the Fiſhing Trade, wherein the Rivers at the Seaſon, are ſuch a Number of Cod, called New-land-fiſh, that with a red Rag and a Hook, a Man may catch forty or fifty in an hour,

which

which dried and falted, are brought into *England* and other parts of *Europe*; befides they Trade fometimes with the Natives for Feathers, Furs and Skins of Beafts; and the moft noted places (for Cities you muft expect none) are fuch as have been named by the *Englifh*, viz. Prince *Henry*'s *Fore-land, Charles Cape, King's Fore-land,* and *Cape Wolftenham* at the end thereof, where the *Streights* open in a large and fpacious Bay, called *Hudfons Bay*; but to come more Southward, the next Region is *Terra Corterialis*.

In *Terra Corterialis*, the people are found to be of a little better Underftanding, Cloathing themfelves more decently in Skins of Beafts, and fuch other Garments as they can conveniently obtain, being generally good *Archers*, getting their Provifion thereby, yet *Strangers* to *Towns* and *Cities*, a. living in Caves and Swamps, or fortified Woods, to which they gave the Names of Towns or Villages; not Marrying, but living Common, moft of them *Idolaters*, and thofe that are their Guides, pretenders to *Southfaying* and *Witchcraft*, much delighting in *Fifh*, which they eat more gladly than any thing, though a *French Colony* fetling here, have built fome inconfiderable Towns, indifferently Inhabited, as *Breft, Cabo-Marzo, Sancta Maria,* and fome others; and this part was firft difcovered by *Sebaftian Cabot* in the Year 1499, at the Charge of King *Henry* the Seventh, though not Improved, but took foon after its name from *Gafpar Corterialis* a *Portugal,* who fome years after, Sailing upon Difcovery, fell in with it; and here are found Staggs, White Bears, and Scut-fifh a Yard long, and fuch fhoals of Cod-fifh upon the Coaft, that they retard the Sailing of the Ships.

NEW-

NEW-FOUND-LAND, another part of this Tract lies on the South of *Corterialis*, parted from it by the Frith or Streight, called *Golfes des Chasteaux*, pretty well Inhabited, though not free from the Extremities of Cold, and has on the Coast such abundance of Cod-fish, Herrings, Salmon, Mussles, with Pearls in their Shells, &c. that it is to be wondered at; as also Thornbacks, Smelts and Oysters; the up-land Country well Manured, producing naturally Roses, and bears Pease in extraordinary Crops, Flourishing with Trees of sundry kinds, as well for Fruits as Shades; and in these Parts the Natives, scaping the Bloody Cruelty of the *Spaniards*, are pretty Numerous, being of a reasonable Stature, broad Eye'd, full Faced, and Beardless, their Complexion the Colour of Oaker, and their Houses for the most part made of Poles, their Tops meeting together, and covered over with Skins, their Hearth, or Fire-place in the middle, after the manner of the *Laplanders*; their Boats, with which they Sail in the Rivers, and on the Sea near the Shoar, are made of the Bark of a Tree, that Country affords, 20 Feet in Length and 4 in Bredth, yet one of them weighs not 1 Hundred Weight; and on this Coast are many curious Bays, safe for Ships; and before this Part, which some term an Island, as being divided by the Frith from the Continent, lyeth a long Bank or ridg of Ground of many Hundred Leagues extent, but not above 24 at the Broadest, and all about Islands, called by some *Cabo Baccalaos*, from the Swarms of Cod-fish found about it, which by the Natives are called *Baccalaos*, so that the Bears frequently pull them out of the Water with their Paws and eat them: As for the Natives (upon the coming of the Christians) they Inhabited the Sea-Coast, but now for the most part have betaken themselves to the Woods and Fastnesses, and used to express their Duty and Reverence

ence towards their King, by ſtroaking their Foreheads, and rubbing their Noſes which if the King accepted, or was well pleaſed with the Party, he turned his Head to his left Shoulder, as a mark of Favour: And at this day the Fiſhery for Ling and Cod, chiefly draws the Engliſh thither, though ſome Furrs and Civit are likewiſe to be found, which the Colonies there ſetled have much improved.

Canada, or Nova Francia, Deſcribed, &c.

ANother part of this Tract, is called *Canada*, from the River of that Name that Waters it; and *New France*, from a Colony of *French* that ſettled there, who at their firſt arrival were gladly received by the Natives, with Singing and Dancing; and this part (as well as *Nova Scotia*, and *Norembegua*) is conſiderably Woody, in the up-land parts full of Stags, Bears, Hares, Martins, Foxes, whoſe Fleſh (till more Civiliz'd) the Natives did Eat raw, as they did their Fiſh, only being dryed in the Sun, or Smoak'd in their Hovels; they have alſo Coneys, Land and Water Fowl in great Plenty, taking great Pride in Bracelets and Chains of certain Shells, called *Eſurgnie*, which they gather on the Coaſt; and here are many great Rivers of freſh Water, which together with Mountains of Snow, render it very cold, yet Wheat and Pulſe grows pretty kindly, though but few Fruit Trees; and here the Women Labour more than the Men, and if ſo the Man (who is allowed two or three Wives) dye, the Widows will not be induced to Marry again, but continue in their ſort of Mourning, which is to daub the naked parts of their Body dy over with Coal-duſt, for in ſome parts of this Tract they go Naked, both Men and Women.

VIRGINIA is a Country ſomewhat more pleaſant than what we have deſcribed; bounded on the North with *Canada*; on the South with *Florida*; on the Eaſt with *Mare del Noort*; and on the Weſt with the Woods of the Country, the end of them not Diſcovered, and is a Colony of the *Engliſh*, along the Sea Coaſt, and conſiderably upland, ſo called in Honour of Queen *Elizabeth*, that Virgin Queen, and Glory of her Sex, by Sir *Walter Raleigh*, in the Year 1584. though by the Natives called *Apalcher*, from a Town of that Name, the Sea-coaſt only being Pleaſant, for as much as what lies more In-land, is full of barren Mountains and rough Woods, where notwithſtanding the Natives Inhabit in poor and miſerable Houſes, under ſundry Chiefs, or Petty Kings, and yet frequently at War amongſt themſelves, for thoſe wretched Dwellings, and ſometimes make Inroads, and Plunder the Engliſh Territories, killing as many as fall within the compaſs of their Power, and then Fly to their Woods and Faſtneſs, where they know they cannot without great hazard and danger be conveniently purſued.

The Country properly called *Virginia* extends from 34 to 38 Degrees of North Latitude, and is very Temperate, by reaſon of the frequent *Breizes*, and refreſhing Gales of Wind that allay the heat, ſo that it affords abundance of Pleaſant Valleys, Spacious Fields, Fruit Trees, as in *England*, yielding a greater Increaſe, and has ſundry Veins of Allom, as alſo Pitch, Turpentine, Cedar, and Olive Trees, with many Pleaſant Hills, which are Planted as Vineyards; ſtore of Fiſh, Fowl, Cattle, and above all ſundry large Plantations of Tobacco, eſpecially upon *James* and *York* Rivers, and have con-

considerable Towns and Villages, many of them well Fortified, to prevent Incursion of the Savages, whose Neighbouring Petty Princes, the Governour obliges to pay Tribute, and to send their Slaves if any outrage be committed by them in the Territories of the *English*, to *James*, *Charles*, or any other Town, appointed to be Punished according to the degree of the Fact; and here the Natives (such as border on the Plantation) are much Civiliz'd, in consideration of those that are more remote, Trading with the *English*, for Furrs, Skins, and Indian Corn, which they set with a Stick, as we do our Beans, which is the work and business of their Wives, as soon as they have bought them of their Parents, and Built them a House, which for the most part is of Poles, pleated on the Sides and Tops Hurdle-wise; and if Female Children be Born, they as soon as they are able, go into the Field to work with their Mother, but the Male goes along with his Father to shoot in the Woods; and so Lazy are the Men, that if they kill any considerable Game, they leave it at a certain remarkable Tree, and when they come home send their Wife to fetch it, who dares not on pain of Death disoblige her Husband. But this is only meant of the Natives, for the English are there, as here, Governed by wholsom Laws, and live for the most part in great Plenty.

MARYLAND lies on the South of *Virginia* in the same Tract, divided from it only by some considerable Rivers, and is as the former a Tobacco Plantation, abounding likewise with Corn, Cattle, and considerable Gardens and Orchards of Fruit Trees, Planted by the *English*. As for the Natives Bordering it, they differ not in manner and quality from the former, going mostly loosly Arrayed in Beasts skins, Feathers compacted, and armed with Bows and Darts.

NEW-

NEW ENGLAND, an *English* Colony in this Tract is bounded on the North-East with *Norumbegua*, on the Southwest with *Novum Belgium*; and on the other parts by the Woods and Sea coast; scituate in the middle of the Temperate Zone, between the degrees of 41 and 44, equally distant from the Artick Circle, and the Tropick of *Cancer*; which renders it very temperate and very agreeable to the Constitution of *English* Bodies, the Soil being alike Fruitful, if not in some places exceeding ours; all sorts of Grain and Fruit trees common with us growing kindly there: The Woods there are very great, wherein for the most part the Native *Indians* dwell Fortefying themselves as in Towns or places of defence, living upon Deer and such other Creatures, as those vast Wildernesses whose extents are unknown to the *English* abound with: there are in this Country store of Ducks, Geese, Turkies, Pigeons, Cranes, Swans, Partridges, and almost all sort of Fowl, and Cattle, common to us in *Old England*; together with Furs, Amber, Flax, Pitch, Cables, Mast, and in brief whatever may conduce to profit and pleasure; the Native *Indians*, in these parts are more tractable, if well used, than in any other; many of them though unconverted, often saying, that our God is a good God, but their *Tanto* evil; which *Tanto* is no other than the Devil, or a wicked Spirit that haunts them every Moon, which obliges them to Worship him for fear, though to those that are converted to Christianity he never appears.

This *English* Colony after many Attempts and bad Successes was firmly Established 1620, at what time *New Plymouth* was Built and Fortified; so that the *Indians* thereby being over-aw'd, suffered the Planters without controul to Build other Towns, the chief of which are *Bristol*, *Boston*, *Barstaple*, and others, alluding to the Names of Sea Towns in *Old England*; and are accommodated with many curious Havens commodious for Shipping, and the Country watered with pleasant Rivers of extraordinary largeness; so abounding with Fish, that they are not taken for dainties: The Religion professed is Presbyterial; and for a long time they were all Governed at their own dispose, and Laws, made by a Convocation of Planters, &c. but of late they have submitted to receive a Governor from *England*.

NOVUM BELGIUM, or the *New Neither-lands*, lies in this Tract on the South of *New England*, extending from 38 to 41 degrees North Latitude; a place, into which the *Hollanders* intruded themselves, considerable Woody; which Woods naturally abound with Nuts and wild Grapes, replenished with Deer, and such Creatures as yield them store of Furrs, as the Rivers and Plains do Fish and Fowl; rich Pastures, and Trees of extraordinary bigness, with Flax, Hemp, and Herbage; the ground very kindly bearing the Product of *Europe*; and here the Natives, such as live in Hutts and Woods, go clad in Beasts Skins, their Houshold goods consisting of a Wooden dish, a Tobacco Pipe, and a Hatchet made of a sharp Flint Stone, their Weapons Bows and Arrows; though the *Dutch* unfairly to their cost, out of a covetous Humor, traded with them for Guns, Swords, &c. shewing the use of them which the *Indians* turning upon their quondam Owners, found an opportunity to send 400 of their new Guests into the other World; and here the chief Town is *New Amsterdam*, commodiously Scituate for Trade, and the Reception of Shipping.

FLORIDA is a large part of the *Mexican* Province, bounded on the North-East with *Virginia*; on the East with *Mare Del Noort*; on the South and some part of the West, with the Golf of *Mexico*,

ico, and the remaining part of the West with *New France*, extending from 25 to 34 degrees North Latitude; and first discovered to any purpose under the Conduct of *Sebastian Cabot* an *English* man, 1497, and now mostly possessed by the *Spaniards* so named from the many Flourishing Trees and Flowers that enammel the Country; the Soil being naturally so Rich, that a long Manuring cannot impair it's rendering 60 fold increase; so that they have two Crops yearly of Maize and Corn; and here flourish most sorts of Fruits, as Grapes, Cherries, Mulberries, Chesnuts, Plumbs, &c. The Country yielding Cattle, Fowl, Fish, and many Medicinal Drugs; likewise Pearls, Precious Stones, and some Mines of Gold and Silver, though not much improved.

The *Indians* Inhabiting this Tract, are of an Olive Colour, great Stature and well proportioned going mostly naked, unless a cover made for their Privity with a Stags Skin, painting their Arms and Legs with divers Colours not to be washed out; their Hair is Black, hanging down to an extraordinary length, cunning and much desirous of revenging injuries; insomuch that they are continually at War amongst themselves; the Women upon the Death of their Husbands, cut their Hair close to their Ears, and Marry not again till it's grown sufficiently long to cover their Shoulders (a very commendable way if used amongst us, to prevent our over hasty Widdows, who are frequently provided before hand;) they have amongst them many Hermaphrodites which they hold in such detestation that they are marked out for Slaves as soon as Born; and though they have a kind of a Glimmering of Immortality, yet they worship Idols, representing the Devil; and when *Ferdinando Sotto* a *Spaniard*, went about to perswade them he was sent from God, to bring them to places of Joy and

De-

Delight; they at that time Reflecting upon the Cruelties of that Bloody Nation, told him they could never believe it, forasmuch as they were assured that God was good, and never would send any amongst them to kill, slay, and do all manner of mischief; which indeed is not one of the least causes, why so many of these poor Wretches, conceiving an Aversation to the Religion for the wickedness of the Professors, remain yet in darkness, and obstinately shut their Eyes against the Marvelous Light that should guide them to Salvation: As for the chief Towns, mostly Inhabited by the *Christians* (for the Natives here, as in other parts, live in Woods and small Cottages) they are St. *Helens*, scituate on a Promontory of that Name; *Charles Fort*, upon the Bank of the River *Maio*; *Port Royal*, a Haven on the Mouth of a River of that Name; *Apalche*, formerly a Town of Forty Cottages, taken by the *Spaniards*, and plundered of great store of Wealth; *Ante*, *Ocalis*, St. *Matthews*, St. *Augustines*, taken by *Drake* 1585, from the *Spaniard*, where he found 18 Brass Pieces of Cannon, and 20000 *Florens* in ready Money: The Mountains here are not very considerable, and the Rivers of note only 11, abound with Fish, where the *Crocodiles* haunt not.

CALIFORMIA is another Countrey of the *Mexicanian* Province or Division of the *West India's*, comprehending a vast Tract of Land, by some branched under divers Denominations; it hath on the East some parts of *Nova Gallicia*, with the vast undiscovered Countreys lying on the West of *Canada*, and *Virginia* on the opposite Shoar, bounded on the North with the unknown parts of the *Mexicanian Province*, on the North West with the Streights of *Anian*; on the West with the Sea interposing between it and the Island called *Mer Vermiglio*; on the South and South West with the rest of *Nova Gallicia*, divided at first into the Provinces of *Quivira* and *Cibola*; the former of these taking up the most Northern parts of this side *America*, being very barren in the extreamest North, yielding few Houses, Trees, or Herbage; the Natives Rude and Savage, eating Raw Flesh without Chewing, Cloathing themselves in Bull and Cow Hides, living in Hoords and Clanns, like the *Tartars*, and are thought to be upon the *Tartarian Continent*; but the Mountains of Snow and Ice interrupts all Communication between the Nations; but more Southward the Countrey appears green and pleasant, Flourishing with Herbs and Trees, breeding store of Cattle, not much differing from those of *Europe*, for bigness, tho in make otherwise, for they have Bunches like *Camels* between their Shoulders, and Bristles, like Logs upon their Backs, their Mains like that of a Horse, and Beards like *Goats*, having short Horns and Legs; insomuch that they look frightful to those that first behold them; but in these the Natives place their greatest Riches, making them serve their turns sundry ways, as their Hides for Cloaths and the Covering Houses; their Bones for Bodkins and Needles; their Hair for Thread, their Sinews for Ropes; their Horns, Maws, and Bladders for Vessels to drink in; their Blood for Drink; and the Calve-skins for Budgets to carry Water in; the people generally Roving from place to place, and seldom being at a stay.

CIBOLA, the second Division of *Califormia*, lying more Southward, is pretty Temperate, so that the *Natives* go Naked, unless a short Mantle of *Beasts-skins* cast over their *Shoulders*, and a Flap to hide their *Pritties*: As for *Fruit-Trees*, they are rarely found, except *Cedars*, of which they make their Boats and Fuel; yet they have Maize and small white Pease growing Naturally, of which they make their Bread; some quantity of Sheep they have,

have, and as for Venison, though they have store, yet they rarely eat it, but rather kill it for the Skins, and so much the Woods abound with *Lyons*, *Bears*, and *Tygers*, that those who border on them are continually obliged to stand upon their Guard; they are very Civil to *Strangers*; however, the *Spaniards*, tho they entered this *Countrey*, withdrew again their Forces, as not thinking the *Countrey* worth their maintaining; as for Cities or Towns there are none of note.

NOVA ALBION, so named by Sir *Francis Drake* Anno 1577. is another part found in this Tract, lying about 38 degrees North Latitude, which renders it considerably Fruitful, abounding in Cattle by reason of the pleasant Pastures it affords, and such store of *Deer* and *Conies*, that it is greatly to be admired; and of the Skins of these, those of most Dignity make them Robes, but the meaner sort go Naked, except the Women, who have only an Apron of Bulrushes to hide their Privities; and here it was the King of the Countrey offered up his Crown of Net-work, and Feathers, to Sir *Francis Drake*, who received it on the behalf of the Queen of *England*, erecting a Pillar and fixing her Arms thereon, as a mark of the Countreys Subjection to her, naming it thereupon *New Albion*.

NOVA GALLICIA, so called from a Province of *Spain* of that Name, to which it is likened for Temperature of Air and Production, is bounded on the East and South with *New Spain*; on the West with the River *Buena Guia*; and on the West with the Gulf of *Californina*; scituate between 18 and 28 degrees of North Latitude, 300 Leagues in Length and 100 in Breadth; the Air is generally very temperate, but rather inclined to heat than cold, and tho often the Inhabitants are disturbed with great Storms of Thunder and Rain, yet is the Air very healthy, so that no Contagious Disease happens amongst them, and when they are deficient of Rains, the Dews refresh the Earth, and the Countrey withal being Mountainous, affords Quarries of Stone and Mines of Brass and Silver, but none of Iron or Gold, and amongst the Metal a great mixture of Lead happens; however the Plains wonderfully abound with Corn, yield Wheat 60 fold, and Maize 200 fold; they have Bees likewise without stings, who make their Honey in Trees of the Woods to great quantities; and here grow Citrons, Figgs, Malacotoons, Cherries, and Olives; the people wavering and inconstant, upon the least discontent betaking themselves to the Woods, and deserting their Houses; their Garments being for the most part Cotton Shirts, with a Mantle over it, given much to Singing and Dancing, and sometimes to Drinking, and have their Tribes, whose Heads Command in Chief, and succeed Hereditarily; yet those Chiefs Commanded by the *Spanish Officers*, inhabiting those parts; and in this Tract are the lesser Provinces of *Cinaloa, Conliacan, Xalisco, Guadalaiara, Zacatecas, New Biscay,* and *New Mexicana*: All of them, as to the Natives and Quality of the Countreys, little differing, the greater part of them Commanded in Chief by the *Spaniards*, to whom the Petty Princes and Governours of the Natives are Subservient and Tributary, and have for their Chief Towns, *St. Philip* and *Jacob*, *St. John de Cinaloa, Pistala, Xalisco, Nombre de Dios*, plundered of great Treasure by Sir *Francis Drake*, *St. Lewis, St. Barbara* and *Chia*, every one the Chief of a Province, and hold some Trade, tho not considerable, the *Spaniards* not desiring to have Commerce with any other Nation, nor suffer the Natives to do it, lest they should be incroached upon; for they hold the poor ignorant people in hand, that they are the most powerful Lords of all *Europe*, and the invincible People of the World.

NOVA

NOVA HISPANIA, or *New Spain*, is another large Countrey, in the *Mexicanian Province*, bounded on the East with an Arm of the Sea, called the Bay of *New Spain* and Gulf of *Mexico*; on the South with part of *Nova Gallicia* and *Mare del Zur*; on the North with the rest of *Gallicia*, some part of *Florida* and the Gulf on the South of *Mare del Zur*; or rather the South Sea, and is so called, in reference to *Spain* in *Europe*, extending from the 15th degree of Latitude to the 26th. Measuring on the East side from the Bay of *Mexico* to the North of *Panuco*, but less by 6 degrees, if the Measure be taken to the West side, and tho it is scituate under the Torrid Zone, yet the Air is very Temperate, by reason the Heats are allayed by the Cooling Briezes that come from off the Seas on Three sides of it, and the Ground being Cooled by the Showers that seasonably fall in *June*, *July*, and *August*, when the Weather is at the hottest; and here are found Rich Mines of Gold and Silver, some of Brass and Iron, great plenty of *Coco Nuts*, store of *Cassia*, and vast quantities of *Cocheneal* growing upon Shrubs or little Trees, planted by the Natives and Spaniards; they have likewise store of Wheat, Pulse, Barley, Plants, Roots, Oranges, Lemons, Pomegranats, Malacotoons, Figgs, Apples, Pears, Grapes, Birds and Beasts, both Wild and Tame, almost of all sorts; and in the hottest part of this Countrey, their Seed time is in *April*, and their Harvest in *October*; but in colder places, lying low and moist, they Sow in *October* and Reap in *May*, by which crossing, they are Supplied with Two Harvests in a Year.

The Natives of this Tract are more Ingenious than any other of the Salvages, giving themselves up to Curious Arts, especially to the making of Feather Pictures, which they perform so lively without Dying the Feathers, but taking them in their

their natural Colours, that they will imitate Men, Beasts, or any other thing, so lively, that at a very small distance, any one not knowing the contrary, would verily believe them to be drawn by the most Curious Master with a Pencil, &c. Working in Gold more neat and dextrous than any *Europeans*, yet so little esteeming it, that at the first-coming of the *Spaniards*, they Barter'd it for Knives, Beads Bells, and such inconsiderable Matters, and not having been used to Ride on Horse-back, they took their new come Guests for *Centaurs*; they were exceeding Populous, which appears by the *Spaniards*, having destroyed Six millions of them in 17 Years, Roasting some, plucking out the Eyes of others, Consuming them in their Mines, and Inhumanly casting them amongst Wild Beasts to be devoured, insomuch that the Women, many of them not only refused the means for Generation, but such as found themselves pregnant, destroyed their Children in the Womb, that they might not be brought up to serve so Bloody a Nation.

In the great Province of *New Spain*, are found the lesser Provinces of *Panuco*, *Mechuacan*, *Mexicana*, *Tbascala*, *Guaxaca*, and *Jucatan*, all plentifully abounding with the pride of Art and Nature; the whole Province taking its name from *Mexico*, a great City upon a Lake, as likewise all that I have hitherto written relating to this *New World*, and because the taking of this City proved of such Importance to the *Spaniard*, we think it not amiss to give a brief Relation of it, *viz*.

Hervando Cortz, born in *Medeline* a Town of *Estremadure*, a Province of *Old Spain*, rising from an obscure Birth to become a private Adventurer in these parts, raised by Industry his Fortune to so high a pitch, that with the help of his Friends, he Manned Eleven Ships, with 550 Men, and after some contending with the Seas, arrived at the I-
sland

stand now called *Sancta Crux*, and passing up the River *Tabasco*, sacked *Potonchon* a small Town on the Banks of it, upon the Inhabitants refusing to sell him Victuals, and by the help of his Horse and Cannon, put to the Rout an Army of 40000 of the Salvages, and so receiving the King a Vassal to the Crown of *Spain*, he passed onwards towards the Golden Mines, Landing at St. *John de Ulla*, where he was met by order of the Governour of the King of *Mexico*, with rich presents of Gold and other rich Things, which so inflamed him, that forgetting the Civility, he found means to pick a quarrel with the King, by building Forts in the Countrey, and claiming it for *Charles* the Fifth, King of *Spain* and Emperour of *Germany*, and getting the *Flascalians* on his part, a party of the Natives who were at variance with the King of *Mexico*, and increasing his *Spaniards* by such as he found in the Countrey, to 900 Foot and 80 Horse, he with the whole Force of the *Flascalians*, being 100000 Men, and the help of 17 Pieces of Cannon, 13 Galliots, and 6000 Canoa's or Boats, besieged that great City by Land and Water, and in 13 Months took, sacked, and burnt it, by which means this Rich Kingdom fell to the *Spaniards*.

GUATIMALIA is another large Tract in the *Mexicanian* Province, bounded on the North with *Jucatan* and the Gulf of *Honduras*; on the South with *Mare del Zur*; on the East or South East with *Castela Aurea*; and on the West with *New Spain*; extended 300 Leagues upon the Coast of *Mare del Zur*, but upon straight measure not above 240, and in breadth about 180 Leagues, comprehending the lesser Provinces of *Chiapa*, *Verapaz*, *Guatimala*, properly so called, and from which the whole Tract takes its Name; *Hondura*, *Nicaragua*, *Veragua*; and has for its Chief Towns *Civida Real*, St. *Augustines*, St. *Salvador*, St. *Jago de Guatimala*,

St. *Maria de Comyagena*, *Leon de Nicaragua*, and *La Trinidada*, with divers others of lesser Note.

This part of *Mexicana*, by reason of its nearness of Scituation to the Line, is Fruitful in all parts, unless where the Rocky Hills thrust up their heads abounding with Fruit, Trees, Corn, Cattle, Foul, Fish, and Mines of Gold, Silver, and Brass; and in the Rivers, which are considerable, much Gold is found, as washed from the Mountains, and here the Natives bear the Spanish Yoke more uneasily than in other parts.

A Description of the Peruanian Province, or the Second Devision of America.

This great Province, divided into many lesser, resembles a Pyramid Reverse more properly so than *Africk*, joyned to that we have mentioned by the Isthmus or Streights of *Darien*, deriving its Name from *Peru* the Chief Province of the whole, which stands thus divided, as far as is hitherto Inhabited by the *Spaniards* or other *Europeans*, viz. *Castela Aurea*, the new Realm of *Granada*, *Peru*, *Chiel*, *Paragnay*, *Brasil*, *Guyana*, and *Paria*, not accounting the Islands, which are reserved for another place; and as for the boundards in general, having already described them; we now proceed to describe the particular Provinces, and of them in their order, viz.

CASTE-

CASTELA DEL ORE, or *Castela Aurea*, is bounded on the West with *Mare del Zur* and some part of *Virginia*; on the South with the New Realm of *Granada*; on the East and North with *Mare del Noort*, called *Castile*, in reference to that in *Spain*, as being discovered by the Influence of those Kings, and *Aurea* added, by reason of the abundance of Gold found there, and contains *Panama, Darien, Nova, Andaluzia, St. Martha*, and the Provinces *De La Hacha*, the Air in most parts is very Healthful, especially to those that have been there for any considerable time, or born there; however the In-land Countrey is thinly peopled, by reason the *Spaniards* upon their first settling there, destroyed in a manner the whole Race of the Natives, whose Assistance now they want to Manure the Soil; there were likewise found at their first Coming, an extraordinary number of Swine, which they also destroyed and suffered to rot upon the ground in such multitudes, that now, tho they would fain retrieve that loss, it is not in their power; however the Earth brings forth a considerable Encrease, where the Fields and Valleys are found, tho the Countrey abounds with barren Mountains and Woods, so that in this Province, besides the Mines of Gold and Silver that are found, enriching the people with great Treasure; they have Corn, Wine, Oyl, Mellons, Balsom, sundry sorts of Drugs and Trees of sundry kinds, producing Fruits different from what are found in *Europe*; and in the Province of *Andaluzia*, the *Spaniards* upon their Arrival, greedy of Gold, found in the Graves of the Dead, which were brought from all parts to be buried there, as held to be the most Sacred ground, so much Treasure, that for a time they took no care to dig it out of the Mountains: As for the People Inhabiting this Tract, they are mostly *Spaniards*, those few Natives that are left, being in a manner their Slaves: The

Countrey is full of great Rivers, as *Rio de Lagartus*, the River of *Crocodiles*; *Sardinila*, *Sardino*, *Rio de Comagres*, *Rio de Colubros*, and others; being in many places overspread by the Spurs of the great Mountain *Andes*, held to be as big as any in the World.

The Chief Towns in this Province are *Panama*, *Darien*, on the bank of the Gulf of *Umbra*; *Carthagena*, scituate in a Sandy Peninsula, and consisting of 500 Houses; *St. Martha* scituate on the shoars of the Ocean; *Lahach*, scituate upon a River of that name; all of them under the Power of the *Spaniards*, governed according to the Laws of *Spain*, to which the Natives are obliged to submit.

NOVA GRANADA, or the New Realm of *Granada*, lies on the North of *Castela Aurea*, being about 130 Leagues in Length, and not much less in Breadth, and is divided into *Granada* and *Popayana*; the Air for the most part well, with a mixture of Heat and Cold, but more of the former; neither differ the days any thing considerably in length; the Countrey extreamly Woody, and somewhat Mountainous, yet stored with Fertile Plains, and breeds a number of Cattle, affording Veins of Gold and other Mettals, and in a part of it called *Tunia*, are found Emeralds of great value: The Natives that are yet remaining, go very decent, and are by their Conversation with the *Spaniards* (amongst whom they live in small Towns) much Civiliz'd; the Women being more White and Comly than in any other part, very Industrious, Tall, and well Proportioned, most of them embracing the *Roman Catholick Religion*, much delighting in Singing and Dancing; and as for the Chief Towns in this Province, are they St. *Foy* an Arch-bishops See; St. *Michael* a Market Town, well Traded to; *Trinidado* seated on the River of that name; whose Fields are full of Vines of Chrystal, Emeralds, Adaments, and

Ca*l*-

Chalcedons; *Tunia, Pampelonia, Papayan,* the usual Residence of a Governour, and a Bishops See: *Antiochia, Carthage, Sebastian de la Plata,* so called from the Silver Mines in its Neighbourhood, with some others of less note: As for the Rivers and Mountains, most of them want names, wherefore for brevities sake, we pass over any tedious Enquiry into them.

As for this Province, it had its Name given by *Gonsalvo Ximenes de Quesada,* in reference to *Granada* in *Spain,* who having Murthered (contrary to Faith given) *Sangipa* the last King of *Bagota,* whom he had made use of in subduing the *Panches,* he seized his Treasure, which amounted to 191294 *Pezoes* of fine Gold, 35000 of courser Allay, and 1800 large Emeralds; by which the Riches of the Province may be guessed.

PERU lying South of the former Province, is accounted in Length 700 Leagues, but disproportional in Breadth, as not exceeding in some places 60 and 40 Leagues, tho in others 100, and is divided into three parts, but so differing in nature and quality, as if they were at a larger distance from each other, being called the Plains, the Hill Countreys and the *Andes*; the first extending on the Sea shore, in all places level, without Hills; the second composed of Hills and Plains, stretching out from North to South; the whole Length of the Province; and the third a continual Ridg of huge Mountains without any Valleys; however, tho the Mountains and Hills are Woody, or otherways Barren, by reason of their Minerals, yet the Plains and Valleys produce store of Corn, Fruit, and Herbage, Flourishing with an Eternal Spring, the Southerly Wind continually blowing on them, bringing no Rain, though on the Mountains all manner of Winds have power, and bring Rain, Thunder, and Fair Weather by turns, as in other

Coun

Countries, and to supply the want of Cattle, they have in the Woods and Mountains, a Beast like a Goat called *Vicagnes*, and a kind of Sheep as big as young Bullocks; bearing large Fleeces, which they use as Horses, to carry their burthens; but if at any time they find themselves over-laden, neither force nor fair means can oblige them to move forward, before they are alleviated, living upon slender diet, and will sometimes Journy three days without Water; and amongst Plants, the Fig-Tree in this Country has a strange effect, viz. the North part looking towards the Mountains, bringeth forth Fruit in the Summer only, and the South part looking towards the Sea in the Winter; and in this Province grow Coco's in great plenty, whose Leaves dryed in little Pellets, satisfie Hunger and Thirst, and are a great part of the diet the *Spaniards* afford their poor Slaves in the Mines, so that it is said 100000 Baskets full of them have been devoured in a year at the Mines of *Petosia*; and a plant they have, by which they try sick Persons, whether they will live or dye, for if the Patient look chearful when it is fast grasped in his hand, then is it a sign of Recovery, but if sad, the contrary; and have Beasts called a *Huanaçu's*, the Males of which stand Centinals upon the Mountains, whilest the Females descend and feed in the Valleys; and if they perceive any man approaching them, they give warning, by making a terrible noise; and hastily running to their assistance, interpose their Bodies till they make their retreat; and many other things are found worthy of note; and the whole Province is divided properly into three juridical Resorts, viz. *Quito*, *Lima* and *Charcas*, these having under them other Divisions of lesser note, as *Las-Quixos*, *Cusco*, *Collao*, &c.

(205)

As for the People they were not so ignorant, upon the first Arrival of the *Spaniards*, of Letters, whereby they might acquaint themselves with other parts of the World, but that they labour to keep them so still, that they through Ignorance may the better brook their Yoak; however they are couragious and industrious, fearless of Death, animated to contemn Life in hopes in the other World to live in Luxury and Riot, and injoy delicate Women; so that when any of their Chiefs or petty Princes die, some of his Servants willingly submit to be Buried with him, that they may wait upon him afterward; some of them dwelling in the most Mountainous parts, go half naked; but the rest have long Mantles reaching to their heels, though in dressing their Heads they differ, each having a peculiar Fashion: And to guess at the Riches of this Country by some part of it, 'tis affirmed, that the Mines of *Petozi*, discovered in the year 1545. afforded for the Kings Fifth's payable to his Exchequer 111 Millions of Pezoes of Silver, every one valued at 6 s. 6 d. of our money, and yet a third part of the whole was discharged of that payment; and in some parts as much Gold is digged as Earth, &c. As for the Rivers of most note, they are St. *Jago*, *Tombez*, *Guagaquil*, and others of lesser note. The Towns are principally *Carangues*, *Peru*, *Cusco*, *Andreo*, *Truxilo*, *Archidona*, *Baeza*, *Lima*, *Collao*, *Potozi*, *Plata*, *Chiquita*, with others; but to draw to a conclusion of this rich Province, we need only say for a further Demonstration, that when *Atabalaba* was overcome by *Pizarro* and his *Spaniards*, he gave (besides what infinite Sums the *Spaniards* had plundered before) for his Ransom, a large Room full of Gold piled up to the Ceiling; yet this prevailed not with those Unchristian like Christians, for falling out about the sharing, and willing to conceal it from the

King

King of *Spain*; they notwithstanding contrary to their Oaths and promises, Strangled that poor *Peruanian* Prince, the last of the Race of the *Inga's*, or Emperors of *Peru*; for which violation and perfidy, God was not flow in punishing them all that were concerned in it, dying a miserable and untimely death: And in this Kings Pallace at *Cusco*, all his Utensils were of Gold and Silver, even to his Kitchen Furniture, and in his Ward-robe were found Statues of Giants, the Figures of Beasts, Fish, Birds, Plants, &c. in their proper shape and largeness of the same Mettal; and thus much for *Peru*, &c. whose Gold proved the ruin of the Natives, and the Impoverishment of *Old Spain*.

CHILE, is on the North bounded with the Desart of *Alacama* Interposing between it and *Peru*; on the West with *Mare del Zur*; on the South with the *Magellan* Streights; and on the East as far as *Rio dela Plata*, with the main *Atlantick* Ocean, Scituate in the temperate Zone, beyond the Tropick of *Capricorn*; if we reckoned to it some other Countries bordering on the *Atlantick*, not yet fully discovered called *Chile* or *Chil* from the extream cold it indures, when the Sun is in our Summer *Solstice*, that it is reported Horses and Riders in the extream parts are often Frozen to death, or lost in the Snows, which extreams on this side, and beyond the Equinoctial demonstrates the Continent of *America* to be larger than *Asia*; the Soil of this Tract in the mid-land parts is Mountainous and unfruitful, but towards the Sea-side, level and full of Trees abounding with Gold Silver, Honey, Cattle, Wine, Maize, Corn, &c. The Natives are of a Gigantick Stature, but very civil, if not too much provoked; cloathing themselves with Skins of Beasts, and Arming with Bows and Arrows; shaggy Haired, and whiter of Complexion than any we have yet spoken of in the *Peruanan Provinces*; and the Countrey is Watered with the Rivers of *Rio de Copayapo*, *Rio de Coquimbo*, *La Ligna*, *Canten*, *Cacapool*, *Topocalma*, and some others of lesser note, especially one, though we find not the name, which falls into the Sea with a violent Torrent all day, but in the night its Channel is dry, and the reason is, it has its Waters from the melted Snow falling from the Mountains, which cease when the Sun is gone down: The Towns of note in *Chile* and *Magellanica*, for into these two parts is the Province divided, are St. *Jago* the Chief, tho not above 80 Houses in it, because it is the Residence of the Governour and Court of Judicature. *Serena* on the Sea-shoar, having in it about 200 Houses, and near it many Mines of Gold Conception. *Delos Confines*, *Imperiale* and some few more in the part called *Chile*; but in *Magellanica*, we find nothing but Capes and Rivers Inhabited, a Savage and Barbarous People afflicted with sharp Winds, and the Mountains continually covered with Snow, wherefore as a Countrey not fit for Commerce, we leave it and proceed to *Brasil*.

BRASIL is a large Tract, reaching from 29 to 30 degrees South Latitude, 1500 miles in Length, and 500 in Breadth, bounded on the East with *Mare del Noort* or the *Main Atlantick*; on the West with undiscovered Countreys, on the North with *Guiana*, and on the South with *Paragua*, or the Province of *Rio de la Plata*, and is a great part of it possessed by the *Portugals* and *Dutch*: The Countrey intermixed with Rivers, Mountains, Woods, and pleasant Plains; the Air wholsome, by reason of the purging Winds which rise from the Southern Coast, every day about Ten in the Morning; the Countrey yielding great store of Sugar Canes, which is brought to perfection by the working of many Thousands of Slaves, so that the *Portugals* brought thence in few Years 150000 *Arobes* of that Commodity, each *Arobe* containing 25 Bushels of our Measure; and here it is the *Brasil Wood* grows, whereof there are Trees of such bigness, that when the Rivers overflow, as frequently they do in the level Countrey, the Inhabitants dwell in the Branches of them, like Birds in their Nests, till the Waters abate.

The People in this Tract nearest the Line, are of a reasonable Understanding, wearing Apparel, but further off they are Barbarous, both Men and Women going stark naked, gladly eating Humane Flesh, insomuch that when they can privately catch any of the Christians, they Roast them, and invite all their Friends, feasting on the Flesh, with great Merriment; and here the Women are wonderful quick, and easie at Child-bearing, never lying by it, but in two or three days seem as well as ever: Beasts are found in this Tract of strange forms; one with the head of an Ape, the Body of a Man, and the feet and paws of a Lyon; a Plant they have called *Copiba*, the back of which being slit, affords a precious Balm, which is so well known by the Beasts of the Forrests, that when they have taken in any Poison, or are bit by Serpents or other Venemous Creatures, they fly to it for succour, as to a Sanctuary for Life, and by sucking in the Antidote, find a speedy Cure: An Herb they have, that being roughly touched, as in Modesty, shrinketh in its branching Leaves, and opens them not till the party who offends is gone out of sight. The People in this Tract, both Men and Women, are good Swimmers, and soused to Diving, that they will remain under Water an hour without respiration, and many of them are so over-grown with Hair, that they seem rather Beasts than Men; the Divisions of *Brasil* are *St. Vincent, Rio de Janeiro, Del Spiritu Santo, Porto Seguro, Des Ilheos, Todas Los Santos, Paraguay, Rio de la Plata, Tucaman, St. Crux de Siera*, a Province full of Palm Trees; *Fernambuck* rich in Tobacco and Sugar; *Tamaraca, Paraiba, Rio-grande, Siara, Maragnon*, and *Para*, being termed *Captainships* or *Præfectures*, possessed by the *Portugals, Spaniards, French, Dutch* and other Nations, who in some places live promiscuously with the Natives, and in others, some coming in search of Adventures, others driven by Distress, as being not suffered to live quietly at home; insomuch that tho the *Brasilians* had but few Houses and fewer Towns, yet now the encrease of them has rendered it in many parts a pleasant Countrey, the Plains enriched like those of *Egypt*, by the overflowing of the Rivers, which are exceeding large.

GUIANA is another Tract of this *Peruanian* Continent, bounded on the East with the *Main Atlantick Ocean*; and on the West with the Mountains of *Peru*, or an undiscovered Countrey interposing between them; on the North with the River, *Orenoque*; and on the South, as some will have it with the *Amazons*; tho indeed we find no such Countrey; however it is undiscovered, and therefore Travellers have liberty to name it as they please.

Tho *Guiana* is scituate on both sides the Line, extending from the Fourth degree of Southern to the Eighth degree of Northern Latitude; notwithstanding by reason of the fresh Winds and cool Air that comes off the Sea and Rivers, it is indifferently Temperate; towards the Sea side it is level, but the Inland swelled with rising Hills, and the Trees and Fields wearing a lasting green, as knowing no Winter, there being always ripe and green Fruits and Blossoms at the same time; so that it may be compared for pleasantness, with any we have yet named in this Tract.

The

The People (Natives of *Guiana*) have no settled Government, yet reduce themselves into Tribes, under several Heads or Chiefs, though this is left to their own discretion, and every one may separate when he pleases, and all the punishment they have for Offenders, is only in case of Adultery and Murther, for which when proved, the Criminal makes an Expiation with his Life; the poorer sort are allowed but one Wife, and the rich two or three; not owning any God, but either not regarding from whence they had their being, and are by Power sustained, or Atheistically ascribing all to Fate and Chance: As for their Accompts they keep them in bundles of Sticks, which they increase or diminish according as the Debt or Business grows more or less; and at their Funerals the Women howl extreamly, whilst the Men on the contrary are Singing and Feasting.

This Country is divided into the Provinces of *Rio-de-Las, Amazons, Wiapoco*, or *Guiana*, properly so called, *Orenoque, Trinidad*, and *Tobago*; and are full of great Rivers stored abundantly with Fish, and wild Fowl, but most of all they refresh the Countries with the Dews that arise from them and the principal of these are *Orenoque, Arrawari, Conawini, Caspurough*, or *Cassipure*, falling into the Atlantick Ocean, *Wiapoco*, the River of the *Amazons*, and a great many of lesser note; and in this Tract are said to be Mountains of intire Chrystal; Mines there are of Gold and Silver, with many strange Plants, Fruits, and Beasts; as also Tobacco and Sugar Canes, and at *Comolaha*, on the South of *Arenoque*, they hold a Fair for the Sale of Women, only where an English-man left by Sir *Walter Raligh*, reports to have bought 8 for a three half-penny red hafted Knife, the eldest not exceeding 18 Years, which he says without making any Burglarys upon their Virginities, he liberally bestowed

in

in Marriage on sundry of the Natives: And near this place is the mighty Water-fall, or Cataract of the River *Arenoque*, whose horrid noise makes the Mountains tremble, which may well fit the Words of the Poet, *viz.*

Cuncta tremunt undis, & multo murmure Montis,
Spumeus invictis albescit Fluctibus amni.

The Noise the Mountains shakes, who roar for spite,
To see th' Unvanquish'd Waves clad all in White.

In an other part of this Province they have a strange custom with their Dead, for when the Flesh is worn off the Bones by Putrefaction, they hang up the Skeleton in the Chamber or House where the party died, decking the Skull with Feathers of divers Colours, and hanging Jewels and Plates of Gold, about the Arm and Thigh Bones. As for the Towns of note in this Tract, they are *Mano*, called by the Spaniards *El' Dorado*, from the abundance of Gold and Silver Coin, Armour, and Utensils found there, held to be the largest of all the Country, though some question the Truth of this place; *Caripo, Gomeribo, Tanparanume, Morequuto,* St. *Thome,* and St. *Joseph,* with some others of lesser note, which they are obliged to build upon Hills, Rocks, or the like advantageous Places, forasmuch as the Rivers yearly overflow a great part of the Country, obliging the Natives to live in Trees with their Families, building them Hutts in the Branches like Birds Nests.

PARIA, another considerable Province, lies on the West of *Guiana,* divided into the lesser Countries of *Cumana, Venezuela,* St. *Margaita, Cubagna,*

bagna, and some *Islands*; and here the Nature of the Soil and People are different, though in general the Country is very Pleasant, being watered with the Rivers of *Rio-de-Cacioas, Rio-de-Neveri, Cumana de Bardones*, and others of lesser note, and has for its chief Towns, *Maracapana* (once a *Spanish* Garrison) *Venezuela, New Cadiz*, and some others; and in this Tract the Pearl Fishery is used, those valuable Commodities being gotten by Diving, and they bring up a Fish much like an Oyster, out of the Shells of which they take the Pearls, supposed to be Ingendred there by the falling of Dews, when the Fish opens to receive the Air upon the Shoar: and though the People in the Province of *Cumana* have Plenty of Fruits and Cattle, with other things whereby to subsist even to Riot, yet they rather chuse to feed upon Insects and Vermin, as Batts, Spiders, Horse-leaches, Worms, &c. each Man being allowed as many Wives as he can maintain, though they never have the Maidenheads of any, prostituting them the first Night to their *Piacos*, or Priests, or their appointment, who for small matters turn over that Drudgery to Strangers; nor do they at any time think their Guests welcome, unless they will do the Office of Men to their Wives, Sisters, &c. blackning their Teeth, and Painting their Bodies of diverse Colours; in this Tract are found diverse Mines of Gold, some of Silver, and other Minerals; and here the *Spaniards* met with many disasters, as well the Ecclesiasticks, as Military, being frequently expulsed or cut off by the Salvages, who are in general a Stout and Warlike People; and here are found the *Capa*, a Beast, the Soles of whose Feet are like a Shooe, and a Hog of monstrous size, with Horns like a Goat, living altogether upon Ants, Pismires, Parrots, and Batts; and could I have added to this Bill of Fair, *Booksellers* and *Printers*, the World
might

might have taken this Monster for a meer *Robin Hog*, &c.

Cattle this Country affords in great Quantities, insomuch that Instructed by the *Europeans*, they make Butter and Cheese of their Milk, in sundry places, which the Natives take as the Prince of Rarities. And thus much *Reader* may suffice for the Empires, Kingdoms, Provinces, and States of the Universe, relating to the Continent of *Europe*, *Asia*, *Africa*, and *America*, from which we proceed (for the greater Satisfaction of the Curious) to the Description of the Islands scattered in the several Seas, attributed to the four Parts of the World; and of these in their Order.

A Description of the Islands of Europe, *and their various Scituations in their sundry Seas*, &c.

Great Britain *Described*.

GREAT BRITAIN, being in a manner known to most that Inhabit it, may occasion some to reflect upon this brief Description as superfluous; however, having undertaken to omit nothing material in this great Undertaking, which indeed wanted nothing but the permission of a larger Scope, to render it more Illustricus, we will not be wanting to give a

mo-

modest Account of the Princess of Islands, or Epitome of the Universe, being properly, and not without just Reason stiled, the World *Minature*; and in this case we must divide it into two Parts, *viz. England, Wales,* &c. and *Scotland,* comprehending the Ocean Islands.

England, *described,* &c.

ENGLAND has for its Eastern boundard the *German Ocean*; on the West the Irish Sea; on the South the British Ocean; and on the North, parting it from *Scotland,* the River *Tweed* and *Solway*; Invironed as to the whole Island, with the main Sea, guarded in most parts by such Rocks, as render it Inaccessible from Forreign Invaders, if the Shoars be but indifferently Defended, though its Walls consists in its many more Powerful and Impregnable Defendants, than those of Stone; which notwithstanding it had not always to defend it, as appears by its becoming a Prey to the *Romans,* its being harassed by the *Picts, Scots,* and wild *Irish,* and the Subjection it was brought under by the *Saxons, Danes,* and *Normans*; but at this day the often Languishing Island lifts up her head as high as the tallest of the Daughters of the Nations upon Earth.

As for the Soil, improved by industrious hands, it is in most parts exceeding Fruitful, as well in Grain as Herbage, Fruit Trees, Rich Pastures, &c. as all other things necessary, and conducing to the support of Life; with Mines of Iron, Tin, Lead, &c. but exceeds other Nations in the Woollen Manufacture; nor is making of Stuffs, Silks, and other Curious Arts wanting in a great measure, but more especially the Traffick abroad, where for our Native

Com-

Commodities, we command the most valuable things in the Universe.

ENGLAND in particular, holds from 50 to 54 degrees of North Latitude; the Air Pleasant and Temperate, by vicissitude of Heat and Cold, as also the varying of Night and Day; but more for the wholesome Laws, good Constitution of the Established Government and Nature of the People, whose Generosity and Valour has famed them in all parts of the known World, and the whole divided into 39 Shires or Divisions, viz. *Middlesex, Essex, Kent, Sussex, Hampshire*, or the County of *Southampton, Surry, Buckinghamshire, Bedfordshire, Cambridgshire, Cheshire, Cornwal, Cumberland, Darbyshire, Dorsetshire, Durham, Glocestershire, Huntingtonshire, Lancashire, Leicestershire, Lincolnshire, Northamptonshire, Notinghamshire, Rutlandshire, Shropshire, Somersetshire, Wiltshire, Warwickshire, Westmorland, Yorkshire, Norfolk, Northumberland, Oxfordshire, Staffordshire, Barkshire, Devonshire, Hartfordshire, Suffolk*, and *Worcestershiye, Herefordshire*; all of them extreamly replenished with Woods, Parks, Rivers, Cities, and Towns of Note, insomuch, that of considerable Rivers there are found 352, and on them 847 Bridges of Note, Cities 25, Market Towns 588, Parishes 8760, Arch-Bishopricks 2, Bishopricks 23. Forrests 61, Parks 752, Chaces 12, and had before the grand unnatural Rebellion, 134 Castles, but during that tedious War, many of them were demolished; the whole Countrey consisting of pleasant Valleys, moderately rising Hills, flourishing Fields and Medows, that it may suffice to live upon its own plenty, without the help or assistance of any other Nation, and for stately Buildings and many other Curiosities too many to be contained in a much larger Volume, if no other Countreys were spoken of: We must wave them, seeing we are at home, and suffer

the

the Experience of the knowing Reader to supply the omission.

WALES is properly a part of *England*, but seeing it is g'nerally divided, or accounted a Principality, &c. we think it not amiss to speak of it by it self, viz. This Countrey is from East to West about a 100 Miles, and from North to South 120; and in it are found 965 Parishes, 55 Market Towns, 4 Bishopricks, 67 Castles, 230 Rivers, 99 Bridges of note, 28 Parks, 6 Forrests, and 1 Chase, and is divided into the Shires of *Brecknock*, *Anglesey*, *Cardigan*, *Carmaerthen*, *Carnarvan*, *Denbigh*, *Flint*, *Radnor*, *Glamorgan*, *Merioneth*, *Montgomery*, *Pembrook* and *Monmouth*, containing both North and South *Wales*, stretching into the Sea like a large Promontory, Fruitful in many places, where the Mountains raise not their Heads, especially the Isle of *Anglesey*, which of it self is held sufficient to feed the whole Countrey, for its store of Cattle and abundance of Corn; this Countrey yielding sundry Commodious Harbours and Landing Places, commercing at once with *England* and *Ireland*; and has for its Chief Towns, *Radnor*, *Carnarvan*, *Brecon*, *St. Davids*, *Cardriff*, *Carmaerthen* and *Monmouth*, most of them very pleasantly seated, and of considerable Trade; the Natives very Industrious and much given to Labour, Frugal, and for the most part Thrifty; nor may we spare to sum up these two Countreys, so mostly distinguished in the Epitome of the Poet, viz.

For Mountains, Bridges, Rivers, Churches fair;
Women and Wooll, they both are past compare.

SCOTLAND is the next considerable part that compacts the *British Empire* or Kingdom of *Great Britain*, separated from it only by the *Tweed* and *Solway*, and the Hills extending from one to the other, and is held to be 406 Miles in Length, tho in
Breadth

Breadth not proportionable, being in some parts but 60 from Sea to Sea, divided properly into two parts by the River *Tay*, *viz*. South and North, the former Division being both Fruitful and Populous, and again sub-divided into the Counties of *Merch, Teviotdale, Lothian, Liddesdale, Eskedale, Annandale, Niddesdale, Galloway, Carrick, Kyle, Cunningham, Arran, Cliddesdale, Lennox, Sterling, Fife, Stratherne, Menteith, Argile, Cantire, Lorn,* all comprehended in South *Scotland*: *Loquabrea, Braidalbin, Perth, Athole, Angus, Merns, Mar, Buquhan, Murrey, Rosse, Southerland, Cathaness,* and *Strathavern*, North *Scotland*; and in this Kingdom are found Two Arch-bishopricks, *viz*. St. *Andrews* and *Glascow*, under whom are Eleven Suffragan Bishops; and here the Chief City is *Edenburg*, a City principally composed of one large Street, about a Mile in length, of very good Building; the rest less considerable, tho throughout the whole Kingdom are many fair Cities, Towns, and Villages.

The Principal Islands lying upon the coast of *Great Britain* and Subject to it, are the Islands of *Wight, Man, Anglesey, Jersey, Guernsey,* the *Orcades* or Isles of *Orkney* 30 in Number; the Chief of which are *Pomania, Hethy,* and *Sheathland,* all very Fruitful, abounding with Cattle and Corn: The *Hebrides* 40 in number, but many of them rather Rocks than Islands, the Chief being *Illa* and *Jona*, the ancient Burying place of the Scottish Kings: *Mulla*, where the *Redshanks* Inhabited, once so frightful to the *English*: The *Sorlings* containing 145 Islands, but none of note, except *Armath, Sansad,* and *Scilly*, after the name of which the rest are called for the most part; some others there are on this Coast, but scarcely worth noting, as yielding little Trade or Commodity.

IRELAND, a Kingdom in Subjection to *Britain* by right of Conquest, separate from *England* only

L by

by a tempestuous Sea, of about a days Sail ; and is as all other Islands of note, scituate in the Ocean, or invironed with Sea, *&c.* containing in Length 400, and in Breadth 200 miles ; and especially divided into four Provinces, *viz.* 1. *Munster*, divided again into the Counties of *Limrick*, *Kery*, *Cork*, *Waterford*, *Desmond*, and *Holy Cross* in *Tipperary*, 2 *Lemster* again divided into the Counties of the *East* and *West Meaths*, *Kilkenny*, *Caterlough*, *Kings County*, *Queens County*, *Kildare*, *Weixford*, *Dublin*, and *Wicklock*; 3. *Connaught*, divided into the Counties of *Clare*, *Thumond*, *Galloway*, *Majo*, *Slego Letrim* and *Roscommon*. 4. *Ulster*, divided into the Counties of *Tyrconnel*, or *Dunhal*, *Tyrone* the upper and nether, *Fermanagh*, *Cavan* or *Cravan*, *Monaghan*, *Colrane*, *Antrim*, *Down*, *Armagh* and *Lough*. And of this Kingdom the chief City is *Dublin*, mostly inhabited by the English, pleasantly seated and very commodious for Trade, which renders it the chief Seat of Justice, and a Bishops See ; besides which are *Waterford*, *Tredagh*, *Limrick*, *Armagh*, and others of lesser note. The Country is in many parts very fruitful but being incumbred with Hills and Boggs, a great deal of it lies waste, and the more for the sluggishness of the Natives, who agree not with Labour, though otherwise Sharp and Crafty, hardy of Temper, and Living upon slender Fare; however the Rivers abound with Fish, especially *Salmon*, and the Hills and Valleys with Cattle ; insomuch that a Cow or a Horse may be purchased at about half a piece of our Money ; and one thing remarkable here is, that no poisonous Creature can live upon this Coast, and of such force is even the Wood brought from *Ireland* into *England* and other Countries, that no Spider will fasten a Cob-web on it.

The Isle of *Oleron*, is scituate against the *French* Province of *Xaintoigne*, South of the Isle of *Rhee*, famous for the Maritime Laws, eſtabliſhed here by *Richard* King of *England*; tho for nothing more than the quantities of Salt ſent hence into *France*, and other parts.

RHEE or *REE*, is a pleaſant Iſland about 10 *Engliſh* Miles in length, and 5 in bredth, and has in it the Towns of *La Butte, de Mont, St. John de Mont, St. Hillary* and *St. Martins*, famous for the defence, the Proteſtants made here againſt the power of *France*, but fatal to the *Engliſh* in their attempt to reſcue them.

ALDERNY is an Iſland diſtant about 6 miles from *Cape Hagge* in *Normandy*, very Rockey and hard of acceſs, and not exceeding 8 miles in compaſs conſiſts but of one conſiderable Town, called from the name of the Haven *Lacrab*; it not containing above 100 Families, nor is the Iſland of any conſiderable Trade.

The *SARK* is an Iſland about 6 Miles in compaſs not much diſtant from the former; and is ſubject to it, being of little Trade or Moment, and theſe being all of note in the Neighbouring Seas, we proceed to thoſe more Northern and Remote, which are

GROEN-LAND under the Frigid Zone, where the Cold is ſo extream that it is ſcarce habitable, though accounted in length 600 miles; yet having *St. Thomas*, and *Alba* for its chief Towns ſupported moſtly by the Fiſhing trade.

ISELAND an extream cold Country, extending 400 Miles, yet thinly Inhabited; and from this Region come the Shock Dogs, ſo much in eſteem; and here contrary to other Countries, the Oxen and Kine have no Horns; the Trade to it being moſtly upon the account of the Fiſhery, and that for Ling; few Trees except Juniper growing in the Country.

FREEZ-LAND is an Iſland reſorted to by the *Engliſh, Flemings, Danes, Scots*, and *Hanſmen*, upon the account of the Fiſhery.

NOVA-ZEMBLA lies extream North, under 78 Degrees, so cold that no Human Creature is capable of Inhabiting of it in Winter, unless driven by Distress, or Fatal Necessity; as were once about 14 *Dutch-men*, who during their abode there, strugled with so many Miseries, as are almost unexpressible; however Bears and Foxes are found here, and great store of Sea Fowl, &c.

SIR *HUGH WILLOUGHBY*'s *Island*, rather infamous than famous, as having its Name only from that Adventurous Gentleman's being found Frozen to Death in his Ship, upon the Coast.

GREEN-LAND, doubtful whether Island or Continent, noted only for the Whale Fishery, &c. otherways so extream Cold, as not to be Habitable after the Season, unless by force; which Fate several *English* found, by overstaying the Ship, &c. and were forced to subsist on the Flesh of Bears, Foxes, and Whale Fretters, in a little Hutt under Ground, induring a lingring Torment, worse than Death, 'till the Ships returned; at what time some of them (though unexpectedly) were found alive.

Having thus far proceeded briefly to the Northern Islands, we now proceed to the more Eastern Islands.

TENEDOS is an Island seated in *Pontus Euxinus*, or the *Black Sea*, so called from the dark Mists that arise, where it charges name into that of the *Hellespont*, not very big, but Fruitful, and pretty well inhabited, famed for nothing more than its being taken upon the *Greeks* Expedition against the *Trojans*.

SAMOTHRACIA, called by some *Samos*, from *Samia* the name of its Chief Town, seated in the *Ægean Sea*, as also are *Lemnos*, *Lesbos*, or *Mittelene*, *Chios*, or *Scio*, *Eubæa*, *Scyros*, *Salamis*, the *Sporades*, and the *Cyclades*, or the Isles of the *Arches*, most of them in the hands of the *Turks*, and of no considerable note, though heretofore divers of them were independant, and notable Sea-faring Islands, famed

for

for many Wonders, and other strange matters by the Poets, tho at this day they are exceeding Fruitful, many of them bearing Lemons, Oranges, Dates, Figgs, Grapes, Olives, Apricocks, Mulberries, &c. affording a great number of Silk-worms, which yield much Silk; the Towns which are generally Havens or Sea-ports, are pretty numerous, inhabited mostly by the *Greek Christians, Turks,* and *Jews*; and f om *Lemnos* is that Earth brought, so much in use for curing Wounds, stopping Fluxes, and expelling Poisons; and indeed all these Islands standing like Studs in the Sea, are so well refreshed and tempered by a mild and healthy Air, that for their Fruitfulness, they may be termed little Paradises of Delight, most of them having Towns or Cities of the same name for their Metropolises or Chiefs. The *Sporades,* tho under one seeming denomination, are in number 125, and the Chief of these are *Milo, Canaton,* and *Assine;* and the Chief of the *Cyclades,* are *Delos* and *Coos,* as likewise *Patmos,* where St. *John* was banished and wrote his *Revelation:* *Giarras* and some few others of little note, lying some in *Greece,* and some in *Asia;* so accounted, as lying farther or nearer the shoar of either Countrey; especially in this case it cannot be distinguished to which of them properly the Island belongs, especially if it be free from the Jurisdiction of any Monarch reigning upon the Continent.

A Description of the Isle of Creet, *and other* Islands.

THe Isle of *Creet* was very famous in former times, for being Mistress of those Seas, nor less for its Fruitfulness, and commodious Scituation for Traffick, as being posited between the *Ionian, Libyque, Ægean,* and *Carpathian Seas,* and is now better known by the name of *Candia,* taken at several times by the *Turks* from the *Venetians*; and is in circuit about 650 Miles, abounding with Oyl, Wine, Corn, Cattle, and many other things of value, which made the *Turks* contend with the loss of much Blood, to possess themselves of the whole, when they had found the sweetness of a part of it: As for Hills, Mountains, and Rivers of note, this Island affords not many, but has for its Chief Cities *Rhetimo*, *Candia*, and *Canea*, or *New Candy*, built by the *Turks* to secure their first possession in the Island; and in this plenteous Countrey *Titus* was Bishop: As for the other *Islands* lying about it there are only *Claudia* and *Egelia*; very Fruitful by reason of their scituation, but not considerable by reason of their smallness.

The Islands *in the* Ionian Sea *described*, &c.

THe Islands in this Sea are chiefly these:
CYTHERA commonly called *Serigo*, held Sacred by the Poets to *Venus*, who took her other name from hence, lying about 5 Miles from *Cape Mello* in *Peloponnesus*; and altho it is not above 60 Miles in Compass, yet it yields such store of Fruits, Corn, and other Commodities of value, that it is esteemed the Jewel of this Sea, and was formerly called *Porphyrus* from the abundance of that sort of Stone digged out of its Mountains; and has for its Chief Town *Capsalo*, scituate on a small Haven, tho not so much frequented, by reason of its shallowness.

The *Strophades* are a brace of Islands, where *Ulisses* and *Æneas* are said to find the Harpy's, and indeed fit for such kind of Creatures only, by reason of their Rockiness, which renders them so barren, that only a few *Greeks*, and some others (out of a desire to exercise their Religion without molestation) possess them.

ZANT, an Island of the *Venetians*, not exceeding 60 Miles in Circumference, is yet so abundantly

ly Fruitful, that it almost exceeds the credit of Report, producing the Grocery sort of Currants, for which it is famed above all other Places; also Pomegranates, Citrons, Oranges, Lemons, Olives, Granadires, Grapes, that make strong Wine, both white and red, and has for the Defence of its Haven a strong City and Castle, Inhabited by *Greeks* and *Venetians*, yet has the Misfortune to be subject to Earth-quakes, though not extraordinary; and indeed the Country is not so Fruitful, but the major part of the Inhabitants are as wicked, not making it a scruple to Murther any, against whom they have conceived a Grudge.

The *Echinades* are five small *Islands*, supposed to be made by the Seas casting up Sand Banks, and the Mud that comes out of the River *Achelous*, according to Poets speaking in the Name of that River, *viz.*

Fluctus Nostriq; Marisq; &c.

The Fury of the Sea Waves, and my own,
Continual heaps of Earth and Mud drew down,
Which parted by the Inter-running Seas,
Made as thou seest the five *Echinades*.

And indeed they are rather Rocks, or hardened Earth, than any *Island* of note and so we leave them.

CEPHALONIA is in Circumference about 155 Miles, and contrary to the *Echinades*, very Fruitful, as yielding Figgs, Olives, Raisins, Currants, Hony, Sweet Water, Mulberries, Pine, Date, Malvaii, Muscadel, Vino Leatico, Wooll, Cheese, Turkeys, Drugs, and Dyes, besides Cattle, Corn, and Rich Pastures; and has for its chief Towns, held under the *Venetians, Guiscardo, Nolo,* and *Argostoli,* Inhabited by *Greeks* and *Venetians*; the people Civil, and very honest Dealers.

CORFU is another Island in the *Ionian Sea*, 44 Miles in Length, and 24 in Breadth; taking its name from the City of *Corfu*, seated at the foot of a large Mountain, on which to strengthen it, tho strong in it self, are two Fortresses, but chiefly out of the natural Rock; and tho the Southern part of this Island be mountainous and subject to hot Blasts, yet the whole in general produces Corn, Oranges, Lemons, Pomegranets, Fig Trees, Olives, Wax, Honey, some Drugs, and many other pleasant Fruits, tho it has not in it any Rivers of note.

ITHACA is a small Island giving a name to *Ulysses*, who born there, tho now it has lost its own name, and is called *Val de Campare*; in compass not above 56 Miles, and of little note, unless for the Reception of Pyrats that haunt this Sea.

St. *MAURO*, formerly called *Leucadia*, is a small Island inhabited mostly by *Jews*, formerly the *Venetians*, but taken from them by the *Turks*; and altho at present it is not much set by, yet formerly was it of such esteem, that the Inhabitants cut an Isthmus of Two Miles breadth, that joyned it to the Continent, and was famous for the Temple of *Apollo* seated in it; from the top of which, those that leaped into the Sea were held to be cured of extravagant Love; better believed than experienced.

Of the Adriatick Sea, *and the* Islands *therein.*

THe *Adriatick Sea* is that at the bottom of which the City of *Venice* is seated, it being accounted 700 Miles in Length, and 104 in Breadth, and has in it these Isles, *viz.*

MESINA, an Island about 150 Miles in Circumference, yielding considerable Plenty, and has only a strong Fortress for its Defence, the Towns being mostly unwalled, and but indifferently stored with Houses or Inhabitants.

LISSA or *Clissa*, is another of the *Adriatick Islands* 20 Miles over, and 60 in Circumference, very Fruitful, and in Subjection to the *Venetians*, who only defend the Sea Ports, and by that means hold the rest in Subjection.

CURZOLA a place not exceeding 60 Miles in Circumference, yet of great moment to the *Venetians* in rendring them Wood sufficient to build their Ships and Galleys; having the Chief Town of the same name with the Island, defended by Two strong Fortresses, Commanded by a Governour, revoked or changed yearly; and altho the Island it self affords no extraordinary Merchandise, yet it lies Commodious for Ships Trading in those parts.

The Mediterranean Sea *Considered, together with the* Islands *therein.*

THe *Mediteranean Sea* is so called from its Midland Scituation, as being environed with the Earth, &c. and in it are found these Islands of Note, viz.

SICILY, about 700 Miles in Circumference, famed throughout the World for its Fertility, producing Oyl, Corn, Wine, Rice, Sugar, Alloms, Salts, Fruits, Mettals, Corral; and of Cattle such abundance, that it feeds not only it self but a great part of *Italy* and other Neighbouring Countries, and was accounted the Granary of ancient *Rome*; nor can the New well subsist without its supplies: And here is found the *Flaming Mount Ætna*, which frequently has such horrible Eruptions, that it not only sends Stones and Cinders with Fire into the Air an incredible height, which scatter over many parts of the Countrey, but to the great Misfortune of the Inhabitants, and many times to the overthrow of Towns and Cities, emitteth streams of Liquid Fire or melted Minerals, which have been known to run in a Fiery Torrent a mile into the Sea, before the Waves could extinguish them; and here the Chief Cities are *Mesina* and *Syracuse*; and the whole Countrey at present is under the King of *Spain*, tho formerly it was an entire Kingdom Governed by a King of its own; the Kings of *Sicily*, lately stiling themselves Kings of *Jerusalem*; and the people are much of the nature of those in *Italy*, from which the Island is divided by a small Arm of the Sea only.

MALTA, anciently *Melita*, the Landing Place of St. *Paul* in his way to *Rome*, when the Viper clave to his hand, and he shook it into the Fire, is a fair Island, tho but little in Compass, yielding store of Oranges, Lemons, Figgs, Citrons, Cottoons, Pomgranats, and many other delicious Fruits; but is so unhappy to be mostly deficient in Wine and Corn, by which it is supplied from *Sicily* and other parts; however it is one of the Chief Sea Fortresses or Bulwarks of Christendom against the Turks, Commanded by an Order of Knights, called the Knights of St. *John* of *Jerusalem*, tho vulgarly termed or named the Knights of *Malta*; the whole Territory being 10 Leagues in Length and 4 in Breadth, yet contains 60 Villages, and 4 principal Cities; the Chief *Valet*, a strong and well Fortified City, wherein the great Master of the Order has his Palace, and the Knights their Chambers; as also a Tower from whence a Prospect may be taken of the whole Island.

CORSICA, Scituate over against *Genoa*, being 325 Miles in Circumference, and of a very Fruitful Product, yielding Corn, Wine, Figgs, Raisins and Hony, and has in it Iron Mines, Mines of Allom, and other Minerals, and has for its chief Cities, *Bastia*, (pleasantly seated on the North East part of the *Island*, on a commodious Haven) *Mara*, *Gallera*, St. *Florence*, St. *Boniface*, and some others of lesser note, and is under the Government of *Genoa*,

and

and affords a Beast, rarely found but in this *Island*, called *Mufoli*, with a Skin like a Deer, but harder by many Degrees, and Horns like a Ram; and here are bred an Excellent Race of good Horses, and is an *Island* much noted for its good Havens, upon the Account of the Reception for Shipping, Trading in the *Mediterranean*.

SARDINIA is another *Island* of this Tract, not above 7 Miles distant from the former, though much larger, as not held to be less than 560 Miles in compass, abounding with Corn and Fruit, as being but little troubled with Hills; and though the Soil is Rich, yet no Poisonous nor Offensive thing is found in the *Island*, having for its principal Cities *Coliaris*, (well Inhabited and Fortified, seated upon a good Haven, being an Arch-Bishops See) *Reparata*, *Boffa*, and *Aquilastra*, and in the whole *Island* are two other Arch-Bishops, and 15 Suffragan Bishops; the People throughout this *Island* demeaning themselves courteous to Strangers, and are very just in their dealings.

The *Baleares* are sundry Islands found in this Sea, and the greatest of these are *Majorca* and *Minorca*.

MAJORCA is an Island about 300 Miles in Circumference, lying about 60 Miles from the Coast of *Spain*, all the Borders of it being Mountainous, and for the most part Barren, but the Inland Countrey Fruitful, bearing Corn, Olives, Grapes, Fruits of sundry Kinds, and has in it the City of *Majorca*, a University; and that of *Palma*.

MINORCA is about 9 miles distant from the former, and 150 miles in Circumference, having for its Principal Cities or Towns, *Minorca*, and *Javan*, and is a Flourishing Island, especially the Inland Parts, both of them under the King of *Spain*: near to these are two other small Islands, *viz*. *Ebrifa*, and *Olibufa*, considerably Fertile, but not large, well Inhabited, or of any considerable Trade,

there

there are moreover the lesser Islands dispersed abroad as the *Vulcanian* or *Æolian Islands*, on the *Sicilian* Shoar; the principal of which is *Lipra*, not exceeding 10 miles in Circumference, and are both properly called the *Liparean Islands*, and abound with Sulphur, Allom, Bitumen, hot Baths, and some Fruits, though not much, as being very Rockey and Mountainous, yet Inhabited by some Spaniards.

VULCANIA, formerly held to be the Forge of *Vulcan*, where he made Thunder-bolts for *Jupiter*, by reason it cast out Fire in three rising Hills, like the Funnels of Chimneys, casting up Stones, and horribly Roaring like a Smiths Forge.

STROMBOLO is another *Æolian Island*, or rather a Burning Mountain in the Sea, carrying its Flames and Fire so bright, that it appears like a Beacon, and may be seen in the dark for many Leagues; held by some who know no better, to be the mouth of Hell; when indeed this and all other Burning Mountains are occasioned by the firing of Minerals, or the unctuous Quality of the Earth; thro the vehement Agitation of Heat and Cold, strugling for mastery in the vacant Caverns, &c.

There are in this Tract 18 Islands, called the Isles of *Naples*, but only *Isica*, and *Capra*, and *Ænaia* are of any moment, and these so small, that they render little Trade: There are others called the *Ligurian Islands*, viz. *Elba* and *Gallinara* and some others, rather Rocks than Islands; wherefore we pass them over as unworthy a place in this Book; and thus much to these Islands.

The *Oriental Islands* are those of the *Eastern Seas*, and to these by many (tho somewhat improperly) are reckoned *Rhodes* and *Cyprus*, Two famous Islands in the *Mediterranean*, exceedingly abounding in all manner of Plenty, and have for their Chief Cities *Famagusta* and *Rhodes*, both Famous for their

Strength

Strength, and the Sieges they sustained against the whole Power of the *Turks*.

ORMUS, lying upon the *Æthiopian Coast*, and a place much frequented, spoken of before.

ZELON, a Famous Island for Plenty, lying not far from the *Indian Coast* called *Cape Comerein*.

MOLOCCOES, Six Islands in Chief, but have many other subject to them, *viz. Tidar, Tarnate, Macir, Rachian, Machin,* and *Bottone,* the only Islands, fruitfully abounding with Cloves, Nutmegs, Ginger, Cinamon, Aloes, and Pepper, for which they are much Traded to by the *Europeans*.

AMBOYNA is an Island Fruitful in Lemons, Oranges, Cloves, Cocoa's, Bonanus Sugar Canes, and other valuable Commodities; and here it was the *Dutch* executed their Inhumane Cruelties on the *English*, and is called one of the Islands of *Sinda* or *Selebes*; the other Three being the *Selebes, Magaffar,* and *Gilolo,* considerably Rich and Plentiful, but Inhabited partly by *Canibals*, and partly by a rude sort of people, little inferiour to them; and next to these is *Banta* or *Banda*, abounding with Nutmegs.

JAVA MAJOR and *Minor*, are Two extraordinary Islands abounding with Spices, Rice, and Cotton, and all other things necessary for the subsistance of Life, Governed by many Kings, which are in continual War with each other; and in this Tract are *Bala* and *Madara, Bocuno, Burneo*.

SUMATRA, is a very pleasant Island of *East India*, as indeed are most of the *Oriental Islands* named, 700 Miles in Length, and 200 in Breadth; and to these of this Tract we may add the *Philippine Islands*, many in number, but most of them small spots or specks in the Sea; and the Chief of these Islands, being in the possession of the *Spaniards*, are *Minbanao, Luffon, Tandain,* and *Pollehan*, abounding with Fruit, Cattle, pleasant Rivers, Fowls, *&c.*

Here

Here are also the two Islands of *Avira*, lying Westward of *Sumatra*.

The Islands of Africa Described.

MADAGASCAR, a large Island of 1000 Miles in Length, and 230 Miles over, Inhabited by Negroes, where either Sex go Naked, and consequently there is no Imployment for Taylors; yet with the Natives the Europeans Trade, tho mostly for Slaves, Copper, Gold, Silver, &c. and in this Tract are found the Islands of *Chameree*, *Meottey*, *Mohelia*, *Mauritius*, *Johanan*, an a Woody Island, called *Englands Forrest*, but of no Trade, though considerably Fruitful.

Socotora, is an Island lying at the Mouth of the Red Sea, 60 miles in length, and 64 in breadth, abounding with Gums, Aloes, Spices, &c. Here are also the Island of St. *Thomas*, the *Princes* Island, and the *Gorgades*, in number 9, viz. St. *Vincent*, St. *Anthony*, St. *Lucius*; *Buenavista*, *Insula*, *Salu*, *Del Fogo*, St. *Nicholas*, St. *James*, and St. *Majo*.

The *Canary* Islands are in number 7, viz. The *Grand Canary*, *La Palma*, *Teneriffa*, *Lancerota*, *Hierro*, *Forte Ventura*, and *La Gomera*; all of them very plentiful, abounding with Fruits, Cattle, &c. But above all, the *Canarys* yield us the Wine, taking its name from the Country; and in one of them is found the Mount *Teneriff*, much transcending the Clouds, as being 15 miles in ascent.

Madera is a famous Island, first discovered by an English Ship, cast away upon the Coast, now abounding with Corn, Wine, Honey, Sugar Canes, and Madder, used in Dying: and upon the Coast is *Holy Port*, an Island, though but 15 miles in compass, very fruitful and pleasant.

The

The *Azores* are 9 in number, *viz. Tercera*, the principal, St. *Michael*, St. *George*, St. *Mary*, *Fyall*, *Gratiofa*, *Pico*, *Corno*, and *Flores*, not being very Fruitful, except the first.

Hesperides, or the *Hesperian* Islands, are 3 in number, *viz. Buanifta*, *Mayo*, and *Sal*, lying about an 100 miles from the Continent of *Africk*, being in themselves not only Fruitful, but exceeding pleasant, by reason of the temperate Air, which occasioned the Poetical Fictions, of their being the *Elizium* Fields, or aboad of happy Souls after their departure.

The American *Islands, &c.*

JAMAICA, now an English Colony, lately taken from the Spaniards, is 170 miles in length, and 70 in breadth, very pleasant and temperate, considerably Fruitful, abounding with Oranges, Lemons, Cocoa Nuts, Pomgranates, and other curious Fruits, abounding with Cattle as *England*, the Trees alwaies Green, *&c.*

BARBADOES, an other English Colony, is very well inhabited, yielding store of Sugar, Cattle, Corn, *&c.* though not exceeding 14 or 15 miles in length.

BERMUDES, called the Summer Islands, are very pleasant, abounding with Oranges, Sugar, and other Commodities, breeding in their Mulberry Trees, great store of Silk-worms, which return to considerable account.

ST. CHRISTOPHERS is a small Island, yet produces store of Tobacco, Cotton, Ginger, full of Woods and steep Mountains, and is possessed by the English and French.

NEVIS, about 18 miles in circumference, is a Colony of the English, and produces Cotton, Sugar, Ginger, *&c.*

AN-

ANTEGO is about 7 Leagues in length, and as much in breadth, with very rocky Shoars, unsafe for Shipping, yet abounding in Fruit, Fish, Venison, Tobacco, Indico, Sugar, &c.

HISPANIOLA, 350 Leagues in Circumference, very Fruitful, as are all the Islands in this Tract, viz. *Cuba, Laba, Balima, Lucayoneque, Abacoo, Bimixy, Labaquene, Viemo, Curateo, Gotao, Oguaato, Samana,* St. *Salvador, Le Triangulo,* St. *Vincent, Dominica, Anguila,* and some others, scarcely taken notice of by Historians, as for the most part not inhabited, yet visited frequently by the Neighbouring Islanders, upon the account of the wild Cattle and Fruits found in them; and for the conveniency of the Fishing Trade. And upon these Coasts of *America,* are lately setled two Colonies of *English,* in *Pensylvania* and *Carolina,* very prosperous and thriving: But not having more room for a further Description, we must, after having thus far proceeded, put a period to this our History of the Universe.

Hoping 'twill find acceptance, since Man
To struggle for the World is much inclin'd.

FINIS.

---

www.ingramcontent.com/pod-product-compliance
Lightning Source LLC
Chambersburg PA
CBHW031733230426
43669CB00007B/339